NETANYAHU

NETANYAHU

The Road to Power

Ben Caspit and Ilan Kfir

Translated and Adapted From Hebrew
by Ora Cummings

A BIRCH LANE PRESS BOOK
Published by Carol Publishing Group

A Birch Lane Press Book
Published by Carol Publishing Group
Birch Lane Press is a registered trademark of Carol Communications, Inc.

Editorial, sales and distribution, rights and permissions inquiries should be addressed
to Carol Publishing Group, 120 Enterprise Avenue, Secaucus, N.J. 07094.

In Canada: Canadian Manda Group, One Atlantic Avenue, Suite 105, Toronto, Ontario,
M6K 3E7

Carol Publishing Group books may be purchased in bulk at special discounts for sales
promotion, fund-raising, or educational purposes. Special editions can be created to
specifications. For details, contact Special Sales Department, Carol Publishing Group,
120 Enterprise Avenue, Secaucus, N.J. 07094.

Manufactured in the United States of America
10 9 8 7 6 5 4 3 2 1

Netanyahu: The Road to Power was first published in Hebrew in Israel by Alfa
Communications—Yehuda Shief; Doni Dor, editor; Moshe Milner, pictures editor.

Library of Congress Cataloging-in-Publication Data

Caspit, Ben.
    [Netanyahu. English]
    Netanyahu : the road to power / Ben Caspit and Ilan Kfir ;
translated and adapted from Hebrew by Ora Cummings.
        p. cm.
    "A Birch Lane Press book."
    Includes index.
    ISBN 1–55972–453–6 (hardcover)
    1. Netanyahu, Binyamin.   2. Prime ministers—Israel—Biography.
I. Kafir, Ilan.   II. Cummings, Ora.   III. Title.
DS126.6.N48K4713   1998
956.9405'4'092—dc21
    [B]   98–37357
                                                                CIP

Contents

Introduction

On May 29, 1996, Benjamin Netanyahu was elected prime minister of Israel. Little was known about the charismatic young man who had taken the country's political right by storm only a few years before. Who was he? What did he believe in, and what did he want?

A few weeks after winning the general election, Netanyahu—"Bibi" to his friends and just about everyone else—offered us a challenge: "You don't really know me," he said. "If you do some homework, you might learn a thing or two."

We accepted the challenge. This book is a long overdue attempt to get to know the man who conquered the Likud party and all of Israel in a period of only eight years. It is our attempt to answer the question: Who are you, Benjamin Netanyahu?

Netanyahu is a human dynamo, a determined and tenacious fighter, forever waging an uncompromising war to attain a goal, and never giving in. We refer to this determination as the "spirit of Bibi." It is the spirit that fired him as a youth in the United States, that drove him during his service in the Israel Defense Forces special reconnaissance unit, that bore him from the embassy in Washington to the United Nations in New York, from there to the Likud leadership, and finally to election as prime minister, against all odds and expectations.

In addition to learning who Netanyahu really is, we also wanted to find out what has happened to the spirit of Bibi. Where has his determination and stubbornness gone during the past twenty months? How could a man who achieved such an improbable election victory turn into someone incapable of replacing an ambassador or choosing an office head or appointing an attorney general? This book attempts to solve the puzzle named Benjamin Netanyahu.

At the beginning of 1982, I called Zvi Rafiah and offered him the post of political attaché in the Israeli embassy in Washington. Rafiah refused. I offered the post to Bibi, who took twenty minutes to accept. When people come to me today and say, "Look what you've done," I have to tell them: Don't blame me! It's Zvi Rafiah's fault.

Moshe Arens, May 1997

NETANYAHU

1

Good Night, Mr. Prime Minister

B enjamin Netanyahu closed his eyes for a moment, took a deep breath, and walked into the hall. After two months of tense campaigning, he was exhausted. Yet his walk remained firm and confident.

Three hours earlier, at ten o'clock in the evening, Israeli television stations had announced that according to the exit polls, Prime Minister Shimon Peres, the Labor party candidate, had pulled out a very narrow victory.

At Labor party headquarters, Peres supporters had already begun celebrating, while across town the Likud headquarters looked as if a bomb had been dropped on it. Many of Netanyahu's supporters had already gone home, and those who remained were in the depths of disappointment. Blame was tossed about and people were crying. The TV announcement had been accepted as final.

At this moment Netanyahu needed all his strength and courage and whatever was left of his famous energy to face his supporters. Shimon Peres had chosen to wait out the results in his Ramat Aviv apartment. Netanyahu, too, could have remained in his suite in the Tel Aviv Hilton. But he didn't.

It was a little before one o'clock in the morning and those who had remained in the main hall of the Likud headquarters were waiting for Netanyahu. They had been working for his cause for months, and now they wanted him there.

And then he appeared. Netanyahu marched in with David Levy—his political archenemy who had suddenly become an ally—at his side. There would be plenty of time for rivalries and grudges within the Likud, but on this night Netanyahu and Levy were united in a larger battle against a common foe.

The entrance of the two men rekindled the crowd. The battle cry of the Likud youth echoed throughout the hall once again. "Here he comes! Here he comes! The next prime minister of Israel!" Young men from the fundamentalist Habad movement formed a circle and started dancing. Netanyahu was taken aback by the current of enthusiasm sweeping over Exhibition Gardens. He waved to the crowd and smiled his familiar lopsided smile, doing his best to conceal his desperation and dread. He hugged David Levy, knowing that this temporary alliance would soon disintegrate, and that he alone would bear the brunt of defeat.

Netanyahu took the podium and turned this moment of crisis into his finest hour. While Labor leaders and activists celebrated their victory across town at Cinerama Hall, Netanyahu resolutely delivered his speech: "We mustn't lose hope. It's not over yet. I want to tell you that I love you, I am proud of you, and I salute you. We must hope and pray that tomorrow morning will bring better news."

Nearby, at his home in Neve Avivim, Shimon Peres sat in front of the television set sipping a glass of good French wine and watching his young opponent with amazement. Two hours earlier, when he received the voting statistics from the Arab sector, Peres had concluded "We've done it. We've won." Yet something about his young opponent's confidence was unsettling to Peres. Toward the end of the campaign, when it became clear that the race would be close, Peres had begun to fear that his underestimation of the Likud candidate might have been a costly mistake.

Netanyahu finished his speech and he, Levy, and Yitzhak Mordechai, another important ally, raised their arms in the air. Netanyahu promised his supporters that everything was going to be all right. The waves of love flowing from the audience restored Bibi's confidence. The feeling of defeat was gone. He was relaxed, rejuvenated, momentarily able to forget the exit polls. A feeling of inspiration washed over the large hall: this was the spirit of Bibi.

*   *   *

Thirty hours earlier, Benjamin Netanyahu climbed out of bed in his Jerusalem apartment. His two children, Avner and Yair, were already awake. Bibi began to prepare for the biggest day of his life. Shai Bazak, his press adviser, had arrived early at his neighborhood voting booth and cast his vote. He then rushed to his boss's home at Sokolov 7, Rehavia, where cameramen and reporters had already congregated to wait for the candidate and his wife to emerge.

Bazak took the stairs two at a time. Unlike his employer, he could not conceal his excitement. This was a change of heart for Bazak—throughout the campaign he had been the prophet of doom, doubting that Netanyahu was capable of defeating Shimon Peres.

At the time, the Netanyahus were living in a cramped rented apartment. There was one room for the two children, a second for Bibi and his wife, Sara, a tiny study, and a small living room. At eight o'clock on this morning, chaos had taken over the whole place. Netanyahu was pacing in the small corridor, fidgeting with his tie. Little Yair was whining, and Bazak picked him up and tried to calm him. Sara was wired with excitement.

Everyone was ready. Bibi and Sara Netanyahu, Shai Bazak, and the security men all left the apartment together. The two children stayed behind with their nanny, Tania Shaw. Bazak whispered the instructions to Netanyahu: smile, wave your hand, and give a brief interview to the press. Netanyahu approached the area cordoned off for reporters and accepted a cup of coffee from Channel 2 reporter Roni Daniel. Bibi tossed out a few jokes and spoke comfortably with the press. He then climbed into his armored car, relaxed and smiling, and he and his convoy set off for the polls, where he would cast his vote for prime minister of Israel. Security around Netanyahu had been tightened significantly in the months preceding the elections. As soon as the campaign was officially underway, he was given an armored car by Shin Bet, Israel's security service. They also doubled his bodyguards. The assassination of Prime Minister Yitzkah Rabin left Shin Bet no choice but to make the Likud candidate one of the most closely guarded men in the country.

The Netanyahus rode in the back sear of the car with Shai Bazak—Bibi to the right, Sara in the middle, Bazak to the left. They made a habit of traveling like this. Less than five minutes after departing, the armored car pulled around the back of the building along a prearranged route and stopped near the entrance to the voting booths.

The Netanyahus entered the building, smiled at the cameras, and made for the voting booth. Sara voted first, and while he waited for his turn Bibi gave a brief interview to the press. He described the itinerary for the whistle-stop tour of Israel he would make on this election day. He would start in Jerusalem, a city that would never be divided under a Likud government, and also visit the Golan Heights, which he insisted must never be given up. It was a short, well-rehearsed speech, written, like all of Bibi's speeches, by his campaign strategists. Bibi then cast his vote, and the convoy took to the road again. This time they headed toward the Knesset airstrip in Jerusalem, where they were scheduled to fly to the Golan Heights in two small civilian helicopters. Because they were running ahead of schedule, however, Netanyahu decided to take a spontaneous break and enjoy the spare time. Bazak suggested stopping for a cup of coffee, and Netanyahu liked the idea. The security men did not object.

They chose a small cafe on the corner of Gaza Street. The other customers were startled to see the Likud candidate and his wife, and looked on with excitement as the couple slid into one of the tables, surrounded by security men. Bazak alerted the press and before long Eli Hershkovitz from Zoom 77 and Channel 2's Roni Daniel showed up. Hershkovitz, who had gone to school with Bibi, joined the Netanyahus at their table. Bibi and Sara were holding hands, smiling, and did not seem as tense as they usually were in the presence of the media.

Back in the car, Bazak wondered out loud how Bibi was keeping his cool. "Listen, Shai," Bibi said, "all my life I have followed a single principle. I do everything I can as long as I have the power to change things. There is no limit to the effort I am willing to exert if I know it will make a difference. But when I reach a stage where nothing I can do will make any difference anymore, that's when I relax. I know that I have done everything I possibly could, my absolute best. Today, it's no longer in our hands."

Bazak believed his boss. For the past few years, he had not left Netanyahu's side. He had been Bibi's press adviser, personal assistant, secretary, confidant, and partner. Bazak knotted Bibi's ties, whispered instructions in his ear, told him which side of his face to show the cameras, whipped out a portable electric shaver whenever necessary, applied his makeup before TV appearances, advised him when to smile, who to wave to, who to speak to, and who to ignore.

Despite his youth—he was in his mid-twenties—and his relative inexperience, Bazak had managed to secure Netanyahu's complete trust through his sheer devotion to the older man. During Netanyahu's most trying times—like when he admitted on TV to an extramarital affair, or when Yitzhak Rabin was assassinated and many blamed Netanyahu's rhetoric—some former friends and associates stopped saying hello to Bibi in the street. But Bazak remained by his side.

Now, Bazak was quite sure that his boss's confidence was no affectation. "Just you wait and see, Shai," Bibi said on the way to the Knesset airstrip. "We're going to win."

Netanyahu had become optimistic three days earlier following his televised debate with Shimon Peres. Likud surveys indicated a clear victory for Netanyahu, and this got his adrenaline flowing. He would need the boost. During the campaign's final three days, Bibi would be forced to muster every ounce of his energy and willpower.

Two helicopters were waiting at the airstrip. Bibi, Sara, senior Likud member Dan Meridor, and several security men crammed themselves into one of the helicopters while Shai Bazak, political adviser Shmulik Cohen, some reporters, and more security men took the other. The helicopters flew northward over the Jordan Valley and landed on a soccer field in the Golan Heights town of Katzerin. The town's mayor, Sami Bar-Lev, was waiting to greet them along with a group of Likud supporters. The welcome was warm. "Look after us, look after the Golan," the supporters called out to Netanyahu. He smiled and waved.

The next stop was Kiryat Shemonah, where the entourage was welcomed by Mayor Prosper Azran and the local Likud branch chairman, Yossi Himi. Himi's wife, Hani, had been badly wounded during Operation Grapes of Wrath in April 1996, when the Israel Defense Forces attacked southern Lebanon to prevent terrorists from advancing to Israel's northern border.

Himi traveled in Bibi's car, but Azran did not; this had been prearranged due to ill feeling between Bibi and Azran. Azran had been the first to leave David Levy's camp after the latter left Likud. This pleased Netanyahu, and he promised Azran a high place on the Likud's

Knesset list. Bibi did not keep his promise and Azran did not forget.

The tour proceeded from Kiryat Shemonah to Hadera and then to Netanya, at which point the helicopters were left behind and the entourage went on by car. At every stop, Netanyahu was cheered on by Likud activists. Throughout the day, Netanyahu communicated every hour with Avigdor Lieberman back at headquarters. Lieberman, whose nickname, Yvette, misleads some into thinking that Netanyahu's closest adviser is a woman, would later become a power player in Israeli politics when Bibi appointed him chief of staff after being elected prime minister.

The reports Bibi received from Lieberman were encouraging. There had been a good voter turnout at the Likud strongholds. On the other hand, the Arab sector, which favored Peres, seemed to be in hibernation. (Late in the afternoon Shimon Peres and members of his cabinet would set off on a desperate "reawakening" mission to the Arab towns and villages and tried to bring voters to the polls.)

Netanyahu was tired. Sara suggested they skip the stop at Benei Berack, a community of religious fundamentalists. "Bibi is exhausted, let's not bother with Benei Berack," she urged Bazak and Cohen. But Bibi's advisers were firm: "We must not disappoint our supporters. We have to go wherever people are waiting for us." They decided not to skip Benei Berack, and it turned out to be the most supportive town on the entire tour.

The town's walls were plastered with banners reading "Netanyahu Is Good for the Jews." There was no sign of support for Peres and the Labor party. Thousands turned out to see Netanyahu in Benei Berack. They danced around his car and chanted "Prime Minister Netanyahu!" They waved a giant yellow voting slip bearing his name. One young zealot, ignoring the security guards, ran up and planted a sloppy kiss on Bibi's cheek.

When he was tired, it was Bibi's habit to retire to a side room, lie down on a sofa, and fall asleep. Bazak would cover him up and wake him a quarter or half an hour later. Sometimes Bibi would beg, "just a few minutes more." On this day, however, it was not possible to stop. Netanyahu ignored his exhaustion and kept going.

The last stop was the twelfth-floor suite at the Tel Aviv Hilton, rented for this occasion. Bibi usually patronized the Tel Aviv Sheraton Hotel, where the Likud party was given a big discount, but on this day he chose the Hilton: "All my American friends are staying there, and I want to be with them."

Bibi made his customary first call—to room service—and took a shower.

The adjoining room in the suite was reserved for the entourage. Bibi's entire inner circle was soon there—Yvette Lieberman, Danny Naveh, Shmulik Cohen, Shai Reuveni, and Nehama Avraham, among others.

Several of Netanyahu's wealthy American friends checked into the Tel Aviv Hilton to be with "their man" on his big day. Morad Zamir, a Jewish millionaire of Persian origin, had come, as had Marvin Idelson, a Jewish American billionaire who had contributed large sums to Netanyahu's campaign. Steve Sheneo, Netanyahu's liaison to the American contributors, was also in Bibi's suite, where the dominant language seemed to be English—with a heavy New York accent.

Optimistic forecasts from the field were flowing in. Activists from the ultra-Orthodox sector called in to report that some of their people had taken part in an exit poll in which they "voted" for Peres as a hoax, "just to teach the TV a lesson." Bibi and Sara sat on the sofa opposite the TV with a couple of Bibi's American friends. Bibi held Sara's hand tightly. Two hours before the preliminary results were to be reported, Shai Bazak was still pessimistic. Toward nine o'clock in the evening the tension increased. Netanyahu asked everyone to leave the suite. He wanted to watch the results with only Sara by his side. Bibi's entourage watched in the adjoining room. The TV report came in—a "tie," too close to call, with a "slight advantage for Shimon Peres."

"Oy vavoy, I can't believe it," Shai Bazak keened. The telephones immediately started ringing—the media seeking reactions, friends expressing support, leading figures from the settlements offering encouragement. Everyone filed back into Bibi's room, except Yvette Lieberman. Immediately after seeing the preliminary results, he had returned to Likud headquarters.

Bibi sat with a grave expression on his face. "It's such a small margin," Bazak reassured him. "It's not over yet. We can still win." Bazak did not believe a word he was saying. The television projections had been accurate over the last few elections, and both major channels were now indicating a close win for Peres.

Netanyahu asked an aide to get Arthur Finkelstein on the phone.

Finkelstein, the secret American adviser of the Likud campaign, had been hired at a rate of one thousand dollars per hour for the sole purpose of putting Netanyahu in the prime minister's seat.

Within minutes Arthur was on the line. Detecting Bibi's panic, Arthur told him not to worry. "I always win the close ones," he assured Bibi.

"Let's do some adding up," Netanyahu said in English. He asked for a sheet of paper and he and Arthur started crunching numbers.

Bazak asked him what he was scrawling, but Netanyahu ignored him. All his attention was focused on the man across the ocean. After filling two pages with complex calculations, he said goodbye and hung up the phone. "Okay, it's not over yet," Bibi declared. "We can still win."

The room full of people did not seem to believe him. The atmosphere was gloomy and no one was smiling. On the television Meir Shitrit, a key figure in the Likud, was admitting defeat and blaming Bibi. Netanyahu smirked and waved dismissively at the screen. "Okay, okay, we heard you."

Images flashed across the television screen—dancing at Labor headquarters and tears at Likud headquarters. "What are they crying about?" Bibi asked with annoyance. "It's not over yet. There's still hope."

At the same time, Shimon Peres was also watching television, also annoyed by the activities at his own headquarters. "What are they dancing about?" he asked angrily. "We haven't won yet."

Netanyahu received a call from Yvette Lieberman at Likud headquarters. Lieberman told him that the people were waiting for him. "Come now," Lieberman advised. Bazak agreed that the time was right. "You have nothing to lose," he told Bibi. "It could be another two or three days until we know for sure, so let's go and get it over with."

Netanyahu reflected for a moment and agreed. Someone suggested calling David Levy, who was one floor below, and inviting him to come along, and Bibi did. "No problem," said Levy. "Let's meet there in fifteen minutes."

Sara stayed behind at the hotel. She was not up to a public appearance. Netanyahu and his entourage went out to the armored Volvo. Bibi smiled and waved to the reporters as he hopped into the car. He was carrying himself like a winner. "How are you keeping this up?" Bazak asked him in the car. Bibi did not answer.

Netanyahu arrived at Ramat Gan and met David Levy. The two embraced warmly. With their arms around each other's shoulders, they entered the hall. After the speeches, Netanyahu returned to his car, where Eyal Arad, the eternal pessimist, was waiting for him—with a smile. Bibi's closest adviser said that he had some new information and for the first time wholeheartedly agreed that the race was far from over.

"What do you mean?" Netanyahu asked.

"There has been a clear swing in our direction. Everything could be upside-down by morning."

Netanyahu was not surprised. "Yes, it is wide open right now."

Arad went on. "If the trend continues, and everything goes according to plan, then after the army vote comes in, you win by one percent."

"So, when do we announce our victory?" Netanyahu asked. He was only half joking.

Arad smiled. Bibi and his closest confidant leaned against the car. The commotion surrounding them did not disturb the intimacy of their conversation.

"Go and get some rest," Arad suggested. "You're tired. You're going to need all your energy later on."

Netanyahu obeyed: "I'm going back to the Hilton to grab some sleep."

A few minutes later, Netanyahu was back at the suite, where bad news awaited. At this late hour, the results had swung decisively back toward Shimon Peres. It looked final now. Netanyahu got ready for bed. The excitement, the tension, the anxiety of imminent defeat—none of this made a difference. He was tired and he wanted to sleep.

Fifteen minutes later, Yvette Lieberman called from Ramat Gan and reported yet another change. The projection was a dead tie, fifty-fifty. A cry of "Yessss!" tore through the twelfth floor of the Tel Aviv Hilton as hope was restored. Shai Bazak, Danny Neveh, Shmulik Cohen, and the others could not believe their eyes. The impossible was beginning to unfold.

Bibi smiled. Sara could not hide her excitement. Half an hour later, the fateful report came. For the first time, Bibi had taken the lead. He jumped up and gave Sara a long, tight hug. More victorious cries pierced the night air.

"You really might win," Bazak said in dazed disbelief.

"What do you mean, might?" Bibi said. "I am winning."

None of Netanyahu's men will ever forget those moments. The fatigue, frustration, and fear evaporated. The room filled with people. The

American millionaires came back in. "We did it," Bazak said aloud, to no one in particular. "It's unbelievable. We did it."

Netanyahu remained calm. At three-thirty in the morning, leading by half a percentage point, he decided to go to sleep.

"Wake me up in the morning," he said.

"As you say, Mr. Prime Minister," someone replied.

He had barely finished his shower when he heard Bazak's knock on the door: "It's six-tenths to your advantage," he reported. Netanyahu smiled to himself, climbed into bed, and was asleep within seconds. "Good night, Mr. Prime Minister," Sara whispered.

Millions of Israelis had gone to bed with Shimon Peres as prime minister. They awakened to the news that Benjamin Netanyahu was now their leader. They were familiar with his name, they knew his face. But that was about all most of them knew.

2

In the Footsteps of Jabotinsky

As a child, Bibi Netanyahu had three heroes. They were his guiding light, and he grew up in their shadow: Yoni, his older brother; Benzion, his father; and Nathan Mileikowsky, his grandfather. Together and individually, the three embodied the ideological template through which Bibi would understand the world and form his own beliefs about modern Zionism, the return to the Land of Israel, and combative right-wing ideology as opposed to leftist defeatism.

Nathan Mileikowsky, scion of a famous rabbinical family, was born in Lithuania in 1880. A wunderkind, he was sent at the age of ten to study at the Volozin yeshiva in Poland and became a rabbi at the age of eighteen. Deeply influenced by Theodore Herzl, the founder of Zionism, Mileikowsky set off at age twenty on a lecture tour which took him as far away as Harbin, China.

A staunch and devoted follower of Herzl, Mileikowsky became one of his greatest opponents in 1903. Seeking a temporary solution to the prevalent persecution of Jews in the Diaspora, Herzl received permission from the British government to form a Jewish settlement in Uganda, in East Africa. Herzl believed that such a swift—albeit temporary—solution was necessary to protect Jews in Eastern Europe from the pogrom massacres being committed by rogue generals and encouraged by the church. The Uganda Plan caused a deep rift among world Jewish leaders. While Herzl insisted that Uganda was only a way station on the road to the

Land of Israel, a young Zionist by the name of Ze'ev Jabotinsky vociferously opposed Herzl's plans.

Nathan Mileikowsky soon joined Jabotinsky. The agreement to form a national Jewish homeland in another country, African Uganda, seemed to Mileikowsky a serious betrayal of the hopes of all those Jews who for millennia had vowed: "Next year in Jerusalem."

In 1905, the seventh Zionist Congress canceled the Uganda Plan, but the issue had compelled young Mileikowsky to solidify his political identity. He was permanently planted on Jabotinsky's side of the Zionist camp, the side to which he would lead his son Benzion, and to which Benzion would lead his children.

Herzl died in 1904 at the age of forty-four. Mileikowsky, then twenty-four, joined thousands at the funeral and delivered an emotional eulogy. The disagreement over the Uganda issue did not detract from his admiration for the founder of Zionism. Four years later, Nathan Mileikowsky moved to Warsaw, where he became principal of his town's Hebrew high school. He also continued his lecture tours, spreading the Zionist message all over Poland.

A Jewish journalist wrote of him:

> Mileikowsky is a genius, a fiery tribune of the people, whose rousing speeches bring to mind those of Homer. His language is rich, bubbling, full of burning temperament. With the breadth of his imagination he has the ability to raise his listeners to the highest ecstasy.... Mileikowsky is a man of stature, upright, tall, his step firm and his head held high. His appearance and speech complement each other in total harmony. It was hard to find a hall large enough to contain the crowds who wanted to hear him speak. People would break down the doors, windows, fight with the ushers—all in order to hear so much as a word from the mouth of the famous man.

Nathan Mileikowsky's son Benzion was born in 1910, the first child in a distinguished family of eight boys and one girl. Though they lived in Poland, where Yiddish was the predominant language among Jews, Hebrew was the only language they spoke at home. In 1914, Nathan was ready to leave Poland and emigrate to Palestine. Unfortunately, a Serbian nationalist shot and killed Archduke Francis Ferdinand of Austria-Hungary, and a month later the First World War broke out.

Poland quickly fell under German domination, and Mileikowsky, one of Warsaw's dignitaries, formed special ties with the city's German governor. One day the governor made him an offer: He would ship Mileikowsky by submarine to the United States, where Mileikowsky would recruit American Jews to oppose American intervention in the war against Germany. The Germans were willing to pay Mileikowsky vast sums of money to help ensure that America stayed out of the war. Mileikowsky did not reject the proposal out of hand, nor did he negotiate over the money. Rather, he attached a political demand to his proposed payment: the German Kaiser Wilhelm II would announce his approval of Herzl's plan for a Jewish national homeland in Palestine, and he would pressure the Turkish authorities to hand over the country—which was under Turkish control—to the Jews. The deal with the governor never materialized, and Mileikowsky remained in Poland until 1920, at which point he took his wife, Sara, and their eight small children, Benzion, Sa'adia, Elisha, Matthew, Amos, Miriam, Erza, and Zachary, and set off for Palestine.

The family traveled by train to Vienna and from there to Trieste, Italy, where four-year-old Amos contracted pneumonia. They were forced to wait a month while he recovered. Nathan and his brood then boarded a ship bound for Alexandria, Egypt, and from there they took another boat to Jaffa.

In his book *A Place Among the Nations*, Benjamin Netanyahu describes his father's family's first moments in Palestine:

> The family got off the ship and rowed to shore in boats, because in those days Jaffa Port did not have an anchorage worthy of its name. After spending some time in one of the first houses in Tel Aviv, they traveled along dirt roads to Safed, a journey which lasted a full two days.
>
> From there, my grandfather and my father took a boat to Tiberius with all their possessions and the rest of the family continued their journey in a horse cart. In the afternoon, a powerful eastern wind started blowing and whipped up the surface of the lake and the boat almost overturned.
>
> After spending the night in Tiberius, the family made its way by horse cart along the way leading to Safed. At Rosh Pina, they changed horses. Apart from Rosh Pina, the whole region was barren,

with the exception of a few bedouin tents which dotted the area from time to time. The journey from Jaffa to Safed, which today takes less than three hours, took three whole days in 1920.

Nathan Mileikowsky was not the first in Bibi's lineage to return to the promised land. Abraham Marcus, grandfather of Bibi's mother Cela, immigrated to Palestine in 1896. Marcus and his fellow members of the Hovevei Zion movement arrived at Rishon le-Zion, at that time a tiny settlement on a large stretch of sandy wasteland, with only a few whitewashed, red-roofed houses.

In *A Place Among the Nations*, Netanyahu writes of his maternal great-grandfather:

> During the day he would plant almond trees and at night he would pore over his Talmud books. By the time my mother was born in nearby Petah Tikva in 1912, the family was already living in the heart of the orange grove which the sons had planted, in a handsome house, which had an avenue of palm trees leading to its front door.

Thus, when Nathan Mileikowsky arrived in Palestine, his future daughter-in-law's family had already been there for a generation. Mileikowsky remained in Safed for two years. He described the town as being "small and neglected, with no electricity or running water. Broken down houses, with no doors or windows." At the beginning of 1922, Nathan got a job that suited his personality: He was made manager of the Jewish National Fund in Europe and later in the United States. He moved his family to Jerusalem and purchased the first house ever built in Bet-Hakerem. The money for their new home was given to Nathan's wife, Sara, by her brother Hovev. Hovev had emigrated from Lithuania to South Africa, as had many Lithuanian Jews. Nathan and Sara had another child at this time and named him Hovev after his generous uncle.

Shortly after arriving in Jerusalem, Nathan Mileikowsky decided to change his family name to a Hebrew name, to signify his break from the past. Many young Zionists were changing their names to signal the new life they had chosen. Mileikowsky chose the name Netanyahu, which in English means "God gave us."

In 1922, twelve-year-old Benzion Netanyahu was sent to a religious boarding school in Jerusalem. In his letters, he described the stern attitude of his teachers, which he believed constricted student creativity.

His father decided to transfer him to a less strict, more secular school.

The Bet Hakerem apartment was soon housing Nathan's parents, Zvi and Gutel; his younger brother Yehuda, and Yehuda's wife and children; and his sister Sara and her husband Dr. David Teitel, whose future grandson, David Shomron, would become Bibi's personal counselor and confidant.

A lesser-known dimension of Nathan Mileikowsky's personality was revealed years later in a diary written by one of his sons, Sa'adia. According to Sa'adia's account, Nathan over the years became a bitter, angry, violent man, and took his frustrations out on his children. In his diary, Sa'adia wrote:

> Father did not have a single moment to spare. He would come home from his journeys to Europe or America and stay for short periods only and I was an open target. And the blows, the blows...in so many cases they were unjustified and I never forgot and it burned my skin, and remained with me forever. Since then I swore an oath, that I should never harm my own children.

Nathan Mileikowsky spread his Zionist message in the United States. A speech he gave in Brooklyn in 1936 thrilled his audience:

> When I first arrived in Safed, I climbed onto a fortress. I was truly enchanted. Everything my eyes could see for far and wide was so clear and sharp. Pure air entered my lungs. I breathed easily, as if I had grown wings and flown to a place where everything is beautiful. Here, the Sea of Galilee is joined to the hills, as if one can jump straight in. And here is Tiberius, the ancient city, and here, just off to the right, is the little settlement of Yavniel. Let's take a walk. It's not far.

In the summer of 1933, the assassination of the Mapai leader Chaim Arlozorov on the shore of Tel Aviv had shaken the population and rekindled Nathan Mileikowsky's political passions. The Mapai leaders had claimed that it was a political murder and blamed the Revisionists.* The

---

*Mapai was the original name of Israel's Labor party. Around the time of Arlozorov's murder, in 1933, there was a political dispute between Mapai, the leading political movement in the country, and the Revisionists regarding the British mandate, which ruled Palestine until Israel's independence on May 15, 1948.

murder created considerable tension between the two parties. Being a good friend and devoted admirer of Ze'ev Jabotinsky, Nathan refused to believe that the murderer came from the right. Twenty-three-year-old Benzion shared his father's view. The issue had awakened Benzion's interest in politics and affinity for Jabotinsky.

Ze'ev Jabotinsky was one of the most important Zionist leaders of the 1930s and 1940s. A staunch political rival of Theodore Herzl, Jabotinsky later opposed Chaim Weizmann, chairman of the Jewish Agency and the first president of the State of Israel. Jabotinsky felt Weizmann was too compromising. Weizmann believed in establishing a governing council in Palestine in which Jews and Arabs would have equal representation. Jabotinsky would not hear of this. He called for a greater Israel, a state through which the River Jordan would flow, instead of that river constituting a border. It was Jabotinsky who formulated the principle of "two banks to the river [Jordan]," which served as the ideological premise for the political right wing in Israel, as represented by Herut and later the Likud.

In 1935, Nathan Mileikowsky died of typhoid and heart disease at age fifty-five. Following their father's death, Benzion and Elisha began academic careers. Their only sister, Miriam, turned to art, eventually becoming a famous sculptor. Brothers Sa'adia, Zachary, Matthew, Amos, Ezra, and Hovev took up careers in business, emigrating to the United States in the 1950s and setting up steel businesses. They anglicized their first names, changed their family name from Mileikowsky to Mylo, raised families, and became millionaires.

Nathan Mileikowsky's sons did not maintain close brotherly ties, and often did not get along. Politically, however, they were in harmony—they all inherited their father's fiery right-wing ideology. The oldest son, Benzion, was the most fervent in his beliefs. Under the influence of his father, Benzion had joined the Revisionist party in 1928 at the age of eighteen. He was a devoted admirer, student, and supporter of Ze'ev Jabotinsky, and would later become his idol's assistant in the United States.

In 1929, Benzion enrolled in the Hebrew University on Mount Scopus to study history, literature, and philosophy. It was the time of the Arab revolt, during which Jews were massacred at Safed and Hebron. Like his father before him, Benzion believed that only Jabotinsky's Zionist principles could protect the Jews in Palestine from further harm. Benzion believed in Jabotinsky's "two banks to the Jordan," and in the necessity of an armed struggle against the Arabs and the British mandate. The intellectual side of Benzion, however, preferred literary combat. He founded and was the first editor of *Jordan*, a Revisionist daily journal, in which he regularly attacked the "tepid" politics of Ben-Gurion and Chaim Weizmann, and recorded armed subversive activity. The British, in accordance with the military censor of the British mandatory government, issued occasional warrants forbidding the publication of *Jordan*.

It was during the 1930s that Benzion Netanyahu discovered his love for history and writing. He tried to establish a career as a researcher and lecturer in Jewish history at the Hebrew University of Jerusalem, but the academic community rejected him. He has always claimed that his rejection was politically based, but the university maintains that it was purely a matter of scholarship.

In 1939, disappointed by his failure to break into the academic establishment in Israel, Benzion packed up his worldly possessions and emigrated to the United States, where his mentor, Ze'ev Jabotinsky, had settled. He served as his assistant until Jabotinsky's death in 1940. The passing of the leader of the Revisionist movement was a hard blow for Benzion Netanyahu. It took him months to recover from losing the man who, in Benzion's estimation, had been the greatest Zionist leader in modern history.

When Benzion arrived in the United States, he knew only a few words of English, but he quickly became fluent. He remained in the United States for ten years and continued Jabotinsky's work, managing the Revisionist movement's offices in New York and spreading Jabotinsky's beliefs throughout the American Jewish community. In New York, Benzion met Cela Segal, a law student and the daughter of a distinguished farming family from Petah Tikva. Cela was married at the time to Noah Ben Tovim, but when she and Benzion met at a Revisionist meeting, a love affair began. Cela, also an enthusiastic Revisionist, continued the secret romance with Benzion for three years, until 1945, when they married in a New York synagogue.

In March of the following year their first son, Jonathan, was born. He was named after his grandfather and also for Col. John Peterson, a personal friend of Jabotinsky's. During the First World War, Peterson persuaded the British government to form the Jewish Brigades, which fought under his command alongside the British against the Turks.

Benzion and Cela's married life began in a small apartment in New York, where Benzion completed the doctoral thesis on the Spanish Inquisition which he had begun at The Hebrew University in Jerusalem. He wrote in longhand, and Cela, with little Jonathan lying in the crib beside her, typed up the thesis.

Cela had maintained close ties with Israel and pressed for the family's return. In November 1948 the Netanyahus moved to Israel, buying a house in Jerusalem's Talpiot neighborhood.

A month earlier, the Israel Defense Forces had conquered Beer Sheva and Menachem Begin, disciple and heir of Ze'ev Jabotinsky in the Revisionist movement, announced the formation of a new political party—Herut, which means "Liberty."

Begin viewed Benzion Netanyahu as an émigré who had turned his back on the struggle against the British and the Arabs. This was why, upon Benzion's return to Israel, Begin did not offer Jabotinsky's protégé a position in the party he had formed. Benzion soon discovered that although he was one of the outstanding spokesmen for Revisionist ideology, there was no place for him in the movement, not even on the Revisionist magazine. Thus began the animosity between Menachem Begin and Benzion Netanyahu. The circle would close forty-six years later with a confrontation between their sons: Benjamin Netanyahu defeated Benny Begin for leadership of the Likud, and Benny subsequently refused a post as minister of science in Netanyahu's government.

In October 1949, a second son was born to Cela and Benzion Netanyahu—Benjamin. Due to his father's political ostracism, Benjamin Netanyahu would be raised to perceive Menachem Begin as the enemy.

Benzion was convinced that David Ben-Gurion, Israel's first prime minister, was incapable of navigating the young state through the perils presented by its many enemies. Benzion's most urgent problem, however, involved not ideology but day-to-day survival: He could not find a job in academia. He blamed the establishment of Mapai, for being "out to get him."

The man who saved Benzion was Professor Yosef Klausner, a distinguished historian, friend of the Netanyahu family and admirer of the Mileikowskys. Klausner was appointed editor in chief of the Encyclopedia

Hebraica, and invited Benzion to be his deputy. Benzion accepted, and several years later became the encyclopedia's editor. In December 1957, leaders of the Labor Federation (Histadrut) complained to the publishers of the encyclopedia, the Peli family, that Benzion was belittling the role of the Labor movement in the founding of the Jewish state and the struggle against the British mandate, while overemphasizing the role of the Revisionist movement.

In 1962, after producing ten volumes of the encyclopedia, Benzion resigned as editor after a quarrel with his publishers.

While Benzion was contending with hostility from both the right and the left, his brother Elisha, a mathematician, was flourishing academically. Elisha had demonstrated mathematical talent as a child, but his father had discouraged it. Now, Elisha was studying at the Technion, a school of technology and engineering in Haifa that was among the most prestigious institutions of higher learning in the country.

During the Second World War, Elisha joined the British army and was responsible for mapping the bombing campaign that preceded the Allied invasion of Sicily. In Israel's war of independence he mapped operations in the Negev region and the south of the country. In 1946, Elisha was accepted as a lecturer at the Technion, and in 1958 he was appointed dean of the sciences faculty. He was an extremely popular lecturer with a great sense of humor. His students fondly recall how on the first day of class he would tell them, his tongue planted firmly in his cheek, that they were unable to add two and two and that he did not understand how they had managed to gain acceptance to such a distinguished institution.

During the next two semesters, he would educate them beyond their greatest expectations. He would test them on the first day of the third semester, and a few days later inform them that they were so good, he had nothing more to teach them.

Benzion could not understand why the kind of scholarly success his brother had achieved in Israel eluded him. In 1962, Benzion was finally welcomed into academia—in the United States. He received an offer from Cornell University to research the history of Spanish Jewry during the Inquisition. He accepted the job and moved his family to the United States once again.

The burden of bringing up the children had fallen on Cela. Jonathan, nicknamed Yoni, Benjamin, known as Bibi, and their little brother Iddo, who was born in 1952, were raised in an atmosphere of deference to their father's scholarly work, which was deemed more important than even the children's education. The thousands of books in their home, including rare volumes that had belonged to their grandfather Nathan, were an integral part of their childhood. Yoni, Bibi, and Iddo would in later years say that they did not remember seeing their father from the front much— his face seemed to be always in his books. The children tiptoed around the house so as not to disturb their father, and on many occasions they were slapped into silence by their mother.

The family remained in the United States for sixteen years. During this time, the oldest son, Yoni, returned to Israel to enlist in the army, volunteering for the paratroopers. In 1967 Bibi followed Yoni's lead.

On July 5, 1976, Benzion and Cela Netanyahu returned to Israel to attend the funeral of their oldest son, Yoni, who had been killed the day before in Entebbe, Uganda, while participating in the daring raid to release Israeli hostages skyjacked by Palestinian and German terrorists in an Air France jet. When the mourning period was over, Bibi's parents flew back to the United States. Two years later they would return to Israel for good.

In neither Yoni's letters, which were published by his two brothers after his death, nor in Bibi's books, is there any mention of the bitterness the Netanyahu boys felt toward their parents for living so far away from Israel. What is abundantly obvious from their writings, however, is the children's desperate need for a kind word from their father and their almost holy reverence for his academic work. In one of his letters, Yoni wrote that he hesitated to take his father's new book with him to the army for fear of damaging the pages.

By the time Benzion and Cela Netanyahu returned to Israel, Menachem Begin had risen to power after twenty-nine years of Mapai and socialist rule. Benzion became polarized to the extreme right-wing fringe, perhaps as a reaction to Begin, perhaps because of his advancing age.

In August 1978, Menachem Begin signed the Camp David accords, which created peace with Egypt and paved the way for Palestinian autonomy. Benzion Netanyahu was certain that Begin had made a huge mistake which endangered the very existence of the State of Israel. He published articles expressing opinions which were similar in their extremity to those of the radical right-wing party Tehiya (which has since disintegrated).

Though Benzion's ties with his brothers weakened over the years, Sa'adia, the historian and diarist of the Netanyahu family, was a mediating force among the brothers. Sa'adia, who to this day lives in an old house in Jerusalem's Katamon quarter, has researched the roots of the Mileikowsky-Netanyahu family, from their Lithuanian origins to the family's arrival in Israel. Sa'adia's politics are similar to his oldest brother's. He is an extreme right winger and a fervent devotee of Herzl, Jabotinsky, and Max Nordau, another of the founding fathers of modern Zionism. Sa'adia was one of Menachem Begin's staunchest opponents, both when Herut was the opposition party and after Begin was elected prime minister in 1977. In Sa'adia's view, Begin was an excellent underground leader, but as a politician he made too many grave mistakes. With all his heart, Sa'adia believed that Ze'ev Jabotinsky, the first Revisionist would have condemned Begin for the things he did had Jabotinsky been alive to see them.

Sa'adia and Zachary, his younger brother, were the first in the Netanyahu family to enter the steel business. In 1946, they formed a partnership with Aaron Rosenfeld, a Haifa businessman who represented foreign companies. Rosenfeld, one of the richest men in Palestine, gave Sa'adia and Zachary the funding to import four hundred tons of steel, and the two brothers sold the merchandise before it was even unloaded at the docks. After paying back Rosenfeld's loan, they had made a profit of 2,000 British pounds, a huge sum in those days.

The fourth brother, Matthew, tried to follow his brothers into the steel business, but found that the market was controlled by a few monopolistic companies which were closely connected to the British authorities and the Yishuv leadership. (Yishuv was the name given to the Jewish settlement in Palestine before the founding of the State of Israel.) Realizing that his opportunities in Israel were limited, Matthew emigrated to the United States. He started up a tin company and sent raw material to his two brothers in Israel, who sold it to companies that manufactured tin cans.

Matthew, Zachary, and Sa'adia had great success in the tin business, and the fifth brother, Amos, decided to join them. A world tin shortage made Matthew, Zachary, Sa'adia, and Amos rich men. In 1958, Amos and Zachary obtained the representation of the Maclaus Steel Works, one of the largest steel firms in the world. Maclaus sold vast quantities of steel, and their clientele included the governments of India and Pakistan.

At the beginning of the 1960s Amos and Matthew had a falling out, and the two brothers never spoke to each other again.

In January 1967, Sa'adia, who was the Israeli arm of the brothers' global enterprise, moved his operation to Edinburgh, Scotland, in order to expand the family's interests to Europe. Ezra, the seventh brother, entered the business at this time.

When the late Pinhas Sapir, former Israeli minister of finance, met Ezra Mileikowsky, he tried to persuade him to return to Israel: "You have all left the country," Sapir said. "Your father Nathan Mileikowsky must be turning in his grave."

"Times were hard in Israel," Ezra replied. "We left to beat the crisis."

While Bibi was a student in America, he grew close to his uncles Amos and Zachary, who often gave him pocket money. Bibi's first wedding took place at Zachary's home in a wealthy New York suburb.

Bibi makes a point of maintaining his relationships with his American uncles. During his first visit to the United States as prime minister, he visited Zachary, and invited his uncle to attend his speech to Congress. Zachary was proud of what he saw, as he said in a press interview: "On several occasions, they stood up and cheered Bibi. He tightened the ties with America. He explained to them how things were. We mustn't let Arafat have any land. Arafat talks about peace but then he tells his friends, 'We'll destroy them.'"

Hovev, another Netanyahu uncle, also a steel tycoon, has chosen to live in Puerto Rico for tax purposes. As a young man, he was a flight engineer in Ezer Weizmann's squadron. After graduating from the Technion he emigrated to America to start a business career. Hovev was also there to hear Bibi's speech to Congress. Afterward, he was quoted by an American newspaper as saying that if Bibi were to run for president of the United States against Bill Clinton or Bob Dole, Bibi would win.

Netanyahu knows the history of his family's steel dynasty. He stays in touch with all of his cousins. Though members of the family live all over the world, most reside in America. Some of Bibi's cousins are steel tycoons in their own right, some are famous lawyers and engineers, one is a successful advertiser and artist, one is a bestselling author, and one is a top gynecologist.

Given his family history, Bibi takes care not to condemn Israelis who emigrate. He has frequently challenged the late Yitzhak Rabin's definition of Israeli emigrants as "weakhearted dropouts."

3

The Boy From Rehavia

Benjamin Netanyahu was born in Tel Aviv's Assuta Hospital on October 23, 1949, eighteen months after Israel declared its independence. It had been a year since the Netanyahus returned to Israel after ten years in America and moved into an old Arab house in the Talpiot neighborhood of south Jerusalem.

When his brother was born, three-year-old Yoni was the happiest little boy in the world. His mother promised him that if he was good and didn't disturb his father, he would be allowed to play with the new baby.

Of his Talpiot childhood, Yoni wrote:

> I told you once that perhaps the most wonderful period of my life (that's how I remember it) was my childhood—when I lived in Talpiot and wandered through fields with anemones and turtles and ladybirds, with an ancient grove of woods and a tumbledown synagogue, with endless inner joy and with wide-open eyes.... We lived in a cool and airy single-story stone house, between pine trees on a slope known as Spirits Hill. My brother Bibi and I used to run up and down the slope and watch the IDF soldiers in Camp Allenby—a military base in the heart of Jerusalem. Bibi loved to peep through the fence at the soldiers and tease them, *"Halalim, halalim!"* [A childish play on words. The Hebrew word for soldier is *hayal*, plural, *hayalim*. The word *halalim* means "casualties."]

As young boys, Yoni and Bibi liked to spend time near the old synagogue next to the neighborhood's pine woods. They were fascinated by the worshipers in their prayer shawls. At home, their father explained the Jewish religion and the meaning of prayers to them.

Yoni's parents sent him to the gymnasium (elementary school) in the town's center. Unlike most of the schools in Jerusalem, this one was not under the influence of Mapai. Benzion preferred that his son travel long distances to get to school every day, rather than send him to a Mapai-affiliated school nearby.

When Benzion was appointed editor in chief of the Hebrew Encyclopedia in 1953, the family's financial situation improved considerably. They purchased a large house in the upscale Katamon neighborhood. The colonial-style house had been built by Armenian immigrants at the turn of the century. The handle on the front door had a bullet hole from the War of Independence, and this captured the imagination of the two brothers. Until the family left for America, the boys spent their childhood in the large backyard of their home, where they would climb a tall poplar tree and hide at the top so their mother could not find them.

Bibi attended the Hadarom Elementary School, which later had its name changed to Henrietta Szold, after the founder of Hadassah. He then attended Rehavia High School. Bibi was a serious boy, but he got along well with other children. He always looked older than his peers because of his large, broad build which he had inherited from his mother.

In those days before television, social activity was conducted outdoors. "We all lived within walking distance of each other," recalls one of the children who grew up in that neighborhood with Bibi. "We would come home from school, eat, and then go right out to play." All the children Bibi played with came from similar backgrounds. They were from "good" families—their fathers were academics, lawyers, physicians, most of them Mapai-affiliated. Netanyahu's close friend Uzi Beller was one of those who, in 1978, signed what was to become known as the officers' letter to Menachem Begin. In this letter officers of the IDF appealed to the prime minister to respond to the overtures being made by Israel's Arab neighbors and to take advantage of the chance to make peace. The Peace Now movement was formed in the wake of that letter. Thus, growing up in this environment Bibi became aware at an early age of a gulf in political opinion, and even as a child he was spouting the rhetoric he heard at home.

Most of Bibi's childhood friends have not changed their political affiliations. Shortly after Bibi was elected prime minister in 1996, Sara Netanyahu called her husband's old friends to find out for whom they had voted. When she heard that almost all of them had voted for Shimon Peres, she furiously replied, "Then you are no longer our friends," and slammed down the telephone. Bibi, calmer and more understanding, spent long hours trying to make amends and restore his old friendships.

Bibi's childhood friends included many who are now successful doctors, lawyers, businessmen, and media people. One of them is TV broadcaster Michael Carpin, Bibi's former scout leader. Carpin is four years older than Bibi, and he remembers him mostly as Yoni's brother. All the children remember Yoni—Bibi followed him everywhere, trying to keep up. "Yoni was always restless. He was forever doing something," one of Bibi's friends recalls. "He would come in for a few minutes, or meet us in the street. Often he would make fun of us. We were younger, so we understood it."

Iddo, the youngest brother, chose a completely different direction. Unlike his older brothers, he wasn't interested in sports. Although he let them drag him into scouts, he preferred to stay at home and play the piano. Of the three Netanyahu sons, Iddo was the only one to play a musical instrument.

Bibi, too, had an artistic bent. His friends and teachers remember his drawings. He had a good hand, but he was embarrassed by his work and avoided showing it to others. At a later stage in his life, he would study architecture at the Massachusetts Institute of Technology (MIT).

On Saturdays, Yoni and Bibi loved to wander among the cyclamens, poppies, and lilies in the Valley of the Cross. Yoni would take his younger brother on long walks away from home. Often, they would disappear for hours and worry their mother, who beat them roundly when they returned. In spite of their mother's threats of punishment if they went too far afield, the two once got as far as Kibbutz Ramat Rahel, very close to the Jordanian border, where they looked out with innocent wonder at the forbidden country. Once, when Yoni was ten and Bibi seven, Jordanian soldiers opened fire on a group of archaeologists on a tour of Ramat Rahel. Their mother heard about it, and for the first time discovered how far her sons would go on their secret walks, and she forbade them to return to Ramat Rahel. However, they would not obey.

Friends remember that the house at 12 Haportzim Street was different from their own homes. The six-room dwelling was forever in gloom, darkly carpeted, with heavy wood furniture and filled with books. It was a home where children were forbidden to run around.

The other youngsters in the neighborhood had no duties. Apart from a weekly music lesson, they were free to play as much as they liked. The Netanyahu children, on the other hand, had obligations, including chess practice and individual tutoring by their father, Benzion Netanyahu. Benzion mainly taught his sons history, but also Judaism. When friends came to visit, Bibi would warn them not to make any noise. One of them has never forgotten the day when Bibi failed to persuade his friends to talk in whispers: His mother slapped his face in front of them. The Netanyahu children were all involved in their father's work. Benzion Netanyahu was always at home, deep in his study.

Bibi's deep respect for his father has always been a part of him. Some years back, Bibi made an appointment with a publisher who was to issue *Self-Portrait of a Hero: The Letters of Jonathan Netanyahu*. Bibi and Iddo arrived early and sat waiting in the office of one of the editors. Before Bibi had a chance to say anything, the door opened and his father walked in. Bibi turned mute. He stood up and offered his seat to his father, and from that moment on, the editor recalls, he did not say a word. The only one who talked, decided, and concluded the conversation, was Benzion Netanyahu.

In 1958, when Yoni was eleven, and Bibi eight, the family moved to America so his father could assume the post of associate professor at a New York college. The family took up residence in a small hotel apartment on 86th Street in Manhattan. The sharp transition from the flower-filled fields of Jerusalem to the noisy streets of New York was especially hard on the two older boys. They were both sent to a grade school on the West Side, which was not as good as the one they had attended in Jerusalem.

While both boys suffered from the move, Yoni was inconsolable. He longed for his friends in Jerusalem and especially for the scouts. He decided to rebel by not speaking English. Bibi suffered less, but this period was hard for him too.

Busy with his research and academic lectures, their father was unaware of his sons' suffering. Their mother, always more attuned to the boys, felt their unhappiness. After a year, the family moved to a larger apartment in

Long Beach, on Long Island, where the greener surroundings brought some color back to Yoni's and Bibi's cheeks and restored some of their youthful energy.

Bibi was ten when the family returned to Jerusalem. He entered the fourth grade and spent the next three years as a straight-A student. On his final report card in 1962, his teacher wrote: "Diligent, active, and quick to understand. Polite, helps his parents and reads a lot, sociable, obedient, spirited, active, and disciplined."

Bibi grew into a serious youth with a political outlook different from that of his peers. He used to join in their talks in Jerusalem's city center, but when they wanted to play, he preferred to discuss the "two banks to the Jordan" principle. All his childhood friends remember that Bibi always wanted to talk politics. They were not interested. "It wasn't on our minds. Politics didn't interest us at all," said one of them.

The Netanyahu family had indeed come back to Jerusalem, but not for long. After three years, Benzion, unable to find his academic niche in Israel (and blaming Ben-Gurion and Mapai for his failure), decided to bring his family back to America. Cela informed the boys that they were returning to the United States because their father had been offered a job at Dropsie College, near Philadelphia, researching the history of Spanish Jewry during the Inquisition, heading the university's Semitic languages department, and editing the Encyclopedia Judaica. For someone who had never succeeded in fitting into the Israeli academic community or achieved tenure at Hebrew University, this was a tempting proposal indeed. Unlike their children, Benzion and Cela Netanyahu had never fully integrated into their Jerusalem neighborhood. They were a solitary, distant couple. When they left for America in 1962, most of their neighbors believed that this time the family was leaving Israel for good.

Yoni was sixteen and a half at the time, a leader in the scouts and an excellent student at school. Bibi was thirteen, and remembers how Yoni begged his parents to let him stay in Jerusalem with relatives, and how he would go to bed red-eyed. It was Benzion who—strangely enough—tended to agree with Yoni, but Cela insisted that he accompany the family to Philadelphia. Years later, Benzion would regretfully admit that he had been unaware of the depth of Yoni's suffering in America and the strength of his longing for Israel.

There was a small problem just before they left, however. In less than two years, Yoni was supposed to be drafted into the Israel Defense Forces and the army would not allow him to leave the country. Benzion Netanyahu appealed to his good friend Shimon Peres, promising that Yoni would be back at the age of eighteen, in time for the draft.

Bibi was an adolescent and Iddo found it hard to read and write Hebrew. Benzion, extremely proud of his sons, pushed them to academic excellence and kept them under a spartan regime.

At this time, the children were further exposed to their father's research work. Their mother, who had always demanded quiet in the home because their father was writing, created around him a sense of awe. Benzion's children perceived their father as one of the greatest men of letters in the Jewish world. From his family Benzion Netanyahu received the kind of recognition and respect he was never given by Israeli academe.

Yoni and Bibi, and later Iddo, also learned to loathe the Mapai establishment under Ben-Gurion, which, according to their beliefs, never allowed their father to take his rightful place of honor in Israeli academe. The fact that Benzion Netanyahu had been rejected by the Hebrew University for purely academic reasons, as well as personal incompatibility, did not prevent the myth from developing. Netanyahu never took the trouble to explain to his children why his good friend, Prof. Yosef Klausner, whose politics were similar to his own, reached a senior position at Hebrew University and in Israeli academe, despite his right-wing ideology.

The Netanyahu children were taught by their mother not to ask embarrassing questions, never to contradict their father's opinions, and to create for him a protected environment. The parents did not tell their children that one of the reasons they decided to return to America was that Benzion had had a falling out with the publisher of the Encyclopedia Hebraica. It was only on their arrival that they learned that their father had stopped working for the encyclopedia and would from now on be focusing on the Spanish Inquisition and the Jews of Spain. Yoni wrote to his friends in Jerusalem, expressing his distress:

> ...I feel I belong to a different world. I'm remote from them, and as time goes by, the distance doesn't diminish, but quite the reverse— it increases continually.
>
> There's not a moment here—even the most precious and beautiful one—that I wouldn't trade for my immediate return to Israel.

My friends in Israel, my social life there, and above all the land
itself—I miss very much.

Longing is difficult to describe. I always used to laugh at the
word; I always thought that you could forget, but I was wrong;
believe me you can't. To adapt oneself to a new life—yes, that's
possible; but to forget the old—that's impossible....

Two things can happen to an Israeli in America—either he
becomes a full-fledged American (something that, I'm sorry to say, I
have seen happen many times), or he becomes, in blood and spirit,
more of an Israeli than he has ever been. I'm waiting for the moment
I can go back—and begin to live again.

Yoni knew that he would be unable to persuade his parents to allow him
to go back to Israel on his own before it was time for his military service.
He told Bibi that on the very day after he graduated from high school, he
would be on his way to Jerusalem. Removed from his sons' feelings,
Benzion Netanyahu inadvertently brought them closer to their homeland
with his stories of the Jewish heroes in the land of Israel. The boys were
especially fascinated by the tale of the Maccabees, the heroic brothers
who led the Jewish revolt against the Greeks and restored the Temple of
Jerusalem.

After graduating with an A average in July 1964, Yoni lovingly embraced
Bibi and whispered to his brother that he would be waiting for him in
Israel. Yoni made him promise to write and flew back home to join the
army. He wrote to his parents and brothers how, on seeing "Israel from
the air, I felt a kind of pull at my heart. With all the bad things in the
country and God knows there are plenty, it is our country and I love it as I
have always loved it."

Bibi read every word of this letter and memorized it. Sometimes he
would place the letter next to his heart, his eyes full of tears. He missed
his older brother.

As a boy, Benjamin Netanyahu avoided mentioning the trauma caused
by his father's decision to emigrate to the United States. His closest
friends have no recollection of any heart-to-heart conversations with him.
None of them can remember any dramatic announcement of the
imminent journey. Bibi probably just mentioned it in passing without
making it an issue.

Bibi would not criticize his parents in front of anyone, whether a stranger or his closest friend. Many years later, he would use a single sentence to mention the trauma: "I remember that my brother and I walked the streets and wept."

But even his closest friends did not see his tears. While Bibi hid his feelings, he decided to act. He did not revolt against his parents' decision to uproot him from his friends and school, but he would do everything in his power to keep in close touch with them.

Throughout his adolescence, Bibi led a double life. In his American school, he was an ambitious, serious, diligent student. Socially, he did not fit in, nor did he make any effort to be part of the local scene. At the end of each school year, he would fly to Israel to spend the summer in Jerusalem with his friends.

At that time, the early 1960s, trips abroad were hardly routine, and only a few people traveled overseas. Young people hardly flew at all. Bibi flew alone, and he made his way to Jerusalem on his own.

Benzion and Cela Netanyahu were not generous and showed no sympathy toward Bibi when he pined for his Israeli friends. In order to finance his annual trips to Israel, Bibi worked all year in Philadelphia ice cream parlors and restaurants. All his summer vacations, including the expensive air fares, were financed solely by himself.

In Rehavia, he was remembered as a young man who arrived at the beginning of each summer and left at the end. During these three months he would do his utmost to make up for the lost time with his friends.

The first summer vacation was spent with his Aunt Shoshana in Tel Aviv, but he soon preferred to stay with the Beller family. Uzi Beller was a very close friend, and during Bibi's annual vacation they were inseparable. Bibi was very fond of the Bellers, and he had a special relationship with Assia, Uzi's mother. He also loved Uzi's father, Professor Uzi Beller. When the latter died in 1996, Bibi went to the funeral and wept openly, as if his own father had passed away.

When Benjamin Netanyahu returned to Jerusalem, he would pick up exactly where he had left off ten months before. He barely spoke of his life in America, nor did he bear any ostensible marks of American culture. He did not exchange sandals for sneakers. He made a point of not mentioning his long trans-Atlantic flights. He tried hard not to stick out—he wanted to remain one of the boys. The only gifts he brought were a Pete Seeger record for Uzi Beller and a T-shirt for Gabi Picker. In Jerusalem, he did

his best to downplay his knowledge of English. He did not show off his
linguistic advantage over his Israeli friends.

Though Bibi tried to disguise his American savvy, it nevertheless
revealed itself at times. When he and his friends went to see a Western at
the Smadar theater, all of his friends watched solemnly as Bibi rolled with
laughter, understanding all the jokes that the filmmakers neglected to
translate into Hebrew.

Bibi and his friends applied to a kibbutz for summer work camp in
1965, when Bibi was sixteen. During camp he was suffering from severe
pains in his knee. Uzi Beller's parents took him to the hospital for tests,
and the doctors recommended physical therapy until the knee healed.
Early each morning Bibi would get up with his friends and put in a day's
work harvesting tomatoes or potatoes. In the afternoon he would do his
knee exercises. Sometimes he did more than was recommended by the
doctor "so it'll get better sooner," he said. He never tried to use his injured
knee as an excuse for getting out of his work.

Bibi stood out as a hard worker. He was always the first one to begin
and the first to complete his quota. "Then he would go around making fun
of us for taking so long to get the work done," recalls one of his friends.
"He had an abnormal competitive urge. He even turned the work in the
fields into a contest. He always had to compete and win, in spite of the
pain in his knee."

Even as a teenager, Bibi talked about a free economy and preached
against socialism. He brought these views with him every summer from
America. His best friends found it hard to hold a conversation with him. He
never discussed or debated; instead, he would give a speech. Said one
friend, "He knew more than we did and he was better at expressing himself.
Anyone who didn't agree with him was automatically wrong. He would end
his speech by determining that we were all wrong and that was it."

Then, as now, Bibi always had to come out on top; he was a compulsive
winner. During much of his first summer back in Israel, in 1963, he and
his friends spent their time in the swimming pool at Moshav Shoresh in
the Jerusalem hills. It was one of the only swimming pools in the region.
"Let's see who can stay the longest underwater," Bibi challenged his
friends, who had no inclination to always be competing.

In the end they would give in and agree to some kind of swimming
competition. "Bibi always had to win," one friend said. "It wasn't always

very pleasant, because we were a close-knit group and there was no real competition among us. Bibi introduced this element into our group early on."

It was Uzi Beller who introduced Bibi to Micki Weissman, the woman who would become his first wife. It was in the summer of 1965 and they were both sixteen years old. Bibi was on summer vacation at Uzi's house when Uzi said, "I'd like to introduce you to the prettiest girl in the class, if not the whole school." From the moment they met, Bibi and Micki were inseparable. It was love at first sight, and distance and time could not overcome it.

Micki was an unrivaled star in a class at Rehavia High School that produced some of the most prominent members of Israeli society. In addition to her intellectual talents, Micki was tall and beautiful. Her nationalistic political views were similar to Bibi's. Each time summer drew to a close and the time came for Bibi to return to America, Micki would become depressed and withdraw from most of her social life. They corresponded obsessively and longed for the time when they would be reunited.

Both Bibi and Micki were extremely ambitious; both had plans for a brilliant future. Both loved challenges and would settle for nothing less than success. Bibi used to accompany Micki on scouts activities and the two could be seen, walking arm in arm, absorbed in a conversation that would last deep into the night.

For ten months of the year, Micki would wait patiently for Bibi's summer visit. She never went out with any of the other boys; she was a one-man woman.

Everyone knew that Micki belonged to Bibi, and vice versa. Micki became part of the group that included Gabi Picker, Uzi Beller, and the others. All summer, they would play in front of her parents' apartment.

Bibi discussed almost everything with Micki—the army, Zionism, politics, the wars which had taken place and those which were to come. There was only one thing he would not share with her—his life in his parents' home in America. Bibi kept his other life on the other side of the ocean to himself.

And Bibi was faithful to Micki. He did not date girls in America—they did not interest him.

Bibi and his friends made sure to keep a clear boundary between themselves and other youngsters, who remembered Bibi's group as being arrogant and aloof. The only time they mingled with other young people their age was when they went to town. Their favorite spot was Cafe Allenby.

One member of their group recalls: "Someone would come up with the idea of going to Cafe Allenby to look down at the locals. It was something to do. We didn't do it often, but if we'd go for an ice cream and run into a group of kids from one of the less successful neighborhoods, they'd say something and we'd say something, and it would often lead to a fight. Having Bibi along was always an advantage. He was big and broad and good at getting into fights."

Bibi was an independent young man. When he was in Jerusalem on his summer vacations, his friends' mothers would treat him as if he were older than their own sons. He and Uzi Beller used to travel together to Tel Aviv to stay with Bibi's aunt. They went to the sea and saw movies. Bibi knew his way about Tel Aviv. Uzi was a more passive companion.

At the end of the summer, it was always taken for granted that Bibi would pack his things and take a bus to the airport, alone, for another ten months of his "other life." He spent those months of each year in America, where the family lived in a two-story stone building with a garden. Bibi and Yoni went to high school in the Philadelphia suburb of Wyncote. Cela and Benzion Netanyahu did not send their sons to a Jewish school, preferring to educate them in an American fashion. Shortly after their arrival in America, the family was granted citizenship. Bibi relinquished his American citizenship only twenty years later, when he was appointed Israel's political attaché in Washington.

At Cheltenham High School, Yoni was remembered as sociable and a brilliant student: His picture hangs on the school's memorial plaque. Bibi, on the other hand, is remembered as having been more introverted and distant.

In class, Bibi always sat on the left side of the front row. His teachers and classmates called him Ben, while in Jerusalem everyone called him Bibi, yet another distinction between his lives in Jerusalem and Philadelphia.

Bibi had no social ties with other boys his age. Dan Selzer, a classmate, said in a newspaper interview that Bibi was never seen at the weekly class party. The only extracurricular activities he took part in were football and chess. Everyone who knew him was aware of his longing for Israel. He never stopped talking about the country, and the only people with whom he had social ties were members of the Zionist youth movement Hashomer Hatza'ir.

Hardly a day passed without Bibi sending or receiving a letter from Jerusalem, which kept him up to date on what was happening in Israel and the lives of his close circle of friends. Every letter he wrote ended with a request: "Write me everything." He corresponded more with Gabi Picker and less with Uzi Beller. After meeting Micki Weissman, he made a point of writing to her almost every day.

Bibi's high school teachers remember him as being an excellent student, not particularly involved in matters which concerned his contemporaries. It was the height of the Vietnam War, young American boys were contemplating the draft, and the peace movement was gaining strength. Bibi was far removed from it all. Unlike his classmates, his clothes were conventional and his hair was cut short. Still, despite his distance from the youth culture of the day, Bibi's Americanization continued. He had managed to get rid of his foreign accent, speaking like a born-and-bred American, and he even developed a love for American history.

Shortly before his 1965 trip to Israel, he got into a fight with a group of local Philadelphia youths. One of them made an anti-Semitic remark, and Bibi went for him. Bibi and some of his Jewish friends gave them a thorough beating. He wrote about the incident with pride to his brother in Israel.

"In my opinion," Yoni wrote in return, "there's nothing wrong with a good fist fight; on the contrary, if you're young and you're not seriously hurt, it won't do you real harm. Remember what I told you? He who delivers the first blow, wins."

It was not the last time Bibi would be involved in a street fight. Years later, when he was serving with the IDF's General Command Reconnaissance Unit, Bibi went with Yoni and some of friends to a movie in Jerusalem. There they were accosted by a group of local youths. Yoni and Bibi arranged to meet them after the movie. They rushed home, changed into their paratrooper boots, and, equipped with batons and chains, returned to meet the youths. They went home victorious, without so much as a scratch.

Bibi graduated from Cheltenham High fourth in his class. Graduation was planned for June 7, 1967, but Bibi was not present. In May 1967, Israel was in mortal danger. The Egyptian army had crossed the Suez Canal and advanced toward the Sinai Desert and the Israeli border. The Syrian army was positioned on the Golan Heights, ready to conquer the northern part of the country. The Egyptian leader, Gamal Abdul Nasser, closed off the Strait of Tiran, thus placing Israel under naval siege.

Bibi finished his exams and informed his parents that he was not going to take part in the graduation ceremony. He had decided to fly immediately to Israel to join his brother before war broke out. On June 2, he was on a plane, and the next day—one day before the Six Day War began—he met Yoni, now a reserve officer in the Eightieth Paratroops Battalion.

Yoni was twenty-one years old and recently released from compulsory national service, but in the last week of May he had been recalled to his reserve unit. The meeting between the two brothers was emotional, and Bibi never stopped worrying about Yoni.

And properly so. Yoni went through the entire war on the front lines. His first night was spent with the paratroops who landed behind the Egyptian lines and, under heavy fire, cleared out all the enemy strongholds.

The unit was then transferred to the Golan Heights, where, three hours before the cease-fire, Yoni led an attack on the Syrian stronghold of Jelabina. A round of machine-gun fire split open the throat of a soldier beside him, and Yoni reaching over to help, was hit by a bullet which splintered his elbow.

Bibi found his big brother in the orthopedic department of Safed Hospital. "See," Yoni told him, "I said we'd win." Bibi had spent the final days before the outbreak of war with his friends, filling sandbags and digging trenches in Jerusalem. A friend recalls:

Bibi was glad to have something to do. He felt he was making a contribution, even if only by filling sandbags. We spoke a lot about the army. We were all eager to enlist, wanted to do our bit. We planned to go together to Battalion Seven's reconnaissance unit... "I remember Bibi and Uzi Beller getting the shelter ready at Uzi's home. They cleaned it out, placed sandbags all around. When they were done, they spray-painted their names on the walls. To this day, the names are there—Uzi Beller and Bibi Netanyahu. "So they don't forget us," they said, without making specific mention of the danger.

Bibi spent the Six Day War in the shelter of Micki's home. They sat there together, holding hands, waiting for the all-clear siren. He wasn't in the United States for his high school graduation, but he had achieved his aim: He was among the top ten in his class.

Two months after the war, he was drafted into the Israeli army. He kissed Micki and made his way to the induction center.

4

Soldier Green

In August 1967 Moshe Dayan, the minister of defense, and Yitzhak Rabin, the chief of staff, were national heroes. Under their leadership, Israel had emerged as the victor in the Six Day War. There was now a feeling of euphoria as victory albums filled bookstores amid a new sense of political purpose. Bibi Netanyahu had his own private hero—his brother Yoni, the paratroops officer who had been seriously wounded.

Bibi and his good friend Uzi Beller decided it was time to volunteer for military service. They both hoped to join the Seventh Battalion Reconnaissance Unit. Yoni persuaded his brother to follow him and join the paratroops. Initially, nobody got what he wanted, as the Israel Defense Forces assigned Bibi to pilot training in the air force. Several weeks before he was drafted, having succeeded in all the stringent tests, he was called to join the most prestigious training group in the Israel Defense Forces.

Bibi and Uzi, who was also part of the group, were asked to take the exams on the same day. Both passed. Then they were informed that if they chose to join the air force, they would have to sign on for an additional two years of military service. Bibi turned to Beller. "Five years altogether? Three's enough for me. Five's too much." They stood up and left the room, and so ended their careers as IDF pilots.

The air force did not stand in Bibi and Uzi's way. Uzi got his wish and joined the Seventh Battalion, while Bibi decided to join the paratroops, as his older brother had originally advised. On his way through the induction center, Bibi was stopped by a tall sergeant in a red beret who introduced himself as Ori Frankel. Bibi was sure he had something to do with the paratroops' recruitment team.

"Would you like to volunteer for the paratroops?" asked the sergeant.

"Yes," Bibi replied, "it's my dream. My brother served there, too."

Frankel said, "Look, drop the paratroops. We've got something much more interesting, something secret and very prestigious." Frankel mentioned no names, but Bibi knew that he was talking about the General Command Reconnaissance Unit. He remembered hearing Yoni speak of "the unit."

Within an hour, Bibi was already being interviewed for admission. He entered a large tent under the shade of a eucalyptus tree, where he met Danny Yatom, who would later become head of the Mossad after Bibi was elected prime minister. Years later, Yatom would be involved in a botched attempt to murder a Hamas leader on a Jordan street and virtually disowned by his old "friend."

The bespectacled Yatom looked Bibi over. "Are you prepared to put in a lot of physical effort, to go without sleep for days on end?" Yatom asked.

"Piece of cake," Bibi said, "I'll do anything you say."

Yatom told Bibi that this was only a preliminary interview, and when he had finished with all of the other candidates, Bibi would know if he had been accepted.

Yoni turned up at the induction center in support of his younger brother. Bibi had been nervous and was looking forward to the weekend when he would receive Yoni's blessing for joining the prestigious unit. Bibi remembers:

> It was two months after being badly wounded in the war, and his arm was still in a cast. He arrived at the induction center dressed in jeans and an army shirt with his lieutenant stripes. It was so typical of him. He went into the place where the recruits were. One of the sergeant majors was giving us a hard time. Fresh recruits, only one day in the army. Today it seems trivial, but at the time it seemed quite bad. He was going after one of the boys and Yoni went up to him and just shouted at him. Showed him up in front of all the recruits. There was no more trouble from the sergeant.
>
> A few minutes later, I went out to meet him. We sat down together. Yoni asked me what I wanted to do. I told him I was

considering joining the General Command Reconnaissance Unit and asked him what he thought about it. Yoni didn't hesitate for a moment. "Go for it," he said. "It's the best thing in the IDF."

Bibi could not have been happier when he learned that he had been accepted into the unit. Another one of the few to be accepted was Doron Salzberg, a tall young man with smiling eyes from Kibbutz Einat. He had wanted to volunteer for pilot training but was disqualified because of imperfect eyesight. His next choice was the General Command Reconnaissance Unit, the secret elite unit of the IDF, which, in those days, comprised mostly people who came from a kibbutz, a communal settlement in which everything is shared, or a moshav, an agricultural settlement whose members sell their produce through communal channels but who live as private families. Today Salzberg is secretary of his kibbutz.

The first thing Doron saw on entering the unit's recruitment tent was a young man sitting in a corner, a stuffed kit bag at his side. At first sight, he looked different from the others.

Doron recalls: "I looked at him and noticed that he was engrossed in a book in English. I believe it was a thriller. He didn't introduce himself or try to join a conversation with the other recruits.

"After a few minutes, he finished reading and left the tent at a run. He came back later, dripping with sweat and started doing a series of push-ups and other exercises. We kibbutzniks, who knew each other from summer camps and our year's service after graduating from school, thought this was rather strange."

It was only after finishing his workout that the strange young man introduced himself. "Bibi Netanyahu, from Jerusalem." During the next few days, they learned that his parents lived in the United States.

Bibi told his new friends how he had wanted to volunteer for the paratroops, but the unit's sergeant had caused him to change his mind. They all laughed. It was exactly what had happened to them. They, too, were looking for the paratroops' recruitment tent and stumbled on the one for the General Command Reconnaissance Unit.

Their first week included meeting with the unit commander, Lt. Gen. Uzi Yairi. Tall and broad-shouldered, Yairi introduced himself but made no specific mention of the unit's name. He said: "You are joining the best unit in the IDF. You have been handpicked from among hundreds of candidates. I expect each of you to give his utmost. Those of you who make it through the course will not regret your decision. Your lives will be interesting, exciting, but hard. You are committed to complete secrecy. At home, with your girlfriends, you must never say a word about your training. Secrecy is the condition we all have to fulfill if we are to succeed."

The team officers, the first lieutenants, saluted. Then General Yairi left the tent, having made a strong impression on Netanyahu and the others.

The unit's volunteers underwent the same basic training as the recruits to the paratroops division. Bibi's company commander was Razi Barkai, today a well-known media personality. Barkai had volunteered for the paratroops after graduating from Haifa's military high school. He remembers Bibi as an excellent soldier in great physical condition. Although he was not particularly skilled with weapons, Bibi asked to be allowed to carry a machine gun, a hard job but one of the most prestigious among the paratroopers.

Bibi was one of the first to get up in the morning. While the others were still asleep, he would go jogging on his own, before the mandatory run, and would do rope climbing, which the group did every morning before breakfast. In sporting competitions, such as running and tug-of-war, he was one of the leaders. He loved field training, camouflage, creeping up on targets, and overcoming unexpected obstacles. Bibi did everything while carrying the heavy machine-gun ammunition on his shoulders.

Like his older brother, he, too, wrote letters to his parents in America, telling them about his experiences in basic training. But his letters lacked the poetry, the soul, the sensitivity, and sometimes even the pain which filled Yoni's letters. And, unlike his brother, Bibi did not like writing, so his parents received fewer letters from him.

Yoni's shadow followed Bibi in everything he did. When the time came for him to take a course in parachuting, Bibi asked to be the first in line, remembering Yoni's stories of how much fun it was to be the first to jump out of the plane. Following his first jump, he wrote to his parents and his younger brother, Iddo, that "the first jump had not been frightening, the second was worse."

On a wet and stormy day in November 1967, a red beret on his head and paratrooper's wings on his chest, Netanyahu arrived at the railway station in Haifa to begin his stint as a fighter in the unit. In Haifa, the soldiers met their team commanders, Amiram Levin and Rafi Bar-Lev, for the first time. Bibi and Doron Salzberg were in Amiram's team. As the young soldiers were looking around for the trucks which would take them to their base, they heard Amiram Levin say, "We're walking to the base."

None of them will ever forget that stormy day. Notwithstanding the pouring rain, Levin turned back and started to lead his men southward along the coast. It was a seventy-five-mile march from the railway station in Haifa to their base in the center of the country. Levin, in the lead, took long, quick steps in the hard-to-maneuver sand. Bibi marched close behind. Physical effort meant nothing to him, and soon the two teams were competing: Who would make it to their base first, Levin or Bar-Lev? It was important to Bibi for his team to be first and not have anyone collapse along the way.

Rafi Bar-Lev's team got some relief when their commander sprained an ankle in the middle of the march. He tried to go on but was obliged to drop out. Before being taken away, he asked Haim Ben-Yonah, one of the trainees, to replace him. With assurance, Ben-Yona took over.

At the end of the twenty-hour trek, Amiram Levin was first to march through the gates of the unit's base. The soldiers were dreaming of cups of steaming coffee and a warm bed, but Amiram had other plans for them. He led his team toward the training apparatus and ordered them to follow him up the ropes and through the other obstacles. Afterward, they dragged themselves, thoroughly exhausted, into the dining room.

Following a few hours of sleep, Bibi was informed that he would be sharing a tent with Doron Salzberg. Both men were pleased. "Bibi and I had become very close," Doron relates. "We shared the same scout tent, ate from the same mess tin, drank from the same mug. It was soon clear to me that I could trust him under the most difficult circumstances."

There was another reason for their new friendship. "We were both about the same height, with broad shoulders. We became partners in stretcher bearing, always at the end, pushing, encouraging the others."

Stretcher marches are the hardest exercises in the choice units. In the General Command Reconnaissance Unit, such marches were held over long stretches of land under harsh conditions in order to train young fighters for the possibility that they would have to retrieve wounded comrades from behind enemy lines.

"Bibi was terrific at the stretcher marches," Doron recalls, "When it became time to change places, he would say, 'Not yet,' that we could go on some more. Sometimes I would ask myself how this guy from Jerusalem, who grew up in America, got to be in such good physical shape. It sometimes seemed that he wanted to test himself to the limit of human endurance, probably to reach the same level as his brother Yoni, whom he considered the all-time greatest fighter in the paratroops division, if not in the world."

In this type of march, it is customary for one of the soldiers to climb up on the stretcher and play the part of the wounded. Not Bibi. It was the one instance when he refused an order; Bibi was not prepared to be wounded. This would have been humiliating. Doron recalls, "He was incredibly motivated to be first in everything, like when we had to run with weapons and all our kit on our backs and on routes which became steadily longer and harder like those in the Negev and the Arava."

On this team, he carried the machine gun. His weapon was always clean, shining, and oiled. At the commanding officer's parade, Bibi was always being praised.

Bibi's competitor for first place on the team was Abraham Feder, from Haifa, later a senior officer in the Israel Police. The competition was fiercest during the twenty-four-mile-long night patrols, when the soldiers carried no maps or navigational guides to help them, and had only the North Star and the constellations to go by. Doron said:

> Before these excursions, Bibi would pore over the maps and learn the region by heart, registering in his mind any special sites. I was always surprised at his determination to complete the course first. Sometimes, after hours of walking, I would say to him, "Bibi, let's stop for a while, take a rest." He would look at me and say; "Doron, if we stop now, Feder will get there first." Other times, he would say, "Let's go on just a little more and then stop." But I knew that the "rest" would come only at the point of arrival. His greatest pleasure was to arrive first and to wait for Feder by the water fountain, with a "hi, I did it again," smile on his face.

In June 1967, in the aftermath of the Six Day War, Moshe Dayan offered the Arab leaders territories for peace. No one, including King Hussein of Jordan, picked up the phone to respond to Dayan's initiative. It was a time of relative political quiet in Israel, when the mood was still euphoric, and there was little to disagree about. Consequently, Netanyahu's teammates knew very little of his political opinions.

Nor did Bibi talk a lot about his family. The others knew that his parents lived in America and that his father lectured in Jewish studies at an American university. They knew everything about Yoni, as if he were one of the team. Later, when Yoni joined the unit, they would discover that Yoni was really something special.

The quiet along the borders did not last long. Terrorists crossed the Jordan on their way to carry out their murderous acts, and the IDF reacted by pursuing them, sometimes losing the finest of its officers. Things were heating up, and the unit knew that it was only a matter of time before they were called into action.

Their chance came on March 21, 1968, a day after a busload of Israeli youth drove over a mine near Be'er Ora in the Arava. The Israel Defense Forces then decided to act against the Palestine Liberation Organization (PLO) strongholds in the Jordanian town of Karameh.

Israeli paratroopers and armored units crossed the border into Jordan. The IDF assumed the Jordanian army would not interfere in the operation, a mistaken assumption that cost many precious lives. Jordanian armored forces took up positions on the Moav hills and opened fire on the advancing Israeli force. IDF tanks were hit, and the paratroopers who rushed in to rescue the tank teams were trapped in the open. The General Command Reconnaissance Unit was called in for a rescue operation, with the unit's young soldiers being sent to rescue the injured tank teams.

This was Bibi Netanyahu's "baptism by fire." At the end of a long day's battle, the IDF counted twenty-eight dead and three missing, and the four tanks which remained in the field were later displayed in a victory parade in Amman, the Jordanian capital.

The Jordanian army and the PLO had more than one hundred dead. The PLO headquarters in Karameh was blown up by an IDF demolition squad, commanded by the young lieutenant Yitzhak Mordechai, currently Israel's minister of defense in Netanyahu's government.

A myth grew around the Karameh operation that Bibi Netanyahu's team had been called in with the express purpose of apprehending PLO leader Yasser Arafat, who was known by the military code name of Abu Amar. In truth, there was indeed a unit assigned the task of capturing

Arafat, but it was not Bibi's team. Rather, a paratroops reconnaissance unit under the command of Capt. Matinee Vilna, was given the Arafat mission. The plan intended for the reconnaissance troops to parachute behind the PLO base in Karameh and to set an ambush for Arafat. However, stormy weather prevented the helicopters from landing in time, and Arafat managed to get away on a motorbike, dressed as a woman.

Before Bibi's team could become operational around the Suez Canal, they still had to complete their course of combat training, navigation, survival treks with no water, exercises under fire, and reconnaissance expeditions in jeeps. Bibi completed the arduous course "with greatest praise." Within the unit, he was often mentioned as a candidate for officers training, but he was undecided. In talks with his superiors, he proposed a candidate better than himself—his brother Yoni.

In his book *Yoni's Last Battle*, Iddo Netanyahu, the youngest brother, reveals that his oldest brother's return to the regular army, where he volunteered for the post of commander of the training platoon in the General Command Reconnaissance Unit, had been Yoni's idea, not Bibi's. Iddo describes overhearing his brothers during one of his vacations in Jerusalem:

> I find Yoni and Bibi sitting on the bed. Yoni is a student of mathematics and philosophy at Hebrew University, following a year at Harvard. There is something of a conspiratorial air in the way they suddenly turn their heads toward the door. When I start investigating the matter, Yoni tells me that he is considering returning to the army, to Bibi's unit, and makes me swear to keep it to myself.
>
> "Tell him [Uzi Yairi, the commander of the General Command Reconnaissance Unit] to take a look at my service record." Yoni goes on talking with Bibi, "I reckon that if he does that, there's a good chance he'll agree to accept me."
>
> "Chance? When Uzi sees your record, he'll grab at you immediately," says Bibi. "That's the trouble," he adds, and there is no joy in Bibi's voice.
>
> Yoni is encouraged by what he has heard, as if he hadn't heard the tone of his brother's voice. "Tell him if he needs an officer and you're refusing to go for officer training. I'll go instead of you."
>
> "I'm not sure you know exactly what you're getting yourself into," says Bibi. "You'll be older than all the other officers, who'll have

parallel jobs to yours. It's not a job for a married man. You'll hardly ever be at home."

"Bibi, I know what I want and what I'm letting myself in for. Tell him [Uzi Yairi] everything I've just said and don't forget my service record."

Bibi is adamant: "Go back to the army, if that's what you want, but to something higher. It doesn't suit you, your age, your experience—this job of team commander."

Yoni warned Bibi and Iddo not to tell anyone about his plans, "Not even to Tutti [his wife]. I'll tell her myself, when I have made up my mind. In the meantime, there's no point in talking to her."

Bibi had known for several weeks that his brother was planning to leave the university and return to the army. The question was not whether he would return, but when and where. Yoni was also quick to share his ideas with his parents in America. He was concerned about the situation on the borders. He believed the atmosphere was similar to that before the Six Day War. Yoni wrote his parents in the United States:

It won't be a war that we'll begin. but one that the Arabs will....

In the light of all this it's not surprising that I find civilian life almost intolerable....It's hard for me to bear the thought that I'm alive thanks to others who protect me with their own bodies while I'm left to play the role, so to speak, of the civilian....

My main problem about going back to the army is not leaving school, but leaving home. I find it difficult to part from Tutti so frequently and for such long periods; but again—I don't plan to do so on a permanent basis.

At the end of 1968, Bibi's team was given the opportunity to take part in one of the more famous IDF actions. The team had almost completed its training when Israel found itself having to face a new kind of threat, terrorism in the air.

On December 26, two Palestinian terrorists attacked an El Al plane on its way from Tel Aviv to Paris while it was making a stopover in Athens. Five months before, terrorists had succeeded in taking control of an El Al airliner in midair and skyjacking it to Algiers. Israel decided to respond.

On Friday, one day after the Athens attack, all leave was canceled in Bibi's unit. On Saturday, the young soldiers, together with veterans, were called for a briefing. The destination: the international airport in Beirut, Lebanon. The objective: an attack on aircraft belonging to Arab airlines in retaliation for the attacks on El Al airplanes.

On Saturday evening, December 28, 1968, the helicopters crossed the coast north of Rosh Hanikra and flew at a low altitude over the sea, skirting the land border between Israel and Lebanon. North of Sidon, the helicopters cut toward Beirut's international airport, which at that moment was busy handling a large number of arrivals and departures of foreign aircraft.

The young General Command Reconnaissance Unit troops, with red berets on their heads and in full fighting gear, prepared for landing. Helicopters carried additional members of the unit's teams as well as paratroopers. The operation was commanded by Col. Raphael Eitan.

Bibi's helicopter landed in an open area, about one kilometer from the Beirut airport runways. The troops made their way quickly toward the airport installations while various aircraft were landing and taking off over their heads.

One of the helicopters landed on the highway connecting Beirut and the airport. The remaining troops spread out among the aircraft on the parking strip. Most of the planes belonged to Lebanese Middle East Airlines, while others belonged to other Arab carriers and some to international companies. The orders were clear: to attack only Arab aircraft. The forces made sure that there were no passengers or flight crews onboard the planes to be destroyed.

It took about a half hour to destroy fourteen planes. In accordance with the plan, each aircraft was blown up separately. Bibi and his young colleagues were involved in blowing up one plane belonging to Middle East Airlines. To Bibi, the operation seemed like something out of a James Bond movie: paratroopers in red berets, without helmets, darting in and out of the aircraft, placing bombs and making a quick getaway before they exploded. Then another force took over the terminal. Not one of the thousands of passengers present was hurt. Colonel Eitan walked around the terminal, giving instructions and ordering his men to withdraw as soon as the operation was completed.

All the Israeli soldiers returned home safely. Not one was wounded.

5

Ambush at the Suez Canal

The escalation in the war of attrition taking place along the Suez Canal caused an alteration in the training program of the young teams. A decision was made to send the young troops to the canal to carry out mainly commando operations on its western, or Egyptian, side.

Shortly before departure, the two teams—Amiram Levin's and Rafi Bar-Lev's—took part in various exercises to prepare them for their new posting. During one of the exercises, a shell exploded as it was leaving the cannon, mortally wounding Zohar Linik and David Ben-Hamo, both of them members of Rafi Bar-Lev's team. Bibi was with a second group of soldiers when the shell exploded. He and Doran Salzberg were among the first to reach the wounded men and offer assistance. The medic used a tourniquet in an attempt to stop the bleeding, but it was no use. Bibi and Amiram Levin carried the two wounded men to a nearby command car, and Levin drove them to the hospital. Ben-Hamo's condition was critical. Linik was fully conscious and crying out in pain. "I can't feel my arm," he said to Bibi, who was sitting beside him in the command car. Bibi told Amiram Levin to hurry up, and in a little while they were at Tel Hashomer Hospital.

While Bibi and Levin were still waiting at the entrance to the emergency room, the doctor in charge came out and told them that the two men had died. Shock had overwhelmed them. This was the team's first encounter with death.

After the funerals the following day, Uzi Yairi gathered his men around him and ordered them to renew their combat training immediately and to return to doing the routine as soon as possible. "We have experienced a terrible tragedy," Yairi said to the young fighters, "but, unfortunately, these things happen in combat units. We shall always remember the friends we lost, but life must go on."

Bibi, who was deeply affected by the tragedy, wrote about it to his brother Yoni, who replied: "It is truly terrible to lose a good friend. Throughout my army service, I had only one really good friend and he was injured during basic training. Life goes on. Nothing changes. You forget, yet always remember."

Bibi's real baptism by fire took place on May 11, 1969, the night the young members of the reconnaissance unit crossed the Suez Canal in rubber boats and laid an ambush for an Egyptian military truck.

The unit's attack came in response to the traps that Egyptians had laid for Israeli patrols, and their attacks on commando units in Israeli strongholds along the Bar-Lev Line, a defensive line along the Suez Canal. The IDF was concerned about the Egyptian successes, and the Southern Command wanted to respond in kind. The General Command Reconnaissance Unit, along with the paratroops unit, was sent to carry out special operations in the canal region. The paratroops laid ambushes in regions vulnerable to Egyptian invasion, while the General Command Unit and the Shacked (which in Hebrew means "almonds"), or Southern Elite Reconnaissance Unit, carried out activity on the west bank of the canal.

On that May 11th night, the reconnaissance unit's holding force, of which Bibi was a member, opened fire on the Egyptian truck at close range. The truck went up in flames. The unit's safe retreat to the canal's eastern bank was lit with Egyptian star shells.

Two days later, on May 13, when they were a short distance from the canal, the two young teams comprising the reconnaissance unit were called by their commanding officers for a briefing. Shortly before, the unit's commander had been replaced by Lt. Col. Menachem Digli. The team commanders were briefed on a planned ambush of Egyptian commando forces west of the canal.

Bibi prepared a special sling on which he laid four boxes of ammunition for his machine gun. He arranged the straps of his ammunition belt to keep them from pressing on his shoulders or making any noise when he was walking quickly. He was ready for action. However, while taking a shower at the army base in Baluza, about ten miles east of the canal, Bibi said to Doron Salzberg, "I'm uneasy about this. I have a bad feeling which I can't explain."

Amiram Levin commanded the operation, known as Bulmus (mania) 13. Forces from the General Command Reconnaissance Unit took part, along with naval commando units that would be responsible for crossing the canal. Levin divided the force into three and assigned each group to rubber boats. Amos Danieli, Uri Gilboa, Amatzia Ben-Chaim, and Haim Ben-Yonah were in the first boat. Haim Ben-Yonah had recently returned to the unit after having completed officer training. The second boat contained Bibi, Doron Salzberg, Moni Oren, and naval commando Israel Assaf. The third boat was taken by Amiram Levin, Avraham Feder, and two sailors from the naval commandos.

As darkness fell, the force set off in the direction of the canal. They left the truck several kilometers from the bank and moved westward, led by Amiram Levin. The men from the naval commandos awaited them at the bank. Doron Salzberg recalls: "We were spotted shortly after we left the east bank of the canal. The sky was lit up as if it was day, and the star shells revealed the boats in the water. The Egyptians opened up heavy fire on our rubber boats, which were several dozen meters away from the Egyptian bank. We were completely taken by surprise. We were in a trap, like sitting ducks."

Paratroopers covering the team opened fire on the Egyptians. Meanwhile, the Egyptians kept shooting at the boats in the water. Bullets whistled back and forth across the canal. Doron further recalls: "The fire from our own holding force frightened us as much as it scared the Egyptians. The whistling of bullets seemed to be getting closer and closer. We pressed up against the sides of the boat. In spite of the noise, I was able to differentiate between the Egyptian fire and our own, the fire criss-crossing [above us]. The first boat to be hit was the first one in the row."

Haim Ben-Yonah, commander of the first boat, was hit in the head by a bullet and fell into the water. He had been sitting in the boat next to Amos Danieli, who recalls, "It happened in a split second. Ben-Yonah was hit and he disappeared from sight. The boat continued to be under heavy fire. Someone called out 'Jump into the water, quick.'"

Amatzia Ben-Chaim, who was also in the first boat, succeeded in changing its direction and pointing it eastward. Then Bibi's rubber boat was punctured by a burst of Egyptian fire. Moni Oren shouted, "Jump into the water!" Bibi tried to remove his heavy ammunition sling, but there was no time. He jumped in and started sinking immediately. All his efforts to pull himself up were useless. Air rushed from his lungs. Israel Assaf, a naval commando, noticed him sinking. Before being hit, the boat had held three General Command Unit troops. Two were now swimming alongside the boat. He could not see the third. Assaf says: "I could see circles of foam on the water. I realized that someone had dived in and was unable to swim back up. The Egyptian fire increased and bullets were whistling overhead. I jumped over into the prow of the boat, which continued to lose air. I bent over into the water and held out my arm toward the place where I had seen the foam circles. I touched a human head. I grabbed it with all my might and pulled it up.

"There was no chance of his coming up on his own. The heavy equipment on his back was dragging him down. With my last remaining strength, I pulled his head up, above the surface of the water, so he could breathe. I released him from his sling and backpack. I tried to inflate his lifebelt, but had no success. It must have been damaged by Egyptian fire."

Bibi had no strength left. He was barely able to hold his head above the water. Doron Salzberg, who was also in the water, swam up to him and held him to keep him from drowning.

Assaf called to the General Command soldiers in the water to swim eastward, to the Israeli side. With a final effort, he managed to hold the boat—which was almost empty of air—above water. He shouted over to Bibi, "Hold fast to the boat. Don't let go. Don't give in. We'll be with you soon."

Bibi held on with his remaining strength while he was dragged along behind the boat. Doron Salzberg swam alongside him and made sure he was not pulled underwater. Bibi felt that he was on the verge of blacking out and about to drown.

Amos Danieli and Amatzia Ben-Chaim were the first to swim to the Israeli side. They noticed the shadow of Bibi's boat making its way slowly toward them. Danieli jumped back in the water and pulled the boat toward the shore. "I could see Bibi hanging on to the boat for dear life. Suddenly he disappeared. I grabbed hold of his head and pulled him to shore."

Bibi sat on the muddy ground and felt his lungs gradually filling with air. He could make out Danieli and Salzberg beside him and, reflecting back on those terrible moments in the water, he concluded that he owed them his life. Only years later, when the story was published in the press, did Bibi learn that the hero who had saved his life was Israel Assaf, one of the naval commandos. A few minutes after Bibi reached the shore, an Egyptian shell exploded close to where the General Command men were lying. Bibi stayed there on the sand. He did not have the strength to move. He was too weak to even thank the men who had saved his life.

The fire went on throughout the night. The naval commandos swam the dank waters of the canal, trying to find Haim Ben-Yonah's body. They were unsuccessful. The search continued for several days and nights, but to no avail. A few weeks later, the Egyptians found the body near Port Said, about ten miles north of the spot where he had been shot and killed. They returned the body to Israel under the auspices of the United Nations.

In his book A *Place Among the Nations,* Netanyahu describes the events of those few days:

It was at the end of a long row of cypress trees at Kibbutz Yehiam in the western Galilee, Haim's home, that he was buried. It was there also that I met Haim's mother Shulamit and discovered that Haim had been born shortly after she and his father had been freed from the death camps of Europe. Had he been born two years earlier, this daring young officer would have been tossed into the ovens, one of the million nameless Jewish babies who met their end in this way. Haim's mother told me that while she felt a great deal of pain, she felt no bitterness. At least, she said, her son had died wearing the uniform of a Jewish soldier defending his people.

I was nineteen years old then, and these words had a profound effect on me. I found myself thinking again and again about the possibility that Haim might not have lived even the short life that he did live. Or, eerily, that he might have outlived the war, but in a world in which Israel had not come into being. Would Haim have come out the same way in another land—a Hungarian-speaking version of the same dauntless Israeli youth, sure of his place in the world, possessed of the same inner calm?

Only after Ben-Yonah's death did Bibi realize how much he missed him. For Bibi, Haim Ben-Yonah was the ideal of an Israeli soldier and officer, the kind of person he himself would have wanted to emulate.

Haim Ben-Yonah had natural leadership qualities. The fact that he had been the first to enter officer training strengthened Bibi's respect for the dead soldier. Bibi and the rest of the team had been offended by the fact that Ben-Yonah had somewhat distanced himself from his peers when he returned to the unit from his officer training course. In time he was able to understand that Ben-Yonah wanted to take a competitive stance with the other officers, and to do this he had to put some distance between himself and them.

There was a pall over the unit after Ben-Yonah's death; he was the first of them to die in action. Over the years, several others fell, but Haim Ben-Yonah was one of the hardest losses.

There was a special sense of loss in Rafi Bar-Lev's team, which included Bibi. Haim Ben-Yonah had been their third overall casualty, and fate continued to attack this team in the years to come. Of the ten original members to start out in August 1967, six were killed: Rafi Bar-Lev, nephew of Chief of Staff Chaim Bar-Lev, died in the 1973 Yom Kippur War when his tank took a direct hit from an Egyptian missile. Amos Ben-Horin was also killed in that war. Amatzia Ben-Chaim, who had taken part in much of the General Command Reconnaissance Unit's activity, was murdered in 1993 in a terrorist attack. These deaths were in addition to those of Ben-Yonah, Ben-Hamo, and Linik.

But life in the unit had to go on. The teams' commanders believed it was essential that their men return to their special training and combat operations. Lengthy navigation exercises under the worst possible conditions were a sure recipe for getting back to a normal state of readiness.

One such exercise took place in the Negev desert in the middle of a *hamsin* (an Arabic word that describes the season, approximately fifty days each year, in which a dry, extremely hot, easterly wind makes the region almost impossible to live in). After several hours of trekking, the team ran out of water. Bibi, Eitan Ziv, and Avraham Feder were in the same group. At one point they met up with the team commander, Amiram Levin, who was semidehydrated and on the verge of passing out. The three gave Amiram their remaining water and went on without a drop among them. Many years later, at a meeting of the unit's veterans, Avraham Feder recalled how they would have given everything they had in the world in return for one canteen of water. Toward the end of the day, the three came across a command car belonging to another team, pulling behind it a container full of water. Feder and Ziv ran toward it with the aim of filling their canteens. Behind them, they heard Bibi calling, "It's not our water. It belongs to the other team. We mustn't drink their water."

Ziv and Feder stopped in their tracks, then went back to Bibi. It took some persuasion for Bibi to agree to fill his canteen and drink the other team's water.

During his combat training, a special relationship formed between Bibi and his team commander, Amiram Levin.* Bibi liked the determined character of his commander, a *kibbutznik* from Lehavot Habashan. Amiram, rather introverted, liked Bibi's own determination and his desire to learn everything quickly.

Unlike the other soldiers in the unit, Bibi was devoid of any natural talent for navigation. Late into the night, long after the others had gone to sleep, Amiram and the Bibi would sit poring over maps, using a classroom ruler to measure out azimuth directions. Amiram explained and Bibi quickly understood. He would memorize certain points on the map and navigate from point to point until he reached the destination.

Bibi never ceased to wonder at the navigational skills of Doron Salzberg and the other kibbutzniks on the team. They could walk about in the darkest of nights as if they were on a daytime outing. After a few months, however, he no longer felt inferior to them. As Bibi said: "During one exercise in the Negev, in which the entire unit took part, we were charging along, covered in dust and sand. I was in the last half-track in the row and Ehud Barak and Yoni were navigating in the first half-track. I had great respect for the two of them, being the unit's commander and his deputy. But they were getting lost. Then, First Lieutenant Bibi Netanyahu came on the line and told them, 'Gentlemen, you have missed the point.' They admitted their mistake, turned the entire convoy back, and we turned on our tracks. For anyone who had any doubt, this was proof that, as far as navigational talents go, I had no problems." Probably because of Amiram,

---

*In the years to come, Bibi would keep in close touch with Levin. In March 1998, Prime Minister Netanyahu appointed Amiram Levin, then commander of the northern front, the head of the Mossad, Israel's intelligence agency.

Bibi discovered a passion for field trips. He loved the navigation treks, which brought him close to parts of the country with which he had been unfamiliar. In his book *A Place Among the Nations*, he writes:

> When I was in the army, we used to hike the distance "from sea to sea" in a day's march. We'd fill up a canteen with sea water from the Mediterranean at five in the morning and empty it in to the Sea of Galilee at five in the evening—twelve hours to cross the country on foot from west to east. This one-day trek crosses Israel in its *present* width. Its previous width lent itself to a brisk run...

Throughout his military service, Bibi never got used to the scruffy way his kibbutznik counterparts dressed; he was always neatly groomed. Even his fatigues were always tidy, while the kibbutzniks looked as if they had just come back from a stint in the barn. His speech was different from theirs, too. Bibi's language was genteel, and he used American expressions. They had no reservations about using vulgar Sabra expressions which were foreign to him.

Bibi had no mechanical ability. The kibbutzniks, who had grown up around tractors in the kibbutz garage or toolshed, enjoyed laughing at his expense. On one of their treks, the team arrived at an orange grove. Bibi unsuccessfully tried to turn on a water tap. One of the soldiers, Arik Tal, who did not recognize him from behind, asked, "Who's that asshole who can't open a faucet?"

Bibi turned and responded quietly: "If you know how to turn on the tap, then by all means do so."

Only after many months in the difficult training course did Bibi's new friends learn of his right-wing ideology and his admiration for Jabotinsky. As far as they were concerned, the country's right was led by Menachem Begin. In those days, the late 1960s, there was no debate over the return of territories or the expansion of settlements. The stormiest arguments concerned the Vietnam War, and Bibi vigorously supported America's intervention in Southeast Asia. Even then, he considered communism tantamount to cancer, which has to be fought before it spreads.

Amos Danieli recalls how one day, after an exhausting combat operation, each member of the team tried to find a tiny corner of their transport truck where they could fall asleep. But not Bibi. He looked for someone to join him in a discussion of world security and the dangers of communism to the free world. He always managed to find someone who would listen to his political theories.

In March 1969, Yoni Netanyahu returned to the army and was appointed commander of the unit's younger platoon. Some months later, Bibi agreed to embark on an officer training course, but not before extracting a promise that, no matter what, he would return to the unit afterward and be appointed team commander.

From his first day at officer training, Bibi was considered an excellent cadet. Although he did not mention it, he felt he had to complete the course summa cum laude, just like his brother Yoni, who had done so several years before. He was presented his Commander's Pin by Yitzhak Rabin, the chief of staff of the Six Day War.

Twenty-six years later, as head of the opposition in Israel, Bibi would lead a vehement and vicious campaign against Prime Minister Rabin, a campaign that would exacerbate political hostilities and create an atmosphere that, arguably, would be partly responsible for the assassination of his former commander.

Bibi, a disciplined cadet, did not argue with his commanding officers even when he was not convinced they were right. "They are the commander and we are the cadets," he said to his friends, graduates of other infantry units. They remember him as an introvert, closed, spare with words, different from most of the other cadets. They did not especially enjoy the days Bibi was on duty. He was much more scrupulous than their own commanders.

His off-duty hours were divided between his girlfriend Micki and his brother Yoni, who easily integrated himself into the unit. From time to time Bibi wrote his parents in America, but much less frequently than Yoni did.

Bibi graduated the course with honors and returned to the unit as commander of a young team just beginning its training, taking them through the same routine he himself had suffered through only two and a half years before.

In January 1970 Bibi was given command of his own team. His first meeting with the soldiers took place near Afula. Most of them were kibbutzniks who had just completed an arduous basic training in the paratroops division. Udi, from Kibbutz Yehiam, remembers that first meeting: "He stood there smiling and called out our names. We replied,

'Yes, sir. No, sir.' He said, 'My name is Bibi.' Then he took us on the traditional trek: 125 kilometers, on foot. A twenty-four-hour hike. Bibi was dragging a leg toward the end, but managed to complete the course.

"We got to know him gradually. He was introverted, controlled, but always ready to lend a helping hand. Nonetheless, he was never ashamed to hand out punishment when necessary."

Bibi liked to ground soldiers. This was the accepted punishment in the unit: for each hour of delay, a soldier would have one hour removed from his furlough.

The "Bibi team" learned to appreciate the special relationship between Bibi and his older brother Yoni, commander of the trainees platoon. Yoni visited often, and Bibi would drop everything to spend time with him. Yoni also liked to take part in Bibi's exercises. One of these involved evacuation in a Yas'ur helicopter.

On one occasion, the helicopter arrived, but its pilots could not land it because of a sandstorm. Bibi decided to give up and return to the base in a truck. Yoni would hear nothing of it. When a second attempt to land also ended in failure, Yoni called back to base and asked for another helicopter to be sent, with a more experienced crew onboard. After the second helicopter landed, Bibi couldn't stop talking about Yoni's talent for making quick decisions.

Bibi wanted his team to be the best in the entire unit and to be given special missions. He was a harsh taskmaster and demanded that his men do more than anyone else in the unit. If other teams climbed up a rope four times, Bibi's men did it five times. Once, during the exercises, Bibi broke his arm. With his arm in a sling, he tried to go on as if nothing had happened.

During this time of intense competition among team leaders, Bibi had very few friends. His fellow officers did not like him, and he made a point of keeping his men at a distance. He would mostly be remembered as an officer who recommended two of his men for officer training, only to see them drop out of the program when they were found unsuitable. This was unprecedented in the General Command Reconnaissance Unit.

He would later defend these two soldiers' failure by explaining that one of them had been through a crisis when two of his friends were killed, and the other had serious problems of his own. Bibi couldn't resist sticking up for his men, a well-known problem in a unit whose special character makes it difficult to draw a line between friendship and authority.

Bibi was considered a good officer in the unit, but not an excellent one. He was too square and lacking in creative imagination, very different from Lt. Col. Ehud Barak, the unit's commander at the time.

Barak had not been with the unit when Bibi arrived as a young combat soldier, though he resumed his position as its commander after having taken a short training course with the armored corps. He was quick to notice the Netanyahu brothers, especially Yoni, who in time became his best friend and soul mate, and one of the unit soldiers closest to him.

Barak showered David Elazar, the chief of staff, with proposals for special operations, even planning one deep behind enemy lines. One such plan was so extensive that it required nine months of training for the troops and officers. Two teams were allocated to the operation, one of them Bibi's. Bibi went into his commander's office and demanded to know which of the two team officers would be responsible for the operation. Barak replied that he had not yet decided. Bibi was insulted. He had no doubt that he was the most suitable man for the job. Since the time had come for his release from the army, he informed Barak that he was leaving the unit. He turned in all of his equipment and went to the Technion in Haifa to get registration papers. Two days later, Barak called to tell him that he was being given command of the two teams and that he would be commander of the operation.

Though the commander of the other team was considered a more creative officer with a talent for improvisation, Barak chose Bibi because of the determination Bibi had shown during the special training exercise. In this operation Bibi saw the mission of a lifetime, and in order to participate, he agreed to sign on for an additional year of military service. In the end, to the great disappointment of Barak and Netanyahu, Golda Meir, who was prime minister at the time, decided not to approve the operation, the details of which are kept secret to this day.

After Bibi was elected prime minister, Ehud Barak admitted that the young Netanyahu had been a good officer: "He successfully carried out any mission he was given. He knew how to follow long-term objectives, like a bulldog, to latch on them and to advance in his own way. Sometimes, he would move forward from the center. At other times, he would overtake his team and turn up from a point where no one expected to see him. This is a man, who, the moment he sets out to do something, will not come back unless he has succeeded."

Ehud, one of the greatest fighters to come from the unit, trusted Bibi and knew he could rely on him in special operations. Later, after having been elected leader of the Likud, Netanyahu referred to the effect that his service in the unit had on shaping his character: "The unit contributed a great deal to my life, the thoroughness and care taken in preparing missions. I learned to understand the need to make changes and improvise. But from a more adult perspective, I realized that the unit has its limits. The entire army cannot operate in that manner. It is impossible to solve all its problems in the same way and with the same methods used in the unit. My experience was unique. I learned not to run away from hardships, that one must overcome them. But life is not always like that. It is no more than a human condition, with its successes, its failures, and its limitations."

If there was one thing Bibi hated, it was having to miss an operation. Sometimes the greatest enemies were the commanders of the other teams, who also did not want to miss out on any action. Like them, Bibi created his own internal information system and made a point of developing a close relationship with Aliza, the commanding officer's secretary. In return, he expected her to keep him notified of anything "cooking." He used to call her My Aliza, and she called him Bibon, a nickname that stuck to him for a long time, but not always with affection.

Bibi also built on the close relationship which had developed between his brother Yoni and Ehud Barak, the unit's commander. He would feel out Yoni, trying to get any information before the others. Bibi, who at first had not liked the idea of Yoni joining the unit, loved every minute of the time they could spend together. They could exchange views on Aristotle and other philosophical works that filled Yoni's bookshelf.

Yoni infected Bibi with his love of Israel. On days off, he advised Bibi to drop everything and go out on a field trip, as he himself did whenever he could.

Although he loved being with Yoni, Bibi tried to persuade his brother to leave the army after a year. His reason: "Just look at poor Tutti [the nickname for Ruth], your wife, all alone at home." But Yoni had other plans. He wanted to command Sayeret Mutkal, the elite reconnaissance unit.

6

Overpowering a Sabena Plane

On May 8, 1972, Bibi's team was training outside their base. A Sabena plane belonging to the Belgian airline was making its way to Israel's international airport, in Lod. The captain, Reginald Levy, was dropping in altitude, getting ready to land in Israel. Levy, a former Royal Air Force fighter pilot, had been born in Blackpool, England, to a Jewish father. His wife, Deborah, a Belgian Jew, was also onboard. The couple had planned to celebrate Reginald's fiftieth birthday the following evening in Jerusalem.

Suddenly a man burst into the cockpit, held a gun to the copilot's temple, and informed Captain Levy, "This is a hijack."

The four hijackers, two men and two women, allowed the pilot to continue the flight toward Tel Aviv, where the plane received ground clearance to land at a distant runway.

Moshe Dayan, Israel's defense minister, was on a flight from Sinai to Tel Aviv, and by the time he landed, a team of combat troops from the General Command Reconnaissance Unit was already in place, under the command of Ehud Barak. Bibi was not there; his team was training elsewhere. Yoni also was not there.

Raphael Eitan, chief infantry and paratroops officer, told Barak to prepare his men to burst into the hijacked plane. The attack could take place at any moment. Under cover of darkness, Barak and a team of flight technicians sabotaged the plane's brakes and oil system so that it would not be able to take off.

In the morning hours, the army began negotiating with the hijackers, who demanded the release of hundreds of Palestinian terrorists imprisoned in Israel. At the same time, David "Dado" Elazar, the chief of staff, was briefing Barak, instructing him to prepare for an attack on the plane.

Barak left a lookout team in the field and took the rest of his men into a larger hanger nearby, where they could rehearse their attack on a Boeing jet which was parked there for maintenance. At this time, extremely valuable intelligence began arriving from the hijacked plane. Captain Levy was sent by the hijackers to the control tower to pass on a message to the Israeli minister of defense: "If Israel does not release terrorists," the hijackers warned, "the plane will be blown up with all of its passengers."

Barak came up with the idea of dressing his men in the white overalls of El Al flight technicians, which would allow them to approach the plane without arousing the suspicions of the hijackers. According to the Belgian pilot's account, the hijackers were located in the cockpit as well as near the plane's back doors. Dayan sent on the message that Israel was willing to release prisoners and asked for an extension of several hours—time that was essential for practicing an attack on the plane.

Meanwhile, Bibi learned of the situation and arrived at the scene, agitated, about an hour before the planned attack. He had made his way at breakneck speed in the BMW belonging to him and Yoni after calling the base and learning that none of the officers were there. He sensed that something was up, dropped everything, and rushed off to Lod. Yoni now arrived too. He had also sensed trouble.

Bibi, angry at not having been called, pressed Ehud Barak to let him join in the action. Barak agreed, although Bibi had not participated in all the operation's practice runs, and ordered him to put on a white El Al overall. Thus, Bibi joined Barak's combat team as an ordinary soldier, assigned to go in through the plane's back door.

During the final rehearsal, Barak witnessed a fierce argument between Bibi and Yoni. Yoni, too, asked to be included in the force, but Ehud refused. "It's out of the question," Barak said. Bibi's commanding officer then, and years later his political adversary, Barak recalled telling Bibi's brother, "Bibi's in the force and I have no intention of including you as well. I won't have two brothers on the same mission. It's a firm principle with me, so you may as well stop wasting time arguing. You'll have other chances."

Stubborn as always, Yoni refused to give up and asked Bibi to change places with him, playing on the feelings of his younger brother. "I'm older, more experienced, and if something should happen to you, I should never forgive myself. And how could I explain it to Mother and Father?"

In return, Bibi argued, "You are married. You have more to lose. You have parents and a wife. Ehud is right, we can't both take part in the operation. Wait for another opportunity."

Barak ended the argument. He called Yoni aside and asked him to give in. "There's no time for any changes," he said. "Everyone knows exactly what has to be done, and I have no intention of waiting a moment longer. Their ultimatum will end at four o'clock in the afternoon. We have to go."

Yoni was on the brink of tears. He hugged Bibi and told him that he would settle their account later.

The attacking force moved toward the hijacked plane on the special tractors used by El Al technicians. The terrorists demanded that they remove the top parts of their overalls to show that they were unarmed. At that moment, a TWA Boeing 707 was moving along the runway and military trucks were making their way toward the plane. The terrorists onboard, sure that Israel had given in to their demands, allowed the white-overalled technicians to approach in order to prepare the plane for takeoff.

At 4:24 P.M., Barak gave the order to attack. All the forces started to act at once, with a special "mattress force" making its way quickly toward the plane to spread mattresses beneath all the openings in case the hostages fell from the wings, or should the need arise to push them off the plane to the ground.

Bibi, who was stationed on one of the wings, waited for the signal—a whistle—from Barak, who was on the ground. The signal was given and the soldiers burst into the plane. Immediately, gunfire blazed at them from short range. Bullets whistled above their heads. One of the passengers was wounded and later died of her injuries.

As they ran, passengers shouted that a female terrorist was sitting in the front of the plane. Bibi made his way to her quickly and grabbed her by the hair. It came away in his hand. It was a wig. He grabbed her again.

Before the operation the soldiers had been warned that the terrorists might activate explosives and blow up the plane, together with the hostages and the rescue force. This was now their main fear. The soldiers did not know if there were any explosives onboard or if they would be activated. Bibi decided to interrogate the female terrorist.

A day before the operation, the soldiers had been issued 22 mm pistols, but none of the men had any experience in using pistols, and Bibi was afraid that in the course of the operation a catastrophe would happen.

He recalled: "Suddenly, one of the unit's reserves, who had been guarding, turned up. His pistol was loaded. I could see the bullet in the barrel and I knew exactly what was going to happen. I didn't have time to call out. I held on to her [the terrorist] and shook her so she would tell me where the explosives were, and then he turned up. The soldier, Marco Ashkenazi, lifted one arm in the air, the one with the pistol, and slapped her with it. A bullet was fired from his gun and tore at my arm. The pain was agonizing. If he'd aimed a couple of centimeters to the side, many of my political opponents would be happy today."

Bibi escaped serious injury, and Barak's team successfully freed the hostages. Yoni was one of the first to welcome the men back. He hugged his younger brother. Bibi was happy, and Yoni was happy for him but could not hide his disappointment that he had not taken part in the successful operation.

At that time the third Netanyahu brother, Iddo, was being recruited into the army, and he too found himself in the General Command Reconnaissance Unit. Until then, only one other family had had all three of its sons serving simultaneously in the unit—the Brug family, whose oldest son is Ehud Barak.

At the beginning of the summer of 1972, Elazar, the chief of staff, decided to carry out an operation which had no precedent in the Israel Defense Forces: to kidnap Syrian officers in order to force Syria to negotiate the release of three Israeli pilots whose planes had been shot down over Syrian territory.

Israeli intelligence learned that the pilots were being held in solitary confinement under appalling conditions, which included horrific torture. All attempts at negotiating an exchange of the prisoners had failed. Even an offer to release thirty-seven Syrian officers and men who had been taken prisoner two years before in an armored invasion on Syrian territory could not sway Syrian president Hafez Assad.

The northern border had turned dangerous. Most of the Palestinians' activity was taking place around Har Dov in the foothills of Mount

Hermon. Information had reached Israeli intelligence that senior Syrian army officers, sons of influential upper-class families, would be making a tour of the region along the Lebanese border. The Israeli general headquarters decided to try to kidnap these officers and use them as bargaining chips in an exchange of prisoners.

Chief of Staff David Elazar called Ehud Barak, the commander of the General Command Reconnaissance Unit, and asked if it was capable of carrying out such a mission. Barak said it could. A few days later, Prime Minister Golda Meir approved the operation, which was given the code name Box. The team commanders started studying the route to be taken by the Syrian officers in Lebanon in order to determine the most suitable spot at which to grab them. To help in planning the details, Barak appointed two officers as his personal assistants—Yoni Netanyahu and Muki Betzer.

After a few tours of the region, the spot was chosen for the kidnapping to take place: a dirt road that led to Har Dov on the Lebanese side of the border. At that spot vehicles were forced to reduce their speed, and that made them an easy target. The unit rehearsed the operation for a few days and waited for confirmation from Elazar. The Netanyahu family was fully represented—Yoni, twenty-six, and Bibi, twenty-three, in the attack force, while Iddo, twenty, was part of the blocking force.

Bibi's team had a key role in the operation: it had been chosen to lay the ambush at the edge of the road on the Lebanese side. Late at night, the men took up their positions close to the road. That morning, the Syrian and Lebanese group did not arrive at Har Dov, however, and Elazar ordered the cancellation of Box One. Box Two was authorized a few days later.

This time the ambush would be set on another road, close to the path leading to Har Dov. Barak personally commanded the operation. Bibi commanded the blocking force, whose task it was to prevent the arrival of Syrian reinforcements and to capture people who tried to escape after encountering Barak's soldiers. The men set off for Lebanon and spread out for the ambush. In the early hours of the morning a Lebanese shepherd arrived at the site. One of his sheep wandered near where Bibi's men were hiding. The shepherd noticed a trip wire and stopped beside it. The commander of the blocking force informed Barak that the shepherd suspected something was wrong. Barak ordered that the shepherd be taken prisoner. The man was frightened half to death. Bibi passed his hand over the man's throat, signaling that one word would be the end of him.

That solved one problem, but another came on its heels when Bibi's men noticed an armored car followed by a jeep full of Lebanese officers. Bibi had no doubt that the Syrian officers were approaching.

The armored car pulled up at an observation point about eighty meters from the position taken by Bibi and his men. Bibi reported to Ehud that the Israeli force had no weapon on hand that could respond to the Lebanese 105 mm cannon. He was told to wait. Three hours went by. The Lebanese patrol halted and did not advance. Meanwhile, Bibi's force lay close to the ground, ready to open fire the moment Barak gave the order. Toward midday, a black limousine, presumably carrying the targeted Syrian officers, approached the place where Barak had set up the ambush. Barak saw the limousine and requested permission from Elazar to give Yoni, who was leading the attack force, the code word to act. Elazar, worried about the Lebanese armored car's proximity to Bibi's men, asked Barak to wait. Barak continued to press for action. Elazar finally decided to cancel Box Two.

Bibi heard about the decision over the wireless, just as he watched the limousine approaching a bend in the road, only dozens of meters from where he and his men were lying in wait.

Bibi ordered his men to pack up and head back to Israel. He did not hide his disappointment. Operation Box Two was supposed to be his going-away present from the unit and from the IDF. The next day, June 19, 1972, he handed in his equipment at the unit's base and was released from the army. Later, as a civilian, he heard from his brother Yoni about the sharp exchange between the chief of staff and the unit's commander.

Barak was in a bad mood and attacked Elazar. "Why did you stop us! We were so close to them! We could have done it easily! We had them in our hands, and we let them go!"

Elazar tried to calm Barak down. "I was afraid the armored car would come across the ambush."

"You're forcing me not to report the truth," Barak replied. "If I had thought you might cancel the operation, I wouldn't have told you about the Lebanese armored car. You should have trusted my judgment. I'm telling you that we could have carried out the mission with no trouble. In the future I won't report things like the armored car and I'll get your approval to go on."

Bibi was convinced that there had been no chance of getting approval to act as soon as the shepherd they captured had been released and revealed to the Syrians the existence of the Israeli force. Two days later, however, when Bibi had already been a civilian for twenty-four hours, the unit received approval to carry out Box Three. This time, fearing another cancellation, Barak decided to take up his position in the command post and appointed Yoni Netanyahu to head the operation. Uzi Dayan was his deputy.

The unit set up an ambush beside the Lebanese village of Ramish. This time everything went like clockwork. Uzi Dayan jumped in front of the white Impala which carried the Syrian officers and signaled for them to leave the car. The Syrians begged for their lives, and one of them took advantage of the commotion and managed to get away. Uzi Dayan took control of the Impala and drove it across the border, where he drew up beside the command post and opened the car doors. Five senior Syrian army officers got out, three of them members of the Syrian General Command Forum.

Syria was in shock. In the diplomatic negotiations that followed, by way of a third party, Israel was offered an immediate exchange of prisoners— the Israeli pilots in return for the officers. Syria's only condition was that the entire incident be kept secret. Israel had a condition of its own—the return of additional Israeli prisoners being held in Egypt. Negotiations became complicated; the incident was exposed by the foreign press and the exchange of prisoners took place only after a year. Bibi, by this time a student at MIT in Cambridge, Massachusetts, read about it in the *New York Times* and smiled.

7

In Boston With Micki Weissman

During his military service, Bibi stopped living in Uzi Beller's Jerusalem house and moved in with his brother Yoni, at Mitodela Street 19. His long-time girlfriend, Micki, lived nearby on Ben Maimon Street. Their relationship deepened. Their love, which had survived distance and time, did not fade, and it was clear to them and to everyone who knew them that the relationship would lead to a wedding. Micki's military service was every bit as worthwhile as Bibi's. She had been an excellent officer and was demobilizing at the age of twenty-one after having signed on for an extra year in the army.

Bibi was still in the army when Micki registered at the Hebrew University of Jerusalem to study her favorite subject, chemistry. She graduated with honors under Professor Israel Agranat, son of Supreme Court Judge Shimon Agranat.

When Bibi was released from the IDF in 1972, after five years of service, Micki was already a university graduate. She wanted to continue toward a postgraduate degree, and he wanted to begin his own higher education. Unlike their peers, they decided to go abroad for their schooling. Up to the last moment, the army tried to persuade Bibi to sign on for further service. He was promised a promotion, a post in the armored corps, rank of battalion commander, and other honors.

Bibi was the driving force behind his and Micki's decision to leave Israel. In those days, it was unusual to go abroad for a B.A. degree, but

Bibi, who had received most of his education in the United States and
believed in the American way, felt that success in America meant success
wherever he went. Besides, his parents were in America, he knew the
language, and as far as he was concerned, this was not a journey into the
unknown. Quite the contrary. Micki did not try to resist. She accepted his
view that studies in America constituted the key to success.

Bibi applied to Cornell University and was accepted easily, after
arriving well equipped with letters of recommendation from Israel. One
was signed by Brig. Gen. Motta Gur, Israel's military attaché in the
United States.

But once Micki was accepted at Brandeis University for a master's
degree, Bibi decided to change plans. He was unwilling to be far away
from his girlfriend; instead, he decided to try to get admitted to MIT. No
one was surprised when he succeeded. His American high school grades
together with his personal attributes left no doubt.

He decided to put his academic career on a very fast track. He had
signed on for architecture. Professor Leon Groisser, dean of students at
the time, recalled his first meeting with the young Israeli student, who
introduced himself as Ben Nitai. He told the dean, "I want you to put
together a program which will enable me to complete a degree in
architecture in four years."

Groisser tried to explain that it was impossible to accomplish those
studies in such a short period of time. "Give me a chance and I'll do it,"
Bibi said.

Professor Groisser allowed him, as a favor, to add courses in order to
shorten the time it would take to obtain his degree. "I am very grateful,"
Bibi said. "You won't regret your decision."

Twenty-four years later, after Bibi Netanyahu had been elected prime
minister of Israel, Professor Groisser told the Israeli daily *Yediot Ahronot*:
"Netanyahu may not have been the most brilliant student I have met in
my life, but he was definitely the most ambitious. He would focus on an
objective and lock himself on it. When he decides he wants something,
there's nothing he cannot achieve."

Bibi completed his B.A. in two-and-a-half years. His grades were high;
in some courses he achieved As. Then he went straight on to get his
master's degree in architecture, and he also obtained credits for a master's
degree in business administration.

Micki, meanwhile, studied organic chemistry at Brandeis, and the two shared an apartment. Yoav Leventar, who became one of Bibi's closest friends and confederates lived on the same floor as did Zvika Livne, now a professor, and the young student Uzi Landau, now a Likud member of the Knesset.

Bibi and Micki decided to get married several months after their arrival in America. They made speedy arrangements and held the *hupa* or marriage tent in the garden of Uncle Zachary's elegant estate in Westchester, New York. It was a Netanyahu family wedding; Bibi's parents, Benzion and Cela, were present, but Micki's parents remained in Israel.

Shortly after the wedding, the couple decided to change their name from Netanyahu to Nitai. Several rumors and accusations surround this change of name, although the truth, as Bibi tells it, is quite simple. One day, when registering for a course, Micki was asked if she was married to an Indian. "What kind of name is that, anyway, Netanyahu?" she was asked. that same evening she passed on the message to Bibi. "What does it mean, really? It's difficult to pronounce, complicated, and raises questions. Let's change it to something simpler and shorter."

Bibi agreed. The name Netanyahu was not originally the family's anyway; his father had changed it from Mileikowsky. About this time, Benzion also had a habit of sending Bibi copies of papers he had written during the 1940s, asking his son to read them. Bibi noticed that the papers were signed with the pseudonym Nitai. Micki called up her father-in-law at once. "What's the meaning of Nitai?" she asked.

"It refers to Nitai Arbeli, who was a famous wise man in the Bible," the professor explained. "It was a name I adopted in my writings at a certain point."

Micki liked the name and called her sister, Meira Shefi, who said, "I think it's a great name. There's a rather gorgeous actor here called Niko Nitai. Why not take the name?"

Micki and Bibi wasted no time in changing their name. Within a few days they were Micki and Ben Nitai. When Yoni arrived at their home a few months later, he noticed the new name immediately. "What's the idea?" he asked. "What kind of a name is this?"

Micki explained, and Yoni fell so in love with the name that he decided to change his own name to Nitai as soon as he returned to Israel. Jonathan

Nitai was the name on his identity card when he was killed at Entebbe. However, by special request of his parents, the name Netanyahu was inscribed on his gravestone.

Ben and Micki led the lives of ordinary students. Micki was a good hostess, and they were soon a popular couple among the Israeli students in Boston. Friends would come over and stay until the wee hours. Conversation focused on political issues. Micki was a terrific cook and an excellent conversationalist, and everyone liked her. On break, the young couple would take off for romantic getaways. Bibi took his wife on a dream holiday to Florence, and they went on to Venice. At that time, he took a great deal of interest in art. He still believed that he would complete his studies and make a name for himself in architecture, a second Frank Lloyd Wright, perhaps.

The time was relatively relaxed regarding his political ambitions, possibly the happiest time of his life. He discovered definite hedonistic tendencies in himself. He ate in the best restaurants, mainly Italian, watched quality movies and plays, and let himself wallow in art. Bibi would spend hours walking through museums, scanning galleries, digging through art centers. In his long talks with Micki, he barely mentioned politics. Bibi was relaxed, at peace with himself. It almost seemed that he was enjoying life.

It was clear to him that his family's flag bearer was his brother Yoni, the beloved and talented firstborn son. Bibi, like the rest of the family, had no doubts that his brother would one day be Israel's chief of staff, after which he would try to get elected prime minister. Bibi himself was a "middle child," always struggling for his father's recognition and his mother's love. Nothing could be taken for granted. All his life he had been burdened with the need to prove himself against the success and glory of Yoni. Bibi often gave up prematurely. While he dreamed of becoming a senior officer or prime minister, he never took those dreams too seriously. He had no choice but to seek another destiny for himself—perhaps as a successful architect, business tycoon, or famous management wizard. He would carve out a career for himself, make money and a name.

In the meantime, Bibi and Micki were not having an easy time financially. Of course, they were both receiving every possible grant. Micki, who was an excellent student, had her tuition paid through a stipend by the school, and another grant covered her living expenses. Bibi had a stipend for his school fees. Their parents also helped, but were not overly generous. Micki had to work as a research assistant at the university in addition to her studies. Bibi did not have a job; his workload was too heavy. No one believed he would succeed in completing his degrees in such a short time.

Micki's parents sent money from Israel and helped them buy their first car, a used Volkswagen, for $500. Uncles Zachary and Amos Mylo, both millionaire steel tycoons, kept in touch with the young couple and slipped them some pocket money from time to time. They were particularly fond of Micki, with her charming personality and intelligence.

At the beginning of 1973, once they had settled nicely into their life in Boston, Bibi was drawn into on-campus Zionist activity. His neighbor, Uzi Landau, son of former Herut minister Chaim Landau and future member of the Knesset and chairman of the Knesset Foreign Affairs Committee, was an engineering student at the time. Uzi Landau was a driving force in the stormy debates that took place on the MIT campus between Israeli and Arab students. Bibi became good friends with Landau, and together with Colette Avital, Israel's consul in Boston, they formed a group that would fight the Arab and Palestinian lobby on campus.

Colette Avital was probably the first one to discover Bibi's talent for rhetoric. In one of their talks at the consulate, she asked him if he would be willing to give lectures in Boston and other cities. "You'll get twenty-five dollars a lecture," she told him, and Bibi was thrilled. What she didn't know was that Bibi would have done it for nothing.

In October 1973 the Yom Kippur War halted Bibi's academic career. Early in the morning, his brother Yoni called to tell him of the heavy fighting along the Suez Canal and in the Golan Heights. Bibi told Micki he had to go back to Israel. He went from Boston to New York and tried to get on a flight. At the airport, he was surprised at the number of Israelis struggling to find a seat on one of the planes. An IDF representative had arrived to put things in order and was giving priority to officers and to combat soldiers in special units and the armored corps.

This told Bibi immediately that the armored corps had been badly mauled, and he fought for his right, as a reserve officer in the General Command Reconnaissance Unit, to leave on one of the first flights out. At one point he even phoned Gen. Motta Gur, military attaché in Washington, for help. He did not succeed in getting on the first jumbo jet, but he did make it on the second. On the plane he met a couple of old friends: Ehud Barak, his former unit commander, who was a student at Stanford, and Uzi Beller, his childhood friend from Jerusalem, who was studying medicine in New York. Uzi Landau, a reserve officer in the paratroops, was also on one of the planes taking troops back to Israel.

As soon as Bibi arrived at Tel Aviv's Lod Airport, he tried to contact Yoni. After much effort he finally got through to his brother and learned of the terrible days Yoni had spent in the Golan Heights. One of the operations in which he had taken part was a bloody battle with dozens of Syrian commando troops who had landed in helicopters, in broad daylight, and dug themselves in not far from the IDF command post. The Israeli soldiers in the post thought these were Israeli troops, and it was only when the Syrian commandos opened fire from close range that they realized their mistake.

Thirty men from the General Command Reconnaissance Unit, led by Yoni Netanyahu, were sent to the rocky hillock, where they fought bravely against the Syrians. After the first burst of fire, which killed one of the Israeli officers, Yoni, together with eight of his men, charged the Syrians. Forty-one Syrian soldiers were killed in the battle. Yoni would further distinguish himself toward the end of the war, when he led a group of soldiers on a rescue of an armored corps officer. Yossi Ben-Hanan, commander of a tank battalion, was surrounded by Syrian tanks when Yoni and his men braved heavy Syrian fire and pulled him out.

Ehud Barak, Uzi Beller, and Bibi arrived at the base near Ashkelon, and looked for a unit to join. For the first couple of days they had nothing to do, so Bibi started organizing the soldiers who were waiting to be sent to their units. One of the soldiers recalls, "He was a nuisance. All day long he was going about writing up lists of people for patrol duty and didn't let anyone, not even Barak, be lazy. He was busy all the time checking that all the guard positions were constantly manned."

Two days later, Beller was sent to join his unit, the Seventh Battalion. Barak, too, was given a tank battalion to command in the south. Bibi went to Sinai with them. He tried to make his way to the General Command Reconnaissance Unit, though it turned out that the unit was not operating as an independent force—its soldiers were divided between the two fronts. Together with other returning soldiers and paratroop officers, Bibi joined an improvised unit, formed during the war, which was equipped with jeeps and armored personnel carriers, and then sent to the southern front. Their mission was to protect parked tanks at night against Egyptian commandos being brought in by helicopters. From the southern front, the force was then transferred to the north. Israel's counterattack was in full force, and in the north there was also a need for trained soldiers who could guard the tanks at night.

At the end of October, immediately following the cease-fire, Bibi returned to America, Micki, and MIT. During the night, he would make up the classes he had missed while he was away fighting in Israel.

Colette Avital, Israel's consul in Boston, waited impatiently for Bibi's return. Although she was familiar with his politics and his criticism of the Israeli government, she did not have a better speaker who could counter Arab and Palestinian propaganda. To a great extent, Bibi owes his first appearance on American television to Colette Avital. A local Boston TV network initiated a confrontation between Professor Edward Said, a Palestinian intellectual and an extremely popular personality among the New York and Boston academic communities, and a representative of Israel. Colette Avital asked Bibi if he was willing to appear and warned him that the adversary was very experienced in TV interviews. Without hesitation Bibi agreed to take on Said.

On the evening of the broadcast, Colette could hardly believe her eyes. The young architecture student appeared with no sign of nervousness or feelings of inferiority when set against the most popular and eloquent Palestinian in the United States. Later, Bibi was approached by local TV stations, asking him to take part in interviews on the situation in Israel and the Middle East. He loved the cameras, and the cameras loved him.

At the height of Bibi's academic career, Professor Groisser suggested that he register for a special program, a shortened, two-year course, at the end of which he would have a Ph.D. in political science. Bibi liked the idea, but preferred to complete his master's in architecture. All that kept him from receiving his degree was a project he had to present to a special committee of professors. Despite his high grades in his chosen subject, Bibi's real bent was business, and he wanted to join one of the large American financial concerns which were courting graduates in business administration. Having studied the American labor market, he decided to focus on the Boston Consulting Group (BCG), one of the oldest in the field. Although some MIT graduates had higher grades than he, Bibi believed he had something to offer a company like BCG. In his interview, he told them about his life, military service, and fighting experience. He could feel that his military background and excellent grades made him an attractive candidate for the position of financial adviser.

In the middle of June 1976, Bibi realized the American Dream. A brief, dry, official letter arrived from the BCG management, stating that they were happy to inform him that he had been accepted for work and wished him luck. He celebrated the wonderful news with Micki at a fancy restaurant in Boston. In addition to his expected high salary—$60,000, not including bonuses—the company placed a new Thunderbird at his disposal. His future seemed rosy.

Bibi's first assignment involved advising the Swedish government on how to improve the function of industrial concerns. Bibi began planning the project, when, in a single moment, a telephone call from Israel ended his American Dream. On July 4, America's two hundredth anniversary, Micki and Bibi were at home in Boston, celebrating with a few close friends. As they stood near the windows, they could hear the popping of fireworks. The telephone rang. Micki picked it up and someone from the consulate asked to speak to Bibi. Micki asked what was the matter, and the voice demanded impatiently, "I asked to speak with Bibi. Where is Bibi?"

8

Entebbe

At midday, Israel time, on June 27, 1976, an Air France Airbus plane took off from Athens for Paris. One hour earlier, the plane had landed at Athens International Airport on its way from Tel Aviv. There an additional eighty-six passengers boarded the plane, including four people who had arrived that same morning on another flight. Two of them, a man and a woman, were European-looking, while the other two were swarthy and Middle Eastern in appearance. As transit passengers, they had no trouble passing through airport security. The four, in their late twenties, were international terrorists, members of the German terrorist organization Bader-Meinhoff and the Popular Front for the Liberation of Palestine, which had joined forces in the struggle against Israel and Zionism.

At a cruising altitude of thirty-one thousand feet, when the Fasten Your Seat Belt sign was switched off, the four terrorists stood up and burst into the cockpit, their outstretched hands holding guns and hand grenades. They informed the French captain, Michele Baccus, that the airbus was being hijacked and that they were now taking over control of the plane and all its passengers. The hijackers instructed the pilot to change course and to land at the Libyan capital, then Bengazi. The Libyan leader Muammar Khadaffi, always an enthusiastic supporter of terrorist organizations, gave the hijackers a warm welcome and allowed the plane to refuel before they set off again. The terrorists permitted one of the female passengers, who claimed to be pregnant, to disembark. The hijacked plane then continued in the direction of Entebbe, Uganda, where it landed late at night.

The Ugandan leader, Field Marshal Idi Amin Dada, dressed in a shiny military uniform, was waiting inside his elegant black Mercedes for the plane to land. He received the terrorists with a warm smile and informed them that they were welcome guests in his country. Ugandan soldiers surrounded the plane and then helped the terrorists transfer the hostages to the old terminal building at Entebbe airport. There all the Israeli passengers and those whose name had a vaguely Jewish ring were separated from the others—just as had happened in the Nazi death camps during the Holocaust thirty years earlier. The captain and his crew insisted on remaining with the Israeli passengers.

In Israel, Prime Minister Yitzhak Rabin convened his government for an emergency session. On his desk lay an ultimatum issued by the terrorist organization, the Popular Front for the Liberation of Palestine. Within twenty-four hours, he had to release three hundred terrorists being held by Israel. If he did not, the terrorists in Uganda would begin executing the Israeli hostages one by one. The cabinet came to a decision: to negotiate with the terrorists, with the aim of gaining time. Prime Minister Rabin stated the principle—Israeli would not bow down to terror. Rabin instructed his minister of defense and chief of the general staff, Lt. Gen. Motta Gur, to prepare for a military option.

Motta Gur looked at the map and measured the distance between Israel and Uganda—about 2,500 miles. In Israel's military history there had been a few supremely daring acts carried out by Israel deep in enemy territory, but never before had Israel acted 2,500 miles from home. The commander of the Israeli air force at the time, Gen. Benny Peled, reckoned that the IDF was capable of carrying out a military assault in Entebbe and flying back to Tel Aviv.

The mission was given to the IDF General Command Reconnaissance Unit, Israel's elite fighting group, which had been brought to the notice of the Israeli public only in 1972 after a series of operations that had amazed the world. At that time, the unit was commanded by Lt. Col. Ehud Barak, later chief of the general staff with the rank of lieutenant general. Today, he is chairman of the Labor party and a candidate for prime minister—making him Benjamin Netanyahu's political adversary. In 1972, within a short period of time, the reconnaissance unit had carried out the successful rescue operation on the hijacked Sabena plane which had been forced to land in Tel Aviv, and in the center of Beirut, Lebanon, the unit had attacked the terrorist leaders responsible for the murder of Israeli athletes at the Olympic Games in Munich, killing three of the leaders while they were in bed sleeping. During that same year, the unit captured the five senior Syrian army officers in Lebanese territory to force Syria to agree to an exchange of prisoners and the return of the three air force pilots who were being held captive and tortured.

In July 1976, under the command of Lt. Col. Jonathan Netanyahu— Bibi's older brother Yoni—the reconnaisance unit was ordered to undertake the mission of saving the Israeli hostages held captive in Uganda. The plan, which was given the name Operation Thunderball, was commanded by Brig. Gen. Dan Shomron, chief infantry and paratroop officer in the Israel Defense Forces. The reconnaisance unit was joined by IDF infantry and paratroop units. Yoni had taken charge of the unit the year before, after having served two years in positions of command in the armored corps.

There was considerable debate in the IDF over how to conduct the operation. Ideas were proposed, and discarded just as quickly. One plan involved parachuting troops over Lake Victoria into Entebbe and attacking the Ugandan air force. In the end the high command adopted the plan proposed by Ehud Barak, whereby the soldiers would land in the airport at Entebbe, burst into the terminal building, attack the terrorists, rescue the hostages, and return to Israel.

The rescue mission belonged to the reconnaissance unit and Yoni Netanyahu. In order to confuse the hijackers, it had been decided that Yoni and other officers would be dressed in Ugandan army uniforms and, after landing at Entebbe, they would drive toward the terminal in a black Mercedes like the one driven by Idi Amin.

On Saturday, July 3, Bibi and his wife Micki were at their home in Boston, studying for exams. In the afternoon, they took a break and went for a walk in one of the pretty parks which dot the city. Bibi and Micki had no idea that at that very moment, Yoni Netanyahu was making his way toward Entebbe in the first of four Hercules cargo planes belonging to the Israeli Air Force.

At 11:01 P.M. Israeli time, Colonel Netanyahu was landing on the runway at Entebbe, followed by the three others in the force. Yoni drove immediately toward the terminal in the black Mercedes. The Ugandan soldiers in his way paid no special attention. They were shot down with guns fitted with silencers.

A few minutes later the reconnaisance unit burst into the terminal where the 109 Israelis were being held. The German and Palestinian terrorists were taken completely by surprise. The battle was a short one. The terrorists were eliminated, one Israeli hostage was killed, and eight were wounded. While commanding the operation from outside the terminal, Yoni did not notice the Ugandan soldiers stationed at the top of the control tower. One of them fired automatic rounds at Yoni, and he fell to the ground in a pool of blood, mortally wounded. Immediately, he was carried by his men and the doctors who accompanied the mission and placed on the first plane. The hostages, dazed from their sudden rescue, boarded another plane, which took off for Israel immediately. Only one hostage remained behind—Mrs. Dora Bloch, an elderly woman who had been taken to a Kampala hospital for immediate medical attention. Shortly after the rescue mission's completion, Mrs. Bloch would be murdered in her hospital bed on Idi Amin's orders.

The remaining three planes followed the first one out of Uganda. The fantastic operation had become a reality. The code name Operation Thunderball, from a well-known James Bond movie, was fitting.

In the plane making its way back to Israel, all efforts to save Yoni's life failed. The doctors were forced to declare him dead. Both the chief of staff Motta Gur and Shimon Peres burst into tears when they received the news over the radio. Prime Minister Rabin closeted himself in his office. It was a heavy loss, and sadness mingled with the joy over the success of the operation and the return of the hostages. Rabin and Peres decided that the operation would be called from then on Operation Yonatan.

Some years after his death, Yoni's younger brother, Iddo, wrote a book titled *Yoni's Last Battle*. In it, Iddo gave a different version of the circumstances of his brother's death. The previous description had come from eyewitness accounts provided by Yoni's fellow soldiers, who were with him in the operation. In his book, Iddo claimed that Yoni was not killed by fire from the rifle of a Ugandan soldier in the control tower but by a shot from one of the German terrorists. Veterans of the General

Command Reconnaissance Unit were furious at Iddo Netanyahu's version of the battle and did not appreciate his attempt to rewrite history.

When Micki answered the phone, she sensed something wrong and called to her husband. Bibi took the receiver, and within seconds he turned pale. Micki saw the expression on his face and realized that something terrible had happened. The woman on the other end of the line had been just as brusque with Bibi as she had been with Micki. "Yoni has been killed," she said. Straight and to the point. Reeling from the news and angry at the way he had been told, Bibi asked the woman from the Israeli consulate not to call his parents. "I wanted to save them from this telephone experience," he would say later.

It was late at night, but Bibi had no doubt that he had to see his parents. The elder Netanyahus were living in Ithaca, in central New York, a seven-hour car ride away. Bibi did not want to drive the whole way on his own, and asked his friend Zvi Livne, who had served with Yoni in the reconnaissance unit, and Zvi's wife, Rutti, to share the driving.

It was the longest journey of Bibi's life. He wept almost all the way to his parents' home, and spoke little, as Micki sat beside him and tried to offer consolation. His life with his older brother flashed before him—he and Yoni, always together, children in Jerusalem, young men in America, soldiers in the army.

Early in the morning, they arrived in Ithaca. Before setting off from Boston, Bibi had made sure there would be a doctor available near his parents' home. He feared the worst.

Bibi walked up the path to the front door of his parents' house. Through the window he could see his father striding back and forth, as he always did, his hands behind his back, deep in thought. Bibi wrote: "Suddenly he looked out and saw me. His eyes lit up. A few seconds later, his expression changed. He understood. Mother came out, saw us, and understood immediately."

Cela looked at her daughter-in-law and said, "It's Yoni, isn't it?"

"Yes," Bibi said.

The flight to Israel was terrible. Benzion and Cela Netanyahu and Micki and Bibi Nitai flew first to New York and from there directly to Israel. They were all deep in shock. Bibi looked like someone whose entire world had collapsed. Yoni and Bibi had loved each other deeply. Yoni was the center of Bibi's world, his teacher and guide. To this day, when he wanders around Jerusalem with his close adviser, Shai Bazak, Bibi reminisces as they go: "Yoni and I used to jog right here," or "Yoni and I used to sit here and talk. It was here that we played..." When he was elected leader of the Likud, the opposition party at the time, Netanyahu took part in a TV special on Yoni. The singer Yehoram Gaon also participated. After the show, when Bibi went to have his makeup removed, Gaon followed him into the makeup room to say goodbye. The makeup artist, waiting by the door, saw Bibi looking into the large mirror, unable to control the tears that were rolling down his cheeks.

During their military service, Bibi and Yoni would go on weekend trips together with Tutti, Yoni's wife, and later Bruria, his girlfriend after Yoni and Tutti divorced. Bibi would take Micki along. The two couples would go on jeep tours to exotic places like Nuweiba, Dahab, Eilat, the Galilee. On these trips Micki learned of Bibi's special relationship with his brother, and she got to know and love Yoni as well.

Yoni's death is without a doubt the worst thing that has ever happened to Benjamin Netanyahu. It left a void in Bibi's life that can never be filled. Yoni had been the family's torchbearer. When he fell, the torch fell. Bibi, who was resigned to being Yoni's follower, hesitated, overcame his shock, and made up his mind. He would pick up the torch. Everything that Yoni was supposed to achieve, Bibi would achieve instead. His political ambition was born with Yoni's death.

Many of Bibi's friends are convinced that the loss of Yoni was largely responsible for the breakdown of his marriage to Micki. Bibi had been happy with Micki as he had never been before. He loved her and saw her as a true soul mate. She provided him, for the first time in his adult life, with a real home. Every Friday they would entertain their friends, sit around eating, drinking, chatting. Micki always made sure that there was something special to eat.

Bibi's affair with Fleur Cates, an English-born Harvard Business School graduate, came shortly after Yoni's death. As always, it was not Bibi who acted first. Fleur made all the moves.

The affair began with a random meeting in the library of Boston University. An exchange of glances led to a cup of coffee at the university canteen, the beginning of a romantic liaison. Later, Bibi would tell his friends that it was Fleur who had initiated the relationship, which developed into an affair and later love. At first, Bibi's allegiance was to Micki, and he did not consider marriage to Fleur, who was not Jewish. But things changed. Bibi started spending more and more time away from home, returning at irregular hours, with weak excuses. One day Micki found a long blond hair on the lapel of his jacket. "Whose is this?" she asked, giving him a long look. Bibi muttered and blushed. Micki knew. At that moment, she made her decision. She had devoted her life to Bibi, waiting many long months for him every year when he was at school in America. She had never dreamed of being unfaithful to him, and was unable to reconcile herself to his infidelity.

Bibi argued, begged, promised that the affair meant nothing and that it would never happen again. But Micki, pregnant with their daughter, No'a, had made up her mind. "You are packing up all your stuff right now and you are leaving this house," she said. Bibi tried to talk to her, but nothing helped. Micki did not shout; she did not make a scene. "Just pack up your things and go," she said. "I admire you, I am your friend, I have come a long way with you, but now it's over. There is no way we can save our relationship."

Bibi left the house with his belongings. At his request, his parents tried to persuade Micki to reconcile. Benzion and Cela loved and respected Micki and found it hard to accept what had happened. They had long conversations with her. Micki spoke patiently, but would not be swayed. "There is nothing to discuss," she said. Micki had left Bibi's life for good.

Bibi was never the kind of man to pick up women. He is by turns apathetic, uninterested, and self-conscious where women are concerned—something of a nerd, in fact. Most of his affairs started when the woman took the initiative. He had been introduced to Micki by his friend Uzi Beller. Fleur met him at the university library and made the first advance. Sara, his current wife, had been an El Al stewardess on a flight to Amsterdam and had slipped him a piece of paper with her telephone number on it. Contrary to common belief, Bibi is no Lothario. Far from being obsessed with women, he is, on the contrary, often uncomfortable in their company.

When their daughter, No'a, was born in April 1978, Micki asked that Bibi not be allowed to visit her, but she did agree to let him see the baby. Micki completed her Ph.D. in Boston and returned to Israel. In July, Micki left America. Bibi's cousin, Uri Mileikowsky, helped her pack the contents of the small apartment and drove Micki and her baby daughter to the airport. A divorce officially ended Bibi's and Micki's marriage, although as far as Micki was concerned, the end had come the moment she found the blond hair on her husband's lapel.

Some years later, Micki Weissman met a young Israeli businessman, Doron Haran, and they were married shortly afterward. For all intents and purposes Doron became No'a's father, and he took an active part in her upbringing.

Bibi saw No'a infrequently, partly because he spent many of the following years on government missions in the United States, first as political attaché at the Washington embassy, and then, from 1984, as Israel's ambassador to the United Nations. The relationship between father and daughter has not been especially close. No'a grew up in a cultured home and, from an early age, showed an aptitude for school. After Bibi married Fleur, he made a point of meeting No'a during his vacations in Israel. Fleur welcomed the girl at their home, and even developed a warm relationship with her. In the summer of 1988, when Bibi and Iddo visited Entebbe as guests of the government of Uganda to see the place where their brother fell, Bibi took No'a with him.

When Bibi began his relationship with Sara in 1989, a rift between No'a and Bibi began to form. Sara did not like Bibi's ties with his daughter, and once she and Bibi were married and their two sons were born, she did everything she could to keep father and daughter apart. On one occasion, before Sara barred No'a from visiting Bibi at home, No'a entered her father's house and called out, "Hi, Father."

"Don't call Bibi Father in front of the little ones," Sara admonished her. "They don't know they have a sister." Sara forbade Bibi to tell his young sons that No'a is their sister.

For a while, Bibi stopped paying child support for No'a, in breach of his agreement with Micki. He had said he would support No'a until after she completed her army service. When Micki and her husband threatened to take Bibi to court and create a scandal, Bibi, who could not afford that sort of publicity, resumed his payments. But he was no longer free to meet No'a whenever he wanted. Sara prevented No'a from visiting her father's home. Even today, Bibi is obliged to use coded entries in his diary when referring to his daughter's visits to his office, because Sara has a habit of reviewing his diary every night to approve his next day's schedule.

When No'a was recruited into the Israel Defense Forces in 1996, Bibi did not accompany her to her military base, as all Israeli parents do when their children join up. He had to make his farewells to his daughter the night before, at his office, unbeknownst to his wife. In a nine-page article titled "The Sara Netanyahu File," published on December 12, 1997, *Yediot Ahronot* revealed to the Israeli public the circumstances of Bibi's relationship with No'a, including Sara's forbidding of Bibi's contact with his daughter. By then, Benjamin Netanyahu's years of innocence were long over. Twenty years had passed since his divorce from his first love, Micki Weissman.

9

Life With Rim Furniture

At the end of 1978 Bibi decided to return to Israel, still hoping he could revive his relationship with Micki. Before leaving the United States, he looked for a company where he could find a suitable position.

He collected information on Israeli firms and located several that seemed interesting. He gathered all the details he could and applied to several firms, particularly those which seemed to be undergoing growth. Among the companies that received his résumé was the furniture concern Rim, one of the most successful and profitable in Israel.

Before applying to Rim, Bibi learned everything he could about the company's owners. He also spread word of his interest in joining Rim to his friends and relatives. Bibi contacted his father's friend Alexander Raphaeli, owner of Jerusalem Pencils. Raphaeli, a veteran Jerusalem industrialist, was happy to help the son of Benzion Netanyahu, his old friend. He called the owners of Rim, Ahron and Rolando Eisen, and suggested they offer Bibi a job. Rolando Eisen recalled, "Raphaeli told me to expect a call from a very promising young man, and that I might be able to help him. He told me that the young man was Yoni's brother, that he was returning to Israel, and that he was interested in working in Jerusalem."

After sending his résumé, Bibi was given an appointment for an interview. He then had a number of meetings with Rolando Eisen, who managed the company under the watchful eye of his father, Ahron. Israel

Amir, who was the company's financial manager at the time, said: "In Israeli reality, then as well as now, it is very strange for anyone to approach a company and offer himself for a job. What usually happens is that the company places an ad in the want-ad sections of the newspapers and people apply. Either that, or we look for outstanding talent.

"I remember that at one of the first meetings with Bibi, before he started to work for us, he said, 'I've checked a number of Israeli production companies undergoing a process of growth and Rim stood out. I found out that your management team is young and good, so I applied to you.'"

Negotiations with Rim were swift. Fortunately for Bibi, the company's marketing manager had resigned and returned to England some weeks before he had applied. Rolando Eisen decided to give Bibi the job. The decision amazed the management team, even those who had been favorably impressed by Bibi. Rolando Eisen said, "His résumé was excellent. Twenty-nine years old, graduated with excellent grades, worked for a very good Boston firm. He had served in the General Command Reconnaissance Unit. He was both arrogant and modest. He made a good impression on me and I was willing to take a chance on him."

During the negotiations, Bibi amazed the Rim people. When they came to discuss his salary, he suggested he take a relatively low salary, which would increase based on his success. He discussed options and the possibility of being made director. This assertive style was unusual for Israel in the late 1970s. Bibi had imported it from America, where such behavior is the norm. Eisen agreed to the terms, and Bibi was appointed marketing manager.

Bibi found it hard going at first. He did not get on with Rolando Eisen, the firm's CEO. To this day, the workers remember the shouting that came out of Eisen's office whenever Bibi went in. Eisen, however, was the only one who shouted. Bibi never raised his voice.

Life was not easy for Bibi at this time. He was living at his parents' house and was not financially well off. His separation from Micki was made official by divorce. Fleur Cates was in America. Most of his childhood friends were either out of the country going to school or busy bringing up young families. Alone, Bibi devoted his energies to Rim.

One other thing occupied Bibi's thoughts and time. Several months after Yoni was killed, Bibi had founded the Jonatan Institute for the Study of International Terror. Bibi hoped to bring hundreds of statesmen, academics, and journalists from all over the world to Jerusalem to take part in a conference on terror. The gathering would be held in memory of his brother Yoni. He sent out hundreds of letters and appeals. Hardly anyone knew the name Benjamin Netanyahu, but everyone had heard of Yoni and knew his story.

The institute's first conference on terrorism took place in July 1979 in Jerusalem. Bibi managed to convene an impressive array of political figures—some were already big names, others were on the cusp of power. Among those who attended the conference were George Bush, former director of the CIA who was about to embark on an unsuccessful campaign for the presidency of the United States, an office he would achieve a decade later; George Shultz, who had been President Nixon's secretary of labor and secretary of the treasury and would later serve as President Reagan's secretary of state; Ed Meese, a professor of law at the University of San Diego who would later become attorney general of the United States; William Webster, director of the FBI and later of the CIA; Jeane Kirkpatrick, a political writer who would soon represent the United States as ambassador to the United Nations; Yitzhak Rabin; Moshe Arens; and many others.

Anyone who did not know Bibi before the conference could hardly ignore him after it. He made sure that the press thoroughly covered the gathering. And he supplied them with a real scoop: Arab terrorists were undergoing training in dozens of military bases in the Soviet Union. The American press reported on the event, making sure to give credit for its organization to Benjamin Netanyahu, brother of Entebbe hero Yoni Netanyahu.

Meanwhile, Bibi remained immersed in his work at Rim. In spite of his quarrels with Rolando Eisen, he got on surprisingly well with the workers and other managers. One of his former colleagues recalls: "In his everyday work Bibi was extremely well thought of. He answered to no one, only to his own interests. If necessary, he was capable of transferring a worker who had been with the firm for twenty years. He didn't fire him, just removed him from his job. Other managers would not have dared touch a veteran employee. He was respected at Rim. Away from work, it was also known that he was the brother of Yoni, the nation's hero."

Bibi brought a number of innovations to Rim. One of his first objectives

(*Above*) Bibi at age thirteen (far right, second row from the top) with his elementary school class in Jerusalem. *Government Press Office*

(*Right*) Bibi (right) with Uzi Beller, his best friend in Jerusalem. *Government Press Office*

(*Right*) A front page cartoon in the newspaper *Hadashot,* December, 1986. Bibi (left) and Ehud Barak, head of the opposition Labor Party. *Government Press Office*

(*Below*) Eighteen years old and standing on his head. *Government Press Office*

בחירות 1996

מועמד בנימין נתניהו

מדובר בתסריט דמיוני, בחומר למחשבה. השנה היא
הליכוד מציג כמועמדו לראשות הממשלה את ב
באו"ם. המערך מציג מציג את אהוד ברק, היום אלוף פיק
זיכרונות. דוד לוי מתמודד מול נתניהו ומפסיד בהו
איפה הם צמחו? איזה אופי יהיה למערכת הבחירו
משתתפים בתרגיל הזה שלא על דעתם, גם אם
שרירותית. לפניך מבט אופטימי מסוף 1986, עשר

(*Opposite*) During his studies in Philadelphia, Bibi (right) spent his summer holidays in Israel. *Government Press Office*

(*Inset opposite*) Yoni (Yonetan) Netanyahu, Bibi's eldest and beloved brother. Yoni was killed in a dramatic hostage rescue mission in Entebbe on April 7, 1976. *Government Press Office*

(*Right*) Bibi as a young officer in Sayeret Matkel, the secret elite unit of the Israel Defense Forces. *Government Press Office*

(*Below*) Netanyahu with Zalman Shazar, late president of Israel, in May 1972, after a heroic and daring rescue of hostages held on a Sabena airline. *Government Press Office*

(*Right*) Bibi Netanyahu during his army service. *Government Press Office*

(*Below*) Training in the Israeli Army. Bibi is on the right. *Government Press Office*

(*Above*) Bibi during a border patrol in Lebanon in 1972. *Government Press Office*

(*Right*) Netanyahu's signature in Hebrew and English. *Government Press Office*

Bibi (center) as a platoon commander in the Sayeret Matkel. *Government Press Office*

Netanyahu (front row, left) with Prime Minister Yitzhak Shamir (front row, right) at the Madrid Peace Conference, where Israel and the Palestinians met in 1991. *Government Press Office*

Netanyahu (right) with Chief of Staff Moshe Levy (left) and General Ehud Barak (center).
The I.D.F. Spokesman

Bibi and his daughter, No'a, from his first marriage. *Government Press Office*

as marketing manager was to prepare a reliable database, so that decisions could be made based on factual analyses, not impressions. Israel Amir gave an example. "If we had placed an ad in the weekend papers, by Sunday morning Bibi would be checking how many people entered the shops. He would gauge the success of the advertisement and build a statistical system based on computerized reports."

The other managers in the firm were often surprised by Bibi's American methods, which were not known in Israel. He spent a lot of time learning, reading books, mainly in English, about marketing. He always had a book in his hands. Often he would forget it in the men's room. Israel Amir said: "I liked him because he seemed honest, courageous and a genuine friend. In the world of business there is a tendency among managers to pass the buck. Marketing problems could be blamed on bad production. Bibi wasn't like that. He took responsibility. He knew when to admit mistakes in marketing. In the management ethic of the time, this was quite unusual. I liked and respected him."

Israel Amir and Bibi became friends. The difference in their politics—Amir was one of the early Peace Now activists—did not bother them. They were at similar stages in their lives. Both were going through a divorce; both were workaholics. Sometimes they would meet on weekends at the home of one of their colleagues. Bibi would often surprise everyone with his theories on the dangers of communism. "We are in a situation in which communism can take over the world," he would say. "Communism is closing in on the free world and the free world has to defend itself."

Bibi fascinated his listeners. He would make his theories meaningful through numerous examples while displaying knowledge on a wide range of subjects. As in his youth, he did not engage in dialogue. He simply lectured. When he finished, he declared that those who disagreed with him were wrong.

The friendship between Bibi and Amir deepened during their joint tours of Rim's nationwide marketing outlets. The two would drive from place to place in Bibi's company car. In the winter of 1980, Bibi asked Amir for help. At the age of thirty-one, he felt it was time to move out of his parents' home and wanted to rent an apartment for himself. Amir owned an apartment in Moshav Bet Zeit, which he offered to Bibi, who gratefully accepted.

One cold, wet Saturday, the two borrowed one of the firm's pickup trucks and transferred a refrigerator from Bibi's parents' home to the apartment in Bet Zeit. In spite of the cold, they were sweating as they lifted the refrigerator onto the truck. Suddenly, Bibi turned to his friend and said, "Listen, one day I'm going to be prime minister." Amir looked at him to make sure he was not joking. "He was quite serious. He meant every word." Amir made no reply. They tied the refrigerator to the truck and drove toward Bibi's new home.

By the early eighties, Rim's annual income had reached $25 million. Bibi controlled a network of dozens of shops and marketing outlets all over Israel and spent many hours on the road in his company car. Almost one hundred people worked under him, most of them in the various stores. The workers liked him. Not a warm boss, he was, nevertheless, a fair one. He initiated a reward system previously unknown in Israel: the outstanding-worker competition, in which excellent performance was recognized with prizes such as weekend holidays paid for by the company. He stirred enthusiasm among employees, giving speeches on motivation and aggressive marketing. In those days, marketing as a profession was not as highly developed as it is today, and Bibi's new approach captivated his listeners. He believed the happier the workers, the more productive they would be, and to this end he organized biweekly parties and conferences in various hotels for his workers. He developed in them a sense of responsibility. He set goals to be met, and they followed him.

Bibi developed countless strategies for selling through special offers, and special sales, but one variable was impossible to control—the rapid inflation under the various Likud governments of the time. Israel Amir said: "The inflation in those years screwed up everyone's life. We were selling in dollars. Prices would go up every day. When we would make a special offer, we would never know if we would make money or lose it. We were working from eight in the morning to eight in the evening and sometimes later. When we had finished our day's work, we were exhausted. We didn't go out for a drink or anything like that. We went home to sleep."

Bibi was never one of the boys at work. He kept his distance. He did not have heart-to-heart conversations with people; he did not involve people in his feelings. He did not flirt with the female workers.

On several occasions, Bibi considered quitting. His first year had been especially hard. He found it difficult to cope with Rolando Eisen's fiery temperament. He jealously guarded his own areas of responsibility and gave no one a chance to interfere with them. Within a year, however, he and Eisen became solid friends, and their friendship has lasted to this day.

At the bat mitzvah party thrown by Eisen's sister for her daughter, hostesses were placed at the entrance to the hall to give each of the entering male guests a flower for his buttonhole. One of the hostesses was especially forward and suggested to Bibi that she would be pleased to meet him after the party. Bibi politely demurred. When one of his colleagues told him off for refusing the attractive young woman's proposal, Bibi replied that he "had too much work to do."

Things got better once the first year was up. His standing in the firm had become stronger and, no less important, Fleur made frequent visits to Israel. He introduced her to Rolando Eisen, who was most impressed. The other managers in Rim could not hold a conversation in English. They remember Fleur, an MIT graduate in business administration, sitting whole evenings without once opening her mouth. Eisen, however, spoke English with Fleur, and their friendship led Eisen to turn her into an unofficial adviser to Rim. Bibi began to consult her before making any big decisions. Eisen, too, often consulted her, sometimes over the phone in Boston, sometimes when she was in Israel. It was Fleur who gave Rim a name for their new mattress line—Paradise—to be marketed as a separate brand.

Fleur started pressing Bibi to marry her, but she wanted to return to America rather than live in Israel. A difficult decision became even harder for Bibi when Eisen suggested making him a director and shareholder in Rim. Bibi said he needed time to think.

During one of his trips to the United States, Bibi married Fleur in a civil ceremony in New York. Later, Fleur, a German born to a Christian mother, underwent a Conservative conversion to Judaism. Later still, when Bibi was appointed ambassador to the United Nations, she went through an Orthodox Jewish conversion.

After the wedding the couple decided to live in two countries, Fleur in America and Bibi in Israel. Every three weeks he would fly to Boston for a week. Rolando Eisen said, "It was very important to him to spend time with Fleur. The compromise we managed to reach was that he travelled back and forth. It was hard, but the management agreed to it. I had pinpointed him to replace me as the company's CEO, and I was willing to wait."

A life divided between Boston and Jerusalem was not easy. There were no fax machines or mobile phones in those days. Bibi would work like a maniac for three weeks and then fly to America. When he was with Fleur, he would call the office every day. Still, his absence was felt. "Although he did his best to keep abreast of things," Eisen said, "we got the feeling that we didn't have a full-time marketing manager. He kept in contact over the phone and received reports, but we had the feeling that he was no longer there."

A close childhood friend of Bibi's remembers that Bibi was not feeling very well at the time. Once again, he found himself torn between Israel and America, leading two lives that seemed disconnected. He knew that the chances were slim that Fleur would agree to move to Israel permanently.

Then came the tempting proposal from Moshe Arens, Israel's ambassador to the United States. At the beginning of April 1982, the telephone rang in Bibi's office at Rim furniture manufacturers. Moshe Arens's personal secretary was on the other end. "Mr. Arens wants to speak with you," she said.

Bibi had known Arens for years. Their first introduction had been made by Benzion Netanyahu, who presented the ambassador as a family friend. In the 1940s, Benzion had been a witness at Arens's wedding when the latter was the Betar (Likud youth movement) representative in America. Shortly after the wedding, Arens took part in the War of Independence.

When Bibi was a student at MIT and on one of his frequent vacations to Israel, his father asked him to visit Arens, then a senior engineer with Israel Aircraft Industries, to convey his regards. Bibi did as he was told. The conversation in Arens's house in Savyon focused around employment possibilities for Bibi once he had completed his studies in Boston. No mention was made of political issues.

Their next meeting came in 1979, during the International Congress on Terrorism. Arens, one of the guests at the conference, was most impressed by young Benjamin's talent for organizing, and especially by the distinguished people he had managed to persuade to take part in the gathering.

At the beginning of 1982, the post of political attaché at the Israeli embassy in Washington was vacant. Arens, then Israel's ambassador, wanted to recruit Zvi Rafiah, who had held the position during the Camp

David talks and was considered an expert on the United States. Rafiah turned down the job. Arens looked for another candidate, and Bibi's name came up.

In spite of his success in Rim's marketing revolution, Bibi felt that the furniture business was too small for him and he had an eye out for more exciting opportunities. Arens's telephone call came just in time. The two met at the Plaza Hotel in Jerusalem. Bibi recalls, "Arens asked me if I would like to come and be his political attaché in Washington. I hesitated for exactly half a minute, then accepted."

Arens recounts the circumstances surrounding the offer: "If Zvi Rafiah had said 'yes,' I would never have offered the job to Bibi. At the beginning of 1982, I called Zvi Rafiah and offered him the post of political attaché in the Israeli embassy in Washington. Rafiah refused. I offered the post to Bibi, who took twenty minutes to accept. When people come to me today and say, 'Look what you've done,' I have to tell them: Don't blame me! It's Zvi Rafiah's fault."

10

Israel's Political Attaché in Washington

On the evening of June 3, 1982, Shlomo Argov, Israel's ambassador in London, was a guest at a cocktail party at the Dorchester Hotel on Park Lane. The hotel was alive with diplomats, foreign ambassadors, and local politicians. Close to ten in the evening, the Israeli ambassador decided to leave the party and descended the elegant staircase into the hotel's Victorian-style lobby. The embassy car was waiting for him at the entrance.

Suddenly he heard a voice behind him, in a foreign accent: "Ambassador Argov?" Before he had a chance to reply, several shots were fired at him from close range. Argov fell to the pavement in a pool of his own blood. His assailants, Palestinian terrorists, escaped in a waiting getaway car. An hour later, they were already on a flight to Lebanon.

The attempt on Argov's life sent shock waves through Israel and the world. The following day the government convened an emergency session. Ariel Sharon, the minister of defense, was on an official visit to Romania at the time, but in his desk drawer lay detailed plans for an invasion of Lebanon to clear out the nests of terrorism in the country.

Sharon returned to Israel that same day. The next morning, IDF fighter jets were on their way to bomb terrorist targets in Lebanon. This time, however, unlike the usual strike pattern, the bombing continued well north of Lebanon's southern border. Israeli jets appeared above Beirut, Lebanon's capital, and bombed the PLO headquarters in the heart of the city, close to the municipal soccer stadium, killing and wounding many Lebanese citizens.

Israel's prime minister, Menachem Begin, called a press conference in Jerusalem and announced that Israel had begun a war of defense against the terrorists in Lebanon. He named the limited military operation the Peace in Galilee War. He said, "We have decided to push back, at all costs, the danger of terrorism from our northern borders. The IDF will push back the katyushas."

President Ronald Reagan and his administration showed some understanding of what Israel was doing. Begin's promise that the operation would be limited to some twenty-five miles into Lebanese territory succeeded in placating the concerns of the Americans.

Meanwhile, convoys of Israeli tanks were crossing the Lebanese border close to Rosh Hanikra and Metulla. The parachute division had landed in the valley of the Awalli River, more than twenty-five miles from the border, with the objective of blocking the Palestinians' escape routes. The IDF started calling up reserves, preparing for possible escalation of the situation.

Bibi Netanyahu was in Jerusalem at the time, getting ready for his imminent departure to Washington, where he would take up the position of political attaché at the Israeli embassy. In the middle of his preparations, Bibi was called up for reserve military service, together with many of his peers, former soldiers in the General Command Reconnaissance Unit. Although he was a reserve officer, he was given no position of command, perhaps because criticism of him from within his unit held that he tended to evade routine reserve duty because of his frequent trips abroad. Even when he was on vacation in Israel, he did not bother to turn up for reserve training. Netanyahu denied such accusations, claiming that whenever he was in the country, he made a point of contacting his unit.

This time, Bibi Netanyahu decided not to join his comrades-in-arms in the war in Lebanon. The other recruits saw him share a brief word with the commander of the reserve unit and then pack his things and leave. Eli Daudi, later called Eli Gill, left the unit along with Bibi. One of the unit's veterans, Gill had volunteered for service although he was exempt from active duty. Gill, however, later made his way back to Lebanon. Netanyahu did not. Years later, in October 1997, Gill would be among the former General Command Reconnaissance Unit soldiers who publicly denounced Prime Minister Netanyahu for comments he made about the left wing in Israel.

Bibi was overheard confiding in the elderly Rabbi Kaduri, one of the spiritual leaders of Jewish fundamentalism, that he believed the "left has forgotten what it is to be Jewish. They want to put Israel's security in the hands of the Arabs...can you believe such a thing?" A large number of Bibi's former comrades in arms were also former kibbutzniks and belonged to the Israeli left. They were outraged by Bibi's comments, and in response published full-page articles in the Israeli press with stinging headlines like: "We do not believe that Bibi was ever in the General Command Reconnaissance Unit."

Bibi's refusal to take part in the Lebanon War came as a surprise to many. He had a reputation as a courageous fighter who never hesitated to join dangerous operations. Most people believed that Yoni's death in Entebbe was behind Bibi's decision not to go into battle again. Some thought he was worried about his parents, who would be unable to handle another loss should anything happen to him.

To this day, Bibi is hurt by criticism of his decision not to fight in this war. He points out that up to the time of the Lebanon War, he always made a point of joining his friends on reserve duty, even volunteering on several occasions, paying for the flight back to Israel with his own money. When war broke out, he did not receive a call-up notice, he explains, but went north of his own volition. In the case of Lebanon, however, he was pressured by Moshe Arens, who demanded that he drop everything and fly to Washington, where he would defend Israel against heavy international opposition.

Netanyahu believed that the war in Lebanon was the most justified of all of Israel's wars. Since Yoni's death, he had come to view terrorism as a spreading global cancer which had to be removed. Bibi felt he could accomplish more to this end in the diplomatic arena than in the military. He believed that the IDF could handle the terrorists, but he also knew that in the corridors of power—in Washington, London, Paris, and the United Nations—equally important battles would be fought.

The appointment of thirty-three-year-old Benjamin Netanyahu to be the political attaché in Washington shocked most of Israel's diplomatic staff. Nahman Shai, who was the embassy's press adviser at the time, recalls that apart from Arens, the ambassador, no one at the embassy had ever heard of Benjamin Netanyahu.

Yitzhak Shamir, then Israel's foreign minister, remembered Bibi's father from years before, when the latter had so avidly supported Jabotinsky. Shamir met Netanyahu for the first time during one of his visits to the United States, in the middle of the Lebanon War. He recalls a talented and enthusiastic young man. Bibi told Shamir about his parents, and Shamir remembered his father and promised Bibi to keep an eye on him in Israel.

The invasion of Lebanon and the photographs which were published in the world press placed Israel at the center of a harsh diplomatic attack, which only escalated when the Israeli Air Force dropped American-made cluster bombs on Beirut and pictures of injured civilians appeared on television. Washington was furious. Against the barrage of criticism stood a small but experienced diplomatic team. To this day, that particular Israeli team is considered in political circles to be one of the finest ever produced by the Israeli Foreign Office. It included Ambassador Arens, whose experience, calm temperament, and fluent English would help mitigate the damage caused to Israel in world public opinion. Other members of the team included the military attaché, Gen. Menachem Merino; the economic attaché, Dan Harpoon; the attaché to Congress, Oded Eran; the press adviser, Nahman Shai; and the adviser on propaganda, Harry Hurvitz. The question mark on the team was Hurvitz, who in the past had written speeches for Menachem Begin. Hurvitz had difficulty fitting in with the embassy's senior personnel. He was something of a "strange bird," a bit eccentric, not the man to lead a counterattack in the media. Into this vacuum burst Bibi Netanyahu.

From the beginning, the embassy staff was aware that they were dealing with a talented, ambitious man. He made it clear that he planned to succeed quickly and on a large scale. Having grown up and attended schools in America, Netanyahu knew that manipulation of the media was the key to political efficacy. Within a few months, Netanyahu became the most asked for interviewee in Washington, a favorite of the leading gossip columnists and the most persuasive of the Israeli embassy's spokespersons. Bibi was ready for television. There was little room for spontaneity.

Each weekend, he and Fleur rented three TV cameras and a large TV spotlight, and their living room became a TV studio. Fleur was the interviewer and Bibi had to reply. Sometimes they would bring in a friend to help. Afterward, they would run through the tapes and analyze how Bibi responded: "I moved my head here.... Here I need more control of my eye movements...." They learned from their mistakes. In time, Bibi became a consummate talking head.

Though not everyone at the embassy was pleased with Bibi's accomplishments, Ambassador Arens was delighted and gave him freedom of action. Arens did not envy Bibi's success. When he was approached by members of his staff who warned him that Bibi was stealing the limelight, Arens refused to listen to their complaints. As far as he was concerned, Netanyahu's ambition made him a valuable asset.

Netanyahu was full of energy. His perfect English, his self-confidence, and the fact that the American way was so familiar to him all helped him excel in Washington. Before long he was a familiar face in the corridors of Congress, and especially in the editorial offices of the leading papers and TV studios. He was confident of his ability to change things, to influence the policy makers in the White House and in the State Department, and to stem the flow of adverse public opinion. He explained that the war in Lebanon was a just one and that the IDF's arrival there was an inevitable event in the cruel struggle to root out terrorism.

Compared to other diplomats, Bibi Netanyahu was like a breath of fresh air. He spoke to the Americans in their own language, using expressions from the world of sports and the college campus. And he was always smiling. Ambassador Arens told his press adviser, Nahman Shai, "Let Bibi appear on TV whenever possible. He's excellent at it, he loves it." Arens was glad to give Bibi the spotlight, preferring to invest most of his own energies in deepening his ties with the Reagan administration. Arens gave his young deputy, who had only just arrived, much more freedom than was common in a relationship between an ambassador and his political attaché. The delegation of work was quite clear: Arens worked the administration, Bibi the TV cameras.

In a very short time, Bibi became a personal friend of Ted Koppel, host of the prestigious TV show *Nightline*; columnist William Safire of the *New York Times*; and George Will, former Washington editor of *National Review* and contributing editor of *Newsweek*, among many others. Once a week, Koppel and Netanyahu would meet for breakfast in a small cafe not far from the embassy. Netanyahu became a regular guest and the most popular interviewee on Koppel's show. Netanyahu also met with the senior managers of the *Washington Post* and introduced himself to the editor, Ben Bradlee, and the paper's diplomatic desk. As usual, he made an enormous impression. He continued on to the other newspapers, and then to prominent TV people, including brothers Marvin and Bernard Kalb, and Sam Donaldson of ABC. They all became Bibi's personal friends.

One of the more interesting friendships formed by Bibi in those days was with the reporter George Nader, editor of a political information sheet which was distributed in diplomatic circles in Washington. Netanyahu's friendship with Nader gave him valuable influence in Nader's publication. Nader, a journalist of Syrian origin, was considered close to his country's governing circles. When Netanyahu rose to power in Israel, he turned Nader into a secret and unofficial mediator between Israel and Syria.

Netanyahu's widespread activity did not escape Nahman Shai. Alone with Arens, Shai warned, "Misha, you should know that Bibi is becoming very popular in the city. He is pulling the rug from under your feet."

"Let him succeed," Arens said. "Sell him wherever you can."

Shai kept a watchful eye on the special relationship between the ambassador and the young attaché. Though Netanyahu's personal agenda and widespread media exposure came at Arens's expense, Shai could find no sign of tension between the two. Shai understood that Arens considered Bibi his personal protégé and was cultivating him to become his successor as Israeli ambassador to Washington. Netanyahu understood. He invested time and energy in cultivating relationships with the leaders of the Jewish organizations in Washington, who were influential in the Reagan administration and in Congress. They were men of respect—and generous budgets. All the Jewish leaders were taken with Bibi, the handsome young Israeli who spoke perfect English, was well educated, a war hero, and the brother of a mythical Israeli figure. Before long, the leaders of the Jewish organizations in New York and the Jewish lobby in Washington found themselves looking forward to the next visit from the young Israeli diplomat. Others awaited his next speaking engagement. Bibi's lectures and study groups were always sold out. The audiences often consisted of large numbers of shiny-eyed women who listened with rapt attention to every word he said.

At the embassy, Netanyahu set out to bolster public relations efforts on Israel's behalf. He employed Yoram Etinger, who produced data sheets and convincing arguments in favor of Israeli policies. Netanyahu molded his p.r. strategy according to military methods. He emphasized speed in responding to hostile publicity, and aggressiveness. He sought ways to "sell" Israel to the American media, even in difficult times. During the Lebanon war, there was plenty of opportunity to implement these strategies.

Moshe Arens was pleased with his protégé and praised him at every opportunity. This only compelled Bibi to raise his sights. Some of his closer acquaintances were beginning, for the first time, to learn of his plans for the future. He started talking about politics and the Knesset and the government. One day he said to his personal secretary, "Just you wait and see, someday I will be prime minister."

The secretary, who often argued with Netanyahu about politics, replied, "It will never happen. And if it does, I will kill myself the same day."

When Netanyahu won the election and became prime minister, that same secretary took a three-day vacation from her job, retreating to a remote rest home in order to recuperate.

In the meantime, Operation Peace in Galilee was running into difficulty in the United States. The early support of the Reagan administration had begun to disintegrate. At the height of the war the IDF pounded the Lebanese capital day after day, and pictures of dead and wounded women and children filled TV screens all over America. The Israeli public relations machine in Washington found itself in serious trouble. American public opinion became decidedly hostile. Israel was perceived as a cruel, aggressive country which did not hesitate to attack women and children in order to advance its political objectives. Israel's defense minister, Ariel Sharon, was the target of most of the hostility. In government circles and on television, Sharon was portrayed as the mastermind of the massacre of innocent Arabs. Some even blamed him for the attempted assassination of Philip Habib, the American special emissary.

Habib, a veteran American diplomat who had family roots in Lebanon, had been appointed by Secretary of State George Shultz to try to find a solution to the crisis between Israel and Syria and the Palestinian organizations. On one of Habib's tours of the region, fierce artillery fire suddenly opened on the observation point where he was standing. Habib said the shells closed in on him, and he was sure that his time had come: "It was a miracle I came out alive from that attack."

Habib had no doubt that this gunfire had come from the IDF and was aimed specifically at him, and that Ariel Sharon had given the order to fire, either to eradicate him, or to "warn" him. Of course, Sharon denied it all, but it was hard to repair the political damage wrought by the charges.

Netanyahu found himself contending almost daily with media disasters like the "attempted assassination" of Philip Habib. Instead of being defensive, he played offense. He ordered his aides to be constantly on the alert for any slipups in Arab "propaganda." When these were discovered, he would pounce. One such instance occurred during the Israeli air force bombing of Beirut. A picture of a small Lebanese girl who had lost an arm in the attack was published in the media. The child became a symbol of Israel's heartless attacks on Lebanon. Ronald Reagan received a copy of the picture and hung it in his office. He was furious and put a call through to Israeli prime minister Menachem Begin, telling him that the attacks must stop. Begin acquiesced and ordered Sharon to put an immediate halt to the bombing of West Beirut.

The decision angered Netanyahu. "We must not give in to American pressure," he told those close to him. "We are at a critical stage in the war. An infantry attack on Beirut would cost us many casualties. We cannot act unless we have control of the air and reinforcements from the air."

Netanyahu suspected that the picture of the one-armed Palestinian child was a fraud. He had it enlarged, and the larger it became, the greater was his suspicion that it was a forgery. Bibi insisted that the photograph had not been taken during the attack on Lebanon. Bibi asked that the child be located. After a search lasting several days, she was found. Her arm had indeed been amputated, but it had happened years before, during the civil war in Lebanon, and had nothing to do with the IDF.

"When I got on to the story," Bibi said, "it was already too late. As far as American public opinion was concerned, Israel was a country which had no mercy, able to bomb civilian targets, including women and children, indiscriminately, in a war which was unjust and unnecessary."

Then there was the massacre in the Sabra and Shatila refugee camps on September 17 and 18, 1982. Hundreds of Moslem refugees—men, women, and children—were slaughtered by the Christian Phalangist forces while IDF soldiers looked on. This resulted in a huge wave of anger and outrage throughout the world.

Israel's image had reached an unprecedented low. Netanyahu found himself facing the media virtually alone. He spent long hours in the television studios and on the telephone, talking to reporters and columnists. He did not succeed in winning this particular war. Not even his most convincing arguments—that the terrible massacre had been perpetrated by the Phalangist forces in revenge for the murder, three days before, of their leader, Bashir Gemayel—were able to vindicate Israel or change public opinion. The hostility of various political pundits was obvious. Netanyahu knew that this battle was a lost cause.

He became very critical of the government of Israel for not setting up a decent public relations mechanism in Jerusalem, which was urgently needed to counteract the image presented by the Arab states. Netanyahu was not averse to criticizing Yitzhak Shamir for this oversight. In a letter to the foreign minister's office, Netanyahu wrote that Israel could not afford to conduct a military operation without having speeches and images to back it up. "In order to balance the many lies being spread about us," Netanyahu wrote, "Israel must recruit the best brains and the sharpest pens. This requires a general overhaul in the government offices responsible for public relations. It is impossible to succeed in an international political struggle without the ability to achieve the support of international public opinion." In his book *A Place Among the Nations*, Netanyahu wrote:

> In a world that has been conditioned to see Israel as the heavy, every Israeli retreat from positions under dispute with the Arabs will naturally be applauded. Israel will be patted on the back and congratulated as long as it continues to make unilateral concessions. But once an Israeli government decides, as it inevitably must, to draw a line beyond which it cannot retreat, the international applause will cease—and pressure will begin again.... The school of thought that holds that Israel's public relations problem would end with the establishment of a Palestinian state is wrong. In such a case Israel would be faced with an existential threat *and* a public relations nightmare, as Arab irredentism turns its focus on the Arab population within the remainder of Israel.

Ambassador Moshe Arens remained supportive of Bibi and did his best to help soften the Reagan administration's stand on Israel, which was very hostile during the Lebanon war. He was aware that certain foreign officers in Jerusalem felt that Bibi was overstepping bounds in his criticism of the Reagan administration and in his attempts to recruit American congressmen.

Bibi's obsession with garnering support for Israel, which included making TV appearances and briefings to commentators and columnists, sometimes caused the Israeli embassy to overlook Washington's inner political activity. Thus it happened that the embassy was caught off guard when it learned of a plan proposed by the administration which called for Israel's unilateral withdrawal from Lebanon and arrangements for evacuating the terrorists. In protest of Israel's bombing of West Beirut, Defense Secretary Caspar Weinberger—one of the sharpest critics of Israeli policy—announced a halt in the supply of American F-16 fighter jets to Israel. Moshe Arens tried to reduce the damage—to rescind the decision or soften it—by making use of his good connections in the American State Department. At first he was unsuccessful. The Americans were furious and determined. Arens's warm personal relationships with George Shultz was of no use in this instance. Political tension between Israel and Washington had reached a boiling point, and not even Netanyahu's media magic could change things. Only after arrangements had been made to evacuate the PLO from Beirut, and Israel announced that it was withdrawing its forces from the region as the first stage of redeployment in the security belt, did the relationship between the two countries return to normal.

At the beginning of 1983, Israel published the conclusions of the Kahan Commission on the massacre at Sabra and Shatila, the two Lebanese refugee camps where Christian Phalangists murdered Lebanese Muslim refugees. The commission declared that Israel's minister of defense, Ariel Sharon, had had ministerial responsibility for the events prior to the massacre, and recommended removing him from his position for not intervening. Prime Minister Begin received the commission's recommendations during a dramatic and stormy government meeting. Sharon fought back, insisting that it was not right that he should be the only one to pay such a high personal price for an event over which he had no control. For years to come, Sharon would continue to fight the recommendations of the Kahan Commission—ultimately unsuccessfully. After many demonstrations and protests—including a Peace Now demonstration in which a key activist, Emil Grunzweig, was killed by a hand grenade thrown by a right-wing fanatic—Ariel Sharon resigned from the government, most unwillingly. Begin offered the post of minister of defense to Moshe Arens. The ambassador considered the proposal, and after some hesitation accepted. In the same breath, he suggested appointing his political attaché, Benjamin Netanyahu, ambassador to Washington.

Begin and Foreign Minister Shamir were not enthusiastic. They respected Bibi but felt he was too young and inexperienced for such a post, and they looked for another candidate. In the meantime, Bibi filled in for Arens, who had returned to Israel.

For six months, Bibi Netanyahu carried out the duties of Israel's ambassador to Washington. He continued to cultivate a special relationship with Secretary of State George Shultz, and the two found a topic of common interest—terrorism.

"One day," Netanyahu recalls, "Shultz invited me into his office in the State Department and told me how worried he was about the spread of terrorism. He showed me some classified information, belonging to the CIA, on terrorism in Libya, Syria, Iraq, and Iran.

"Those terrorists," Shultz said, "are wild animals and not human beings. I have decided to change American policy toward terrorism."

Shultz told Netanyahu about the sharp debate between himself and Caspar Weinberger, who opposed the use of American and international force against terrorism. Surprised by the willingness of the secretary of state of the largest nation in the world to take a stand against terrorism, Bibi said, "It is possible to wipe out international terror, on the condition that the West adopts two basic principles as guidelines against it. First, never give in to terrorist demands, and second, be prepared to fight countries which support and protect terrorism."

Bibi suggested to Shultz that the United States adopt a firm policy against countries which support terrorism—including economic sanctions and, where necessary, military force. It was during this talk with Shultz that Bibi realized that the time was ripe to introduce an idea he had been nurturing for a long time, an international conference on terrorism, in Washington. He told Shultz of his plan and explained that such a conference could be held under the auspices of the Jonathan Institute. Shultz seemed supportive.

"Will you give a lecture at such a conference?" Netanyahu asked.

"You can bet your life on it," Shultz replied. "I'll be there."

Netanyahu was determined to turn the war on terrorism into a major story in America. It was a timely issue. American marines stationed in Beirut had been killed by suicide bombs, and hundreds of bodies of G.I.s had been sent home in coffins. Moreover, relations between Israel and the United States were back on track following the IDF withdrawal from Beirut.

Netanyahu envisioned the conference on terrorism as a truly grand affair that would attract a large number of distinguished participants, create headlines in the media, gain prime-time attraction on TV around the world, and generate a great deal of prestige for himself. He began to search for suitable candidates for organizing his conference and asked for a recommendation from Douglas Faith, a special assistant to the American secretary of defense, as well as a friend of Netanyahu's. Faith knew just the man: an Israeli living in America who was both talented and popular, a pianist named David Bar-Ilan.

Netanyahu had heard of him. Several years before, not long after Yoni's death, Bibi had found himself in Bar-Ilan's elegant drawing room on Manhattan's Upper West Side. Bibi was trying to explain to a distinguished group of wealthy Americans why they should supply the funds for a heroism museum in Jerusalem. It would enshrine the heroes of Jewish history, and among these heroes would be his brother Yoni. Bibi had flown to New York in order to raise funds for the project. The improvised meeting at the Bar-Ilan home did not produce impressive results, but those present were taken by young Netanyahu's charisma and enthusiasm.

Now, in November 1983, Bibi Netanyahu and David Bar-Ilan met once again. Bar-Ilan went to Netanyahu's Washington office and responded enthusiastically to the idea for a conference on terrorism. During the next seven months, Bar-Ilan devoted all his free time to organizing and coordinating the event. It was no easy matter. The idea was for fifty lecturers from twenty-five countries to take part in the conference. They all had to be persuaded to appear, and then Bar-Ilan had to coordinate a complicated schedule as well as find suitable lecture topics for the distinguished guests. He also had to raise funds, advertise, and arrange publicity.

The 1984 conference took place in the prestigious Four Seasons Hotel in Washington and lasted three days. The success of the event surprised even Netanyahu himself. Five years after the first conference, he had succeeded once again in bringing together the political and media elite of the United States and the rest of the world around the issue of terrorism. Attendees of the second terrorism conference held under the auspices of the Jonathan Insititute included Charles Krauthammer, senior editor of the *New Republic*; Daniel Schorr, head of the CBS office in Moscow; Winston Churchill, grandson of the great leader; senators Patrick Moynihan and Al D'Amato of New York and Alan Cranston of California; historian Paul Johnson; and Jack Kemp, future Republican candidate for vice president. Returning from the first conference were George Bush, who had since become vice president of the United States, and George Shultz, who was now secretary of state. The Israeli contingent was back too, led by Yitzhak Rabin and Moshe Arens. Shultz delivered the keynote speech, which was broadcast live internationally, and in which he signaled a change in America's policy regarding terrorism. Senators, congressmen, and professors gave lectures on terrorism. Ted Koppel spoke and also conducted a special panel discussion with leading media personalities.

"The amazing thing," Bar-Ilan recalls, "is that there was no need for me to persuade any of them to come. For Bibi, they said, they would come."

The conference received enormous international attention and acclaim. Everyone involved became a friend and admirer of the man who made it happen, the recently appointed political attaché Benjamin Netanyahu.

A little over a year after the conference, Netanyahu published *Terror: How the West Can Win*. Though it was a great success, the book was no more than an anthology of essays on terrorism gleaned from the two conferences on terror (in Jerusalem, three years after the death of Yoni Netanyahu, and in Washington in 1984) and featuring contributions from Secretary of State George Shultz and others who attended.

The two conferences and the book, published in Hebrew in 1985 and in English in 1986, raised international awareness of the issue of terrorism. President Reagan and Secretary of State Shultz read Netanyahu's book and were profuse in their praise. Terrorism, which had been mainly an Israeli problem during the 1970s, had become over the years an issue which involved Americans no less than the rest of the world. During the years preceding the publication of Netanyahu's book, there had been several terrorist attacks on American and European citizens—the hijacking of a TWA plane to Beirut, the hijacking of the cruise ship *Achille Lauro*, the murder at sea of an American, Leon Klinghofer; the attempted explosion of an American plane on a flight from Rome to Athens; and the attack on passengers at airports in Vienna and Rome, which was prevented by Israeli security guards.

In his book, Netanyahu revealed data, supplied by the Israel security services, that supported the claim that terrorism was not the initiative of private terrorist organizations, but was nurtured and financed by countries such as Libya, Syria, Algeria, and Iraq, mostly under the patronage of the Soviet Union. Documents taken during the Lebanon war in 1982 revealed the widespread organization of Islamic terrorism under the auspices of the Soviet Union. The conference reinforced Netanyahu's view that the PLO, the umbrella for all Palestinian political activity, was nothing more than a terrorist organization.

In his book, Netanyahu called on the free world, particularly the West, to organize against terrorism because they were its main victim. A series of political, economic, and military responses had to be adopted in order to fight back.

One result of the publication of *Terror: How the West Can Win* was that Bibi was given constant protection by Shabak, the Israeli general security services, who were later replaced by American bodyguards. At a Jewish charity event in which two thousand enthusiastic, wealthy Jews gathered in New York's Waldorf-Astoria Hotel, George Shultz, a guest speaker, told the audience how Bibi's book on terrorism and the lectures at Bibi's conference brought about a change in American foreign policy. Shultz revealed that during a flight to California with President Reagan on Air Force One, he showed the president a copy of the book and urged him to read it. Reagan did and was deeply impressed. "I have decided to reconsider our policies regarding terrorism," he said to Shultz. "I think Netanyahu is right." Several months later, American jets attacked Libya in response to that country's involvement in a terrorist attack on American soldiers in Germany. Shultz hinted that the attack, which represented a change in policy, was influenced by Bibi's book. The audience burst into wild applause.

By this time Bibi's friends were beginning to glimpse his political future. "I will be prime minister," Bibi would announce. Bar-Ilan recalls, "At this stage, we were already saying among ourselves that if he does not get to be prime minister, there must be something wrong with the system." His friends would introduce him at official events as "the future prime minister of Israel."

After the international conference, Netanyahu was a star. Almost all the American Jewish organizations, including Bonds for Israel, made use of his fund-raising services. He traveled throughout the United States, participating in charity events. His presence always ensured that fund-raising expectations would be met. Netanyahu was considered a human "money pump." He knew how to talk, what to say, when to smile, and when to shed a tear. He knew how to open the pockets of wealthy American Jews.

David Bar-Ilan founded an organization whose purpose was to bring members of Congress, particularly liberal Jews from the East Coast, closer to Texas oil tycoons. It was the time of the oil crisis, and America's pro-Israeli policies correlated with heavy losses for oil companies, which caused some resentment toward Israel in the American oil business. Enter Netanyahu. Through Bar-Ilan's organization, Bibi managed to rally the oil tycoons around a single, common enemy—OPEC (the Organization of Petroleum Exporting Countries). Before long, several rich, hard-line Texas oil magnates became dyed-in-the-wool Zionists. A few of them even embarked on a guided tour of Israel.

Netanyahu's connections with American media heads became stronger. He seemed to know everyone. His small, powerful clique of journalist friends is to this day called the Gang of Four. It includes A. M. Rosenthal and William Safire, two influential columnists for the *New York Times*; George Will, from *Newsweek;* and Charles Krauthammer, from *Time* and the *Washington Post*. Will, the only non-Jew in the "gang," is the most ardent Zionist of them all. On the rare occasions he attacks Netanyahu it is only for being too moderate. Krauthammer remains one of Netanyahu's closest friends in the American media. Even after being elected prime minister, Bibi continued to receive much-needed support from Krauthammer. During the Western Wall tunnel crisis, when the rest of the world media were up in arms against Bibi, Krauthammer wrote an article in *Time* in favor of Israel's young prime minister.

These four newsmen shared a neoconservative outlook, a political niche that suited Bibi and brought him close to them. Some right-wing Democrats, usually supporters of Israel, also fell into Bibi's crowd. He would listen to their views on America, while they were willing to hear him out on Israel.

Some, however, were not impressed by the young political attaché. In the Israeli embassy in Washington, Netanyahu did not have many admirers. His Israeli coworkers saw a side of Bibi that was hidden from American eyes. "We saw him as hollow, spineless," says one of the embassy workers. "He had a powerful aura, he was ambitious, he knew how to take advantage of circumstances, how to charm people, but everything he did was only for his own good. His will to succeed was enormous, and it was this will that governed his life, his behavior. Nothing else interested him."

The Netanyahu known to the embassy workers is a self-involved man who does everything for his own benefit and believes that other people exist only to serve his interests. A story involving his personal driver, Moshe Hanini, is typical.

Netanyahu, as usual, was late for an urgent meeting. Though his tardiness did not usually bother him, this time he told Hanini to step on the gas. Hanini obeyed. Unfortunately, they were caught in a speed trap and pulled off the road by Washington policemen.

The cops asked Netanyahu and Hanini to get out of the car. They saw at once that the driver was carrying a concealed gun. Hanini showed them his permit to carry it. The police, however objected to the fact that the gun was concealed, and, permit notwithstanding, they promptly handcuffed Hanini.

"Bibi, what are we going to do?" the frightened Hanini asked.

"Don't worry, I'll drive myself to the meeting," Bibi replied. Hanini, in shock, watched his boss get into the car and drive off.

Hanini was taken to the police station. Netanyahu forgot all about the incident and did not bother to report to anyone at the embassy that his driver had been arrested. Fortunately for Hanini, he was allowed one phone call several hours later. He called the embassy's security officer, who intervened and pulled a few strings, and at the end of the day Hanini was released from custody.

Netanyahu returned to the embassy in the evening, still without having reported the incident. Late that night one of the security guards asked Netanyahu where Hanini was; Bibi raised his head from some papers and murmured, "Ah, Hanini, there was some problem this morning. I think he was arrested, or something..."

And he said no more.

11

Ambassador to the United Nations

The years Netanyahu spent in the United States in the service of the Israeli government were probably the most important in shaping his career. The two years in Washington as a political attaché and four as Israeli ambassador to the United Nations thoroughly prepared him for his future. He formed important ties, met the big donors, Jewish and non-Jewish financial tycoons, Jewish community leaders, and, no less important, the most influential people in the American media, whom he would need more than anyone else. During this period, he also developed his political, social, and economic theories.

Then the "Reagan Revolution" came to America. The liberal Democrats, like Jimmy Carter, were replaced by conservative Republicans. Reagan had inherited an economy in crisis, with rising unemployment, and a society which was apathetic and pessimistic.

By the time Bibi left America in 1988, Reagan was at the end of his second term, rich with honors and achievement, enormously popular, and surrounded by an aura of success. Netanyahu had watched the American president's journey with admiration. For him, Ronald Reagan was an enlightening example of someone who made the establishment his own.

During his term as political attaché in Washington, Netanyahu lived with his wife, Fleur, at the embassy's official residence on Connecticut

Avenue. They behaved like a young couple in love. Fleur was beautiful, with her porcelain skin, wonderful features, and lovely figure. She made an immense impression on everyone she met. She had presence and was a great conversationalist.

It was obvious that she was head-over-heels in love with her husband. In all his public appearances she stayed close by his side. On such occasions, Netanyahu would usually be surrounded by attractive women who stared in admiration at the young Israeli diplomat and hung on his every word. But Fleur was almost always with him, watching.

Apart from her good looks and social grace, Fleur, a graduate of Harvard Business School, was extremely talented. She was a first-class financial adviser and received many lucrative job offers. During Bibi's first year in Washington, she worked for a large firm in Boston.

The couple spoke for hours on the phone almost every night, and spent weekends together, usually somewhere between the two cities. At that time Bibi only had eyes for Fleur. People believed he was truly happy with her.

Fleur also served as Bibi's personal editor. She worked on his terrorism book, organized all his speeches and articles, and did research and collected material for him. In this respect, Fleur was a real treasure. Netanyahu, who usually expects and demands excellence from his subordinates, is himself untidy and disorganized. His desk is always covered with piles of papers. He is the kind of person who is forever writing himself notes, which he invariably loses. He valued Fleur's organizational skills and consulted her about everything he did. For her part, she looked after him like a Jewish mother. During the first years of their marriage, she had complete control of his life and he gave himself willingly to her ministering.

Fleur was born in Germany to a Jewish father and a Christian mother. Her parents had escaped Germany and found refuge in England, where Fleur won a local beauty contest when she was eighteen. About five years older than Bibi, her rather old-fashioned style in clothes made her look older than her age and much older than her husband.

At the beginning of their marriage, Fleur was not much of a hostess, and the couple did little entertaining in their Washington home. They usually preferred to eat out with their friends. When Netanyahu was interested in impressing a journalist or politician, he would invite him to dinner at a restaurant—preferably Italian.

As a diplomat's wife, Fleur was faultless. Her impressive style made the combination of Fleur and Bibi especially welcome in Washington drawing rooms.

Fleur had a special rapport with TV's Ted Koppel—a friend of Bibi's and a Jewish Holocaust survivor who had spent time in England. Koppel and Fleur shared a common background: Both had known exile, having to move to another country, Koppel as a Jew and Fleur as a half-Jewish German.

Netanyahu often went on trips around the country, not always on official embassy business. He spent a considerable amount of time raising funds for Bonds for Israel and other Jewish charities. Everywhere he went, he cultivated new connections. He soon had influential friends in every large American city.

In the wake of his success with the international conference on terrorism, Bibi was accused, behind his back, of having used embassy resources to organize it. There was also a lot of nasty gossip about Fleur's origins and the need to look into the activity of her non-Jewish German relatives during the Second World War. Rumors were also circulating that Fleur had converted to Judaism only after Bibi's appointment to the post in Washington. Netanyahu denied all the rumors. He was briefly embarrassed by the charges, but soon got over it. He was very confident in his relationship with his wife and never tried to hide her or keep her at a distance.

When Moshe Arens returned to Israel to take up the post of minister of defense, Netanyahu hoped to be appointed ambassador in his place. For eight months he served as acting ambassador, convinced he would eventually be given the job. But Yitzhak Shamir, then foreign minister, had doubts about Bibi's youth and inexperience. Despite pressure from George Shultz and Arens, Shamir, an extremely stubborn man, continued to refuse to elevate Netanyahu. He appointed Meir Rosen, legal adviser to the Foreign Office, to the post of ambassador to Washington. Rosen, an older man, was experienced and reliable, and a staunch believer in the ways of the Likud.

Rosen had quite a time with Netanyahu in Washington. Bibi had no inhibitions about undermining Rosen and stealing headlines from him. It seemed that whenever Rosen was out of town, Bibi appeared on *Nightline*. This drove Rosen crazy. Once, George Shultz sent Rosen an invitation to a meeting; Netanyahu turned up instead. Rosen had never received the invitation.

Rosen sent hundreds of letters, wires, and complaints to Jerusalem, but nothing helped. No one dared confront Netanyahu, an invaluable media asset. The ambassador's wife, Vera Rosen, also suffered and complained bitterly, but to no avail. So relentless was Bibi that the ambassador was actually relieved when he heard that the first decision made by the national unity government, convened in Israel in 1984, was to name Netanyahu the Israeli ambassador to the United Nations. Yitzhak Shamir, the new foreign minister, had had his own candidate for that post, Elyakim Rubinstein. But when Moshe Arens intervened and suggested that Shamir appoint Bibi, Shamir brought the proposal to Prime Minister Shimon Peres and Peres agreed.

However, a problem remained: What to do with Rubinstein, who really wanted to sit in the ambassador's chair in New York? Shamir sent Arens to him. "Bibi has a terrific TV presence," Arens said. "He is more suitable for the post at the U.N. You'll have to give in."

Usually a pleasant, easy-going man, Rubinstein took it very hard. He later recalled that the incident left him deeply scarred. He was unwilling to give up and, defying Shamir's and Peres's decision, formally applied for the post. It was no help. He formally lost to Netanyahu.

Years later, in 1997, Rubinstein became attorney general in Netanyahu's administration. At the height of the Bar-On affair, which involved unsavory wheeling and dealing between Netanyahu and his justice minister, Rubinstein would be forced to decide whether to put Netanyahu on trial. After much deliberation, Rubenstein would save Netanyahu's political career by deciding not to recommend bringing charges against him.

When Bibi heard of the decision to appoint him ambassador to the United Nations, he upped the ante and offered to serve in two positions. "I will do both jobs from New York, ambassador to the U.N. and ambassador in Washington."

The farewell party organized by Ambassador Rosen for his political attaché was swiftly arranged. The workers gathered in the ambassador's office, drank a toast, Rosen said a few words, Netanyahu added a few of his own, and that was it. Everyone sighed with relief.

No one was surprised by the fact that Benjamin and Fleur Netanyahu took New York by storm. Bibi's reputation as a winner preceded him. The

Israeli delegation to the United Nations was suffering a moral crisis. Four harsh years of declarations, anti-Israel decisions, and successful Arab forays had left the delegation worn out. The retiring U.N. ambassador, Yehuda Blum, had carried out his job in a professional and efficient manner, but he was a rather uninspiring man.

Enter Bibi Netanyahu, young, dynamic, energetic, a smooth talker, overflowing with adrenaline. In a short time he became a local media favorite. The Jewish community was totally enchanted by him. The members of the Israeli delegation suddenly found themselves arriving at work full of enthusiasm, waiting impatiently for the morning meeting. Netanyahu paid no attention to the Arab bloc, ignored threats, and enjoyed challenges.

During Bibi's first few months, his excitement was obvious. He worked hard on his speeches, carefully editing the work of the delegation's official speechwriter, and then locking himself in his office for hours on end and practicing. He would then call David Bar-Ilan to read long passages, make amendments, consult, and deliberate. Bar-Ilan, Bibi's good friend, was also his ghostwriter. Aside from his meteoric musical career, Bar-Ilan was also a talented speechwriter. He wrote speeches for senators, members of Congress, and other key American politicians, usually on the right. Netanyahu, who had complete faith in Bar-Ilan since the successful terrorism conference, employed him as his full-time secret adviser.

People who know Bibi well are convinced that had he not entered politics, he would surely have become a literary editor, or even the editor of a newspaper. His favorite hobby is editing. He does not like for others to write his speeches. He writes out what he wants to say, develops the thoughts into a speech, and edits it over and over again. In most cases, it takes three drafts before he is satisfied.

If a speech is written by someone else, he will edit it dozens of times, going back to the speechwriter repeatedly with questions, suggestions, and amendments. Bibi will often send an article to a newspaper and then call the editorial office at two in the morning, frantic about a comma which has been moved or removed. As far as he is concerned, if the mistake is not remedied, the article is of no value.

Meir Rosen, the Israeli ambassador in Washington, soon learned that the name Netanyahu would continue to haunt him, even from New York. Before long, letters and wires were flowing once again from the embassy in Washington to the prime minister in Jerusalem, complaining about the initiatives being taken by the new ambassador to the United Nations and his "intrusions" into areas reserved for the ambassador in Washington.

Several times Foreign Minister Shamir reprimanded Bibi, but the new ambassador did not worry too much. Meir Rosen learned what others knew—that internal wars against Bibi are a lost cause.

In the meantime, Fleur became involved in furnishing their official residence. The house, in a dreamy location on Fifth Avenue overlooking Central Park, had been bought shortly before their arrival through an especially worthwhile deal arranged by Yehuda Blum. Fleur furnished it with impeccable taste, taking months to do so. She also spent time editing Bibi's book on terrorism. She always made a point of accompanying her husband on social occasions. They continued to hold hands in public and appeared to be in love.

Bibi became a regular guest on *Larry King Live*. After each visit Larry King was astonished by the number of calls that poured in from women wanting to speak to the young ambassador and wondering if he was married. King was impressed. He said years later, "On a scale of one to ten, as a guest star on my program, I would give him an eight. I'd have made it a ten if he'd had a sense of humor."

Fleur started to entertain, proud of the elegant official residence, whose interior she had designed. The Netanyahus were a popular and compelling couple. Then rumors started to emerge about affairs Bibi was having with famous women, but there was never any proof.

In New York, Bibi succeeded in assembling an efficient and loyal team of workers, as he had not done in Washington—Judy Vernai, his spokeswoman; David Granit, his political adviser; and his assistant, Raffi Gevir. Vernai arranged his appointments with media people and tours of newspaper editorial offices. They had a close relationship and she did not hesitate to criticize Bibi when necessary. Gevir, on the other hand, was a supremely loyal employee. He never said a critical word and was usually delighted with his boss. Bibi's staff also included Bernard Lewis, the highly respected historian on the Middle East.

Netanyahu continued to cultivate his ties with journalists and leading politicians. He used to meet them for breakfast or lunch at expensive Italian restaurants. Bibi made a habit of not paying, even for himself.

In addition to Italian food, Bibi also enjoyed Indian cuisine. Most of the dinners served by Fleur in the ambassador's official residence consisted of Indian food. He also developed a penchant for fine cigars. To this day, he makes a point of smoking one after dinner and considers himself a connoisseur on the subject. In the past there had been a permanent supply of quality Cuban cigars in his office, and he would go to great lengths to ensure that he was never without them. Recently Bibi announced he would cut back on his beloved cigars when the treasury revealed his habit cost Israeli taxpayers $40,000 a year. He has never smoked cigarettes, nor does he inhale cigar smoke. It is the smell he enjoys, the aroma, and the style.

He rarely drinks alcohol, only an occasional glass of wine. He would never touch a drop of whiskey, vodka, or other spirits. In a pressing social situation, a formal event or a cocktail party, he might sip a glass of wine or beer.

In New York, he found time for his old love—action movies—and for reading. Bibi likes biographies and history books. He has read most of Western philosophy, beginning with Plato, and tends to sprinkle his conversation with quotes from the more famous philosophers. A great admirer of Winston Churchill, he has read all his writings. As far as Bibi is concerned, Churchill exemplified the man who believes in himself and his views, defies the accepted wisdom of the moment, and is proven right. Of all gentiles, Churchill is the man Bibi admires the most.

Most of Bibi's energy is expended at night. He blooms in the wee hours and barely functions in the morning. He has always hated to get up early, but does so if the need arises. He is a reticent man, with very few—if any—close friends. He is not one of those people who make a point of keeping in touch. Bibi can call someone up suddenly, after years of silence, as if the two had spoken only yesterday. And it works the other way, too— someone can contact him after years of silence, and he will be most receptive.

He demands perfection from his workers, but does not raise his voice. When he reprimands them, it is in a cold, low voice, and the effect is devastating.

One thing has never changed. Bibi is a chronically late, no matter how important the event or the people he is to meet. Being late does not bother him. "Don't worry, Judy," he would say to his faithful spokeswoman, "it'll be okay." It is hard for those delayed by his tardiness to stay angry with him. He will smile and murmur some made-up excuse and be forgiven immediately. Nevertheless, anyone who has ever worked with Bibi has spent endless hours waiting. When it comes to meetings with world leaders, Bibi's lateness can be a problem. Even when he makes use of his famous smile and charm, he sometimes fails to appease those he kept waiting.

At a conference in Lisbon in 1997, Bibi was very late for a meeting with Russian foreign minister Yevgeny Primakov. The Russians became so annoyed that they almost left the meeting place. Some were seen kicking the wall, furious at the Israeli prime minister. Bibi's excuse that he had been held up by French president Jacques Chirac did not impress the Russians.

Throughout his term in New York, Netanyahu would often phone his daughter, No'a, who lived with her mother in Israel. Fleur, too, developed a warm relationship with the girl, and each time No'a came to visit, Fleur would make the house comfortable and arrange a schedule of activities for her. Bibi missed No'a and spent as much time as he could with her on his visits to Israel. His ex-wife, Micki, was always cooperative and allowed him to see her when he could.

However, as Bibi's career flourished, his relationship with Fleur began to fall apart. Because of Bibi, she went through years of painful and expensive fertility treatments at a Harvard hospital. The treatments failed. Later, Fleur said to one of her friends, "They fucked up." The failure of the treatments, which produced enormous weight gain, also caused health complications. Eventually Fleur and Bibi had to face the fact that she would never be able to have children. By the end of their stay in New York, the two were sleeping in separate bedrooms.

12

"You're My New Spokesman"

At the beginning of 1985, the Israeli delegation to the United Nations began recruiting new staff for various positions. The additional personnel were meant to reinforce the existing team during the opening of the General Assembly. Among the applicants was a young student named Eyal Arad.

Eyal, the son of two journalists and the brother of Yael Arad, who would make history seven years later as the first Israeli to win an Olympic medal, in judo, had recently completed his theological studies. He was waiting for his wife, Heidi, to earn a degree in architecture at Columbia University. Not particularly interested in politics, Eyal was only barely aware of the existence of an Israeli embassy in the United Nations, and he did not know the ambassador. But he was looking for a job, something temporary, and a friend told him that the embassy was seeking students to fill a few posts, mainly security positions. Eyal took himself to the offices of the Israeli delegation and sat opposite a man named Gevir, the personnel manager at the embassy. Gevir sent several candidates for the job, including Eyal, to the ambassador for a final interview.

Eyal Arad entered the ambassador's office and was surprised to see a young man sitting in the chair opposite him. He did not know Benjamin Netanyahu. He had heard of him but knew nothing about his background.

"Where in Israel are you from?" Netanyahu asked. "Jerusalem," replied Arad, who then told Bibi a little about himself.

"What did you do in the army?"

"Officer in the armored corps."

As the conversation continued, Netanyahu was much taken by Arad. The fact that Arad had been a combat officer gave him additional points. They had a common topic of conversation.

"Do you speak English?"

"Yes," Arad replied.

"Do you mind if we continue this conversation in English?"

"No," Arad said.

When they started discussing accents, Arad noted: "Nobody will think I am from Massachusetts."

Netanyahu could barely conceal his pleasure. The ease with which Arad had pronounced the name of the northeastern state proved that the bearded young man in front of him could indeed speak English, and well.

The interview lasted five minutes. "The job's yours," Netanyahu said, and he sent Arad off to the delegation's offices.

Arad was appointed Israeli representative to the United Nations Economic Committee. It was a junior post, but Arad was pleased. He was not thinking about a career in politics. All he wanted was to pass the time while his wife finished school and then go back to Israel.

For four months, Arad worked at the embassy and rarely came across Netanyahu. They once ran into each other by chance. "How's it going?" Netanyahu asked.

"Fine." Arad replied. That was the extent of the conversation.

Then one of the clerks in the office of public affairs went on leave, and Arad replaced her for a month. It was here that the ambassador started paying attention to the new employee. Netanyahu knew that the Foreign Office was eliminating the post of his spokesperson, Judy Vernai, and that he personally would be obliged to hire a local spokesperson. As he started search for a replacement, he thought of Arad.

Bibi liked Eyal Arad's personality attributes, and fluent English, and began keeping an eye on him from afar. Arad did not know that he was the subject of the ambassador's interest. One day, he was walking down a corridor when he ran into Netanyahu.

"Good morning, Eyal," Bibi said.

"Good morning," Eyal replied, surprised that the ambassador remembered his name.

"Can you do me a favor?" Netanyahu asked.

"Of course."

"Go to the phone. Call Elimelech Ram, Israel TV's Washington correspondent. Tell him there's going to be special debate in the Security Council on the Lebanon issue. Tell him you're my new spokesman and join me in the plenum in fifteen minutes."

Arad recovered from his shock and answered, "I'd be delighted to speak to Elimelech Ram," he said, "but I'm not sure if you're aware that in two days I'll no longer be working here. I'm flying back to Israel."

Netanyahu smiled that old familiar smile, knowing that Arad would not be going anywhere.

"It's going to be just fine," Netanyahu said. "Get yourself a tie."

Eyal Arad took up his new position in January 1986. He had never done anything like it before and here he was, suddenly responsible for the media affairs of public relations whiz kid Benjamin Netanyahu. At the time he was unaware that he was not Bibi's first choice. In 1985, Danny Naveh, a law student, volunteered to assist the minister without portfolio, Moshe Arens. On one of his visits to Israel, having heard great things about Naveh, Bibi met with him, and offered him the job of spokesperson. Naveh declined. He wanted to complete his internship and knew that he would never do it if he went on a mission to America. They shook hands and parted friends, keeping in touch until Bibi's return to Israel in 1988.

In one respect, Arad's job was a fairly easy one. Netanyahu was already well known to the American media and enjoyed a wide network of connections in all its various sectors. Netanyahu felt right at home on all the important talk shows, and many of the leading columnists would call him up seeking background information.

The chemistry between Bibi and Arad was immediate, notwithstanding their basic differences—Netanyahu is usually conservative in his way of thinking, while Arad is more bohemian in character and more freewheeling, never hesitating to gamble or take a chance.

Shortly after Arad, twenty-eight, took up the position as spokesperson, Bibi's book on terrorism was published. His publishers had invested a great deal of money in promoting the book, and it paid off. Almost overnight, thirty-six-year-old Benjamin Netanyahu became a star. Invitations to talk shows flooded his office. The book was a big seller and was heralded in the press and on TV. *Time* magazine devoted seven pages to the book, including two written by Bibi himself.

It was Netanyahu's finest hour yet. He had become an expert on terrorism. His service in the General Command Reconnaissance Unit, his relationship with the legendary Yoni, his rhetorical talents, his impressive appearance—all these factors made him a star. His celebrity also produced threatening phone calls and hate mail.

One of the lesser known secrets from those days was that Bibi employed two special advisers, experts in their field—David Garth and Lilyan Wilder. Garth was responsible for building Bibi's political image, while Wilder focused on improving his speeches and TV appearances. Before any importance appearance, Wilder would advise him on what to wear, how to look at the host and the camera, and where and when to emphasize important points in his speech.

Bibi had become so well known in New York that Israeli Shabak, the general security services, decided to provide him with a local bodyguard. The Americans reached a similar decision, and in the end the Israeli bodyguard was replaced by three Americans who took turns protecting him.

One day, Arad, Netanyahu, and the bodyguard were walking down Second Avenue, not far from the consulate. A car traveling down the other side of the street, several lanes away, suddenly swerved wildly and pulled up, brakes screeching, alongside them. Bibi's bodyguard pulled out his gun. As he started to pull the trigger, Arad recognized the car's driver and shouted to the bodyguard, "Don't shoot, I know him."

The man waved his hand and called out to Netanyahu, "Mister Ambassador, you're doing a great job, we're with you."

On another occasion, Netanyahu and Arad were on their way to a lecture in Canada. The Americans were securing Netanyahu's safety only within the borders of the United States; the Canadians were responsible for his security on their own soil. Thus it happened that between the United States and Canada, on a commercial flight from New York to Toronto, Benjamin Netanyahu was left exposed in a no-man's-land, sans bodyguard. The American bodyguards had left him at the American airport. The Canadian bodyguard, who would take over for them, was waiting at the Canadian airport. In the air, Netanyahu and Arad had no protection.

Just before takeoff, Bibi and Arad noticed a couple of suspicious characters onboard the plane, which was half empty. The two, mustached men in their thirties, were sitting close to one of the exits.

"Who are those characters?" Bibi asked.

"I've got no idea," Arad said.

Bibi was worried. "They look a bit suspicious, don't they?"

"I don't know. You're the expert on these things, not me."

Netanyahu peeked at the mysterious pair and told Arad, "Go into the bathroom for a minute. Go past them and try to figure out what's going on."

Arad strode toward the two men and saw that they were trying to fill out a Canadian immigration form. "Just write that you're from Jordan. What can they do to us?" one of them told the other.

Arad returned to his seat and reported what he had heard. In the meantime, the plane was beginning to take off. Shortly afterward, one of the men got up and locked himself in the bathroom. Netanyahu and Arad exchanged concerned glances. Arad's heart started beating wildly. Netanyahu was also tense. He called the stewardess and ordered two bottles of wine—most unlike him. Arad looked at him in amazement.

"It's okay," Bibi murmured. He managed to disconnect his seat belt, and told Arad to do the same. "Do as I do," Bibi instructed, and he wrapped the broad belt around his right arm.

Arad followed his boss's orders to the letter. "Do you know how to break a bottle with a single strike?" Bibi asked.

"Yes," Arad replied.

"This is what we'll do. If anything happens, we break open the bottles and attack them with the broken bottles and the seat belts."

Arad nodded. And thus the two traveled, Israel's ambassador to the United Nations and his press secretary, all the way to Canada, each with one arm wrapped in an airplane seat belt and one hand grasping the neck of a wine bottle, ready for combat. Arad imagined the press conference they would hold after successfully overcoming the two skyjackers and making it possible for the plane to land safely. As it turned out, the two passengers were innocent tourists.

Netanyahu was so successful an ambassador that he could hardly be ignored back home. The Israeli press could not avoid paying him the attention he deserved. The first serious profile, by Akiva Eldar in *Ha'aretz*, was published at the time of Netanyahu's appointment to the United Nations. It was full of vicious criticism. The second was by Eli Tabor in *Yediot Ahronot* and came in the wake of Netanyahu's book on terrorism. This time the article was extremely favorable. It was followed by the famous prediction in *Hadashot,* in which Hanan Kristal and Ilan Kfir claimed that Netanyahu would be the Likud candidate for prime minister and that his opponent would be Labor's Ehud Barak. They were almost right. Bibi eventually ran against Shimon Peres, but since Barak subsequently took over the leadership of Labor, a Bibi-Barak confrontation is possible in the very near future.

From New York, Netanyahu operated a very effective public relations network. Through Eyal Arad, he made sure that all the shapers of public opinion in Israel were made aware of his success and the support he was engendering in the United States. Undermining Meir Rosen, the official Israeli ambassador, was an easy matter. The media preferred Bibi to the rather nondescript Rosen, who was obliged to watch time after time as Bibi represented Israel on TV and radio, ignoring the existence of an official embassy in Washington. Rosen was furious, but he knew there was nothing he could do.

For the public relations network Netanyahu created, he hired Ralph Swarman, an American Jew with excellent connections among the American intelligence community. Swarman prepared Netanyahu for his public appearances and equipped him with lengthy intelligence files. Disciplined and thorough, Netanyahu did his homework the evening before each appearance and was always fully prepared. He would arrive for a discussion of a violent incident involving the IDF well briefed, and carrying an exhaustive file on the affair. The file would also contain material on events in Lebanon, Iraq, Sudan, Egypt, Syria, and Saudi Arabia—hundreds of incidents of violence, border disputes, skirmishes, and revolts—not one of which had anything to do with Israel. The Israeli Embassy would take the trouble to distribute these reports as special U.N. documents prior to the debate. As a result, Netanyahu was able to get up on the podium and declare, "Look at how much violence there is in the Middle East. Every year there are hundreds of incidents, hundreds of casualties, not one of them connected with Israel. Nonetheless, a special debate is convened here to discuss Israel's behavior, as if Israel is the unstable element which is pushing violence into the region."

The relationship between Netanyahu and Arad deepened. Netanyahu developed an almost blind faith in his assistant. When he took long, fast hikes, as in his army days, Arad would accompany him, huffing and puffing and trying to keep up with his boss.

From time to time, Netanyahu would recruit other people from the office to go jogging with him or join him on one of his long walks. Some of the staff would simply disappear from sight when they knew Bibi was on the rampage, looking for a walking partner. Those who were not nimble enough to escape remember that Bibi always turned the hike into a contest. Sometimes, when he was joined by a staff member whom he knew was faster runner than him, Bibi would say, "Today we're not competing for speed. This time we're competing for distance."

Bibi would walk quickly, in silence, hardly looking at his surroundings, focusing on reaching his destination. At that time, during the U.N. days, Netanyahu still had a youthful and sportsmanlike physique, solid and muscular, broad shouldered and swift-footed. For a while, after he returned to Israel, he continued to enjoy walking. Over the last few years, however, he has let himself go physically. His once youthful figure has turned to fat. One year short of his fiftieth birthday, Netanyahu has become heavy jowled and thick waisted.

In New York, Bibi liked to eat with Eyal Arad. Over a plate of pasta and a glass of mineral water, followed by a fine cigar, he would describe his plans for the future. The words "prime minister" were not mentioned, but Arad had no doubts that his boss was destined for greatness.

On the way to the top, however, there was a huge hurdle which almost ended Netanyahu's diplomatic career. While he was making enormous efforts to expose the PLO as a terrorist organization, and its leader, Yasser Arafat, as an arch terrorist, Netanyahu discovered in early 1985 that Israel's national unity government, under Shimon Peres, was conducting secret negotiations to free Israeli prisoners of war in return for the release of terrorists. More than one thousand PLO members, many of whose hands were stained with the blood of Israelis, were to be set free in return for three Israeli prisoners of war being held in Lebanon by Ahmed Jabril, head of a group of Palestinian terrorists, and his men.

Netanyahu was furious. From the moment he learned of the deal, he did his best to torpedo it. He claimed the government was pulling the ground out from under him. In the future, how could he repeat his mantra, that no concessions will be made to terrorists? He used all the resources at his disposal to try to rescind the government's decision. He talked with Foreign Minister Shamir, a Likud leader, sent telegrams to Peres, and asked for the intervention of American Jewry.

On the morning of the prisoners' release, Netanyahu gave an interview to the Voice of Israel morning program, in which he condemned the exchange of prisoners. It was seven o'clock in the morning and Netanyahu knew that his words would soon reach Prime Minister Peres and the government ministers. Peres indeed heard the interview on the radio of his official car, on the way to his office in Jerusalem. Furious, he demanded that his foreign minister order all Israeli ambassadors in the world to refrain from discussing the issue. Everyone knew that the order really referred only to Benjamin Netanyahu. Netanyahu also knew this, but told Eyal Arad that he had no intention of keeping quiet and was planning to attack the issue at every opportunity. Bibi reckoned that it was only a matter of time before Peres gave Shamir the order to fire him. He told Arad, "I expect that if they fire me, they will also act against everyone who is close to me."

Arad knew that meant him. That same morning he told his wife, Heidi, that this might be his last day with the Israeli embassy in the United Nations.

A letter of dismissal never arrived. Netanyahu kept right on attacking the "mistaken and miserable decision of the government of Israel." It was not the last time Netanyahu would show complete disregard for the directives of the Israeli government. During the unity government, shared by Likud and Labor, a power rotation took place, with Shamir replacing Peres as prime minister and Peres being appointed foreign minister in Shamir's government. Peres appointed Yossi Beilin as the Foreign Office's political general manager. One of the first directives issued by Peres and Beilin to all the Israeli embassies declared that Israel was not interested in any intervention in Lebanon and would never return there with a large military force, as had happened in 1982. The directive was not to Netanyahu's taste, and in his interviews and speeches in the General Assembly he continued to warn Syria and Lebanon that Israel had not dropped the military option. Peres was annoyed, but soon discovered that Prime Minister Shamir happened to agree with Bibi.

In 1988, Peres and Beilin sent out a new directive from the Foreign

Office to Israel's ambassadors abroad: to cease all verbal attacks on Arafat and to use the term West Bank instead of Judea and Samaria. Once again, Netanyahu chose to ignore the directive and continued to call Arafat a terrorist with blood on his hands. Once again, Prime Minister Shamir agreed with Bibi.

13

A Star Is Born

In March 1988 Benjamin Netanyahu began preparing for his departure from New York. It had been clear to him from the start that his position as U.N. ambassador was a springboard for greater things. Now, after having taken America by storm, his thoughts turned to Israel.

He knew exactly what was waiting for him. His frequent visits allowed him to become very familiar with Israel's political jungle: the conspiracies, the quarrels, and the power of his potential adversaries, the Likud "princes." In his frequent talks in New York with his faithful spokesman Arad, Netanyahu made it clear that he was looking ahead.

"I am not sure if he was thinking of the prime ministership at that time," Arad said. "But it was quite clear that he was going a long way."

Two years earlier, in 1986, *Hadashot* published an article by Hanan Kristal and Ilan Kfir on the projected candidates for prime minister in the 1996 general elections: Ehud Barak, the young army general, for Labor, against Bibi Netanyahu for Likud. Netanyahu, already well known and popular in New York, was almost unknown to the Israeli public. The article increased public awareness of Netanyahu as someone worthy of consideration for the position of prime minister, or at least someone who should be listened to. Eyal Arad felt it was Kristal and Kfir's article that turned Bibi into a legitimate candidate for the post of prime minister.

Netanyahu had been one of the more popular Israeli ambassadors to the United Nations, and almost everyone in the diplomatic corps wanted to say goodbye personally. The leave-taking was as hard on the Jewish community as it was on Netanyahu himself. While not always agreeing with his hard-line views, America's Jews were proud of the brilliant representative of Israel.

Financial tycoons, people in the media and in finance, wealthy industrialists, and others had become very fond of the young Jew, whose natural talents included the ability to tell everyone exactly what they wanted to hear.

It was an emotional time for Bibi, leaving behind a warm home, considerable support, and an immense source of power. There were official parties and private farewell events. Over the years, he made many friends in New York and Washington and other centers of power.

Yet while his leaving saddened many people, it also made many others happy, especially the Arab ambassadors and the PLO representatives to the United Nations. Netanyahu was their deadly enemy—a dominant and charismatic ambassador—and they hated every minute of his public appearances.

Several thousand miles from New York, a large gathering of people awaited Netanyahu. At Metzudat Ze'ev, the Likud headquarters in Tel Aviv, the atmosphere was charged with anticipation of the return of the ambassador superstar after his six years in the U.S. No one knew exactly what his impact would be, but the nervous tension was palpable.

The Likud party leadership, which had been governing the country since 1977, was tight-knit. There was no room for another charismatic leader. The Likud leadership was made up of the party's "princes" who enjoyed the support of Yitzhak Shamir. There were also several potential heirs, such as David Levy and Ariel Sharon. None of them were inclined to clear the road for anyone else.

Moshe Arens, one of the party's leaders, had known all along that the United Nations was a stepping stone for Netanyahu. It was Arens who had discovered Bibi, believed in him, and gave him his first chance. Arens continued to harbor great hopes for Netanyahu. He saw in Bibi an important reinforcement for the party and a real asset in the approaching fight between himself, as representative of the Shamir-Arens camp in the Likud, and the opposing camps, of Ariel Sharon and David Levy.

All this was not lost on Levy and Sharon. Though they appeared nonchalant, they were definitely concerned. Levy, a Moroccan Jew, represented Israel's underclass. A resident of Bet-Shean, a small village near Jordan in Northern Israel and a former construction worker, he would not allow anyone, especially someone who had only just arrived, to harm his seniority or his position.

A veteran politician, Levy decided to make Netanyahu an offer he could not refuse: Upon his resignation from the United Nations, he would be appointed chairman of the Jewish Agency. The proposal came shortly after Yitzhak Shamir and Shimon Peres had rotated the prime ministership.* Roni Milo, the current mayor of Tel Aviv, who was chairman of Herut at the time, let Bibi know about Levy's interest.

Bibi sent Eyal Arad to do some research. "Find out what the job is all about, the responsibilities, power, status," he said. Arad did as he was told and reported back to his boss. "It's a waste of time. It's the kind of job that's aimed at burying people, not pushing them forward." Bibi and Arad discussed the matter with Tsahi Hanegbi, who was Shamir's private secretary at the time. Hanegbi, too, recommended not taking the job. Then they went to Shamir, who as usual was noncommittal: If you want the job, I'll support it. If not,...do whatever you think is best for you.

And then David Levy materialized. The minister of housing was on a trip to New York, and a meeting was planned with Bibi at the Plaza Hotel. Levy was accompanied by his aide, Albert Ben Abu. Bibi came with Arad. The two aides remained in one room while Levy and Bibi closeted themselves in Levy's suite.

Levy laid out the proposal, which he insisted was an excellent proposition. "The job suits you, and you'll be able to get ahead, with your English and all your connections with world Jewry." Uncharacteristically, Bibi did not even bother to play along. Instead of being polite and grateful, he simply said, "I'm not interested."

This was the first time Bibi insulted David Levy, but far from the last. He was Levy, a senior cabinet minister, leader of a huge Likud camp, offering a prestigious job to an almost anonymous diplomat, and the diplomat had simply refused it in three words. Levy swallowed the insult, but remembered it. The seed of the conflict between Levy and Netanyahu was planted.

---

*The 1984 general elections were a tie and the two leading parties, Labor and Likud, agreed to form a national unity government, with their leaders, Shimon Peres and Yitzhak Shamir, taking turns serving as prime minister.

Levy genuinely wanted Bibi to take over the Jewish Agency for the Likud. He was at the peak of his power and did not really fear Bibi. The Kfir-Kristal prediction of Bibi's candidacy was an eye-opener, but not of immediate concern. At that time, Levy could not have imagined what would happen in just a few short years.

Bibi had other job offers at that time. He was offered the post of general manager of the prime minister's office. Yossi Ben Aharon, who had been asked to assume the position, was hedging. The job was offered to Bibi, who deliberated and then refused. "I have no interest in becoming a government clerk," he said.

The next proposal, initiated by Eyal Arad, was to appoint Bibi traveling ambassador on the issue of terrorism. In this capacity he would also be special adviser to the prime minister. This proposal never took off, mostly because it did not capture Bibi's imagination.

Then came a tempting offer from the Tsomet party leader, Raphael "Raful" Eitan. This one proposed that Netanyahu join the young party in the number two position of leadership, after Raful. Bibi would become the heir to the throne and help Raful capture thousands of votes from the Likud in the next Knesset elections. This offer was tempting. It surely meant a seat in the Knesset—maybe even a government portfolio—as well as status and a powerful political springboard. Moreover, in those days Raful and Bibi saw eye to eye on many issues, especially those affecting the economy. Like Bibi, Raful is an outspoken believer in privatization, market power, and war on bureaucracy. Politically, too, they shared a similar outlook.

But Netanyahu rejected this proposal too. He seemed to be confronting a fundamental decision: whether he wanted to be leader of the pack in a small, less influential party, or work his way up from lower down in a large party.

Eyal Arad left New York two months before his boss, at the end of February 1988, immediately after the birth of his son, Alon. He took a position with an advertising firm in Tel Aviv, but his real job was to set about forming a Netanyahu camp in the Likud party. He received instructions to renew contact with the Likud activists he had met on his trips to Israel and to recruit their support for Bibi. "Talk to Moshe Arens, talk to other people, and get to work," Bibi instructed him.

Arad's first recruits were Ya'akov Akset from the Ariel branch, the largest town in the Shomron in the occupied territories, Baruch Netah from Tel Aviv, Sami David from Kiryat Ono, and Benny Dahari from Ramat-Gan. They were joined by Yaffa Motil from Bet Horin, who later became Bibi's headquarters secretary. It was not a clearly defined camp, just a random collection of people with a common admiration and respect for Bibi Netanyahu, some of whom were also close personal acquaintances of his.

Ya'akov Akset opened a clinic run by Red Magen David, (similar to the Red Cross) in his hometown of Ariel. The clinic was being named after Yoni Netanyahu, and Bibi, who was in Israel on a visit from America, was invited to participate in the opening ceremony. Afterward Akset and his wife invited him home for coffee. Netanyahu, in high spirits, asked Akset what he did for a living and was told: "I run the Likud branch in Ariel."

"So what's it like in politics?" Bibi asked jovially. "I'm thinking of joining myself."

"Then do," Akset replied. "We're waiting for you. As soon as you get back from America, give me a ring and we'll all help you get started."

Netanyahu heard, noted, and remembered. Arad made the call and by the time Bibi arrived in Israel, the foundation was laid. At the same time, another man was announcing his intention of standing for election as leader of the Likud. Dr. Benjamin Ze'ev Begin, a real Likud "prince," son of the late prime minister, Menachem Begin, announced his intention to give up his work in geology at an American university and join the Likud. This announcement, however, did not arouse enthusiasm in Israel, as did the arrival in Tel Aviv of Benjamin Netanyahu.

Bibi's arrival had been prepared in advance. The media would play a critical role. He needed the dramatic impact and exposure that only the media could give him.

Bibi reserved his opening shot for the most prestigious interview show on Israeli television, *Moked* (Focus). Before his appearance, he kept silent, refusing to be interviewed or even photographed. Expectations were raised, and the country's politicians eagerly awaited Bibi's first public words.

Netanyahu arrived at the Jerusalem studios accompanied by a battery of photographers and reporters. He took his place opposite Yoram Ronen, the veteran correspondent. It took Ronen only seconds to realize that he was facing a real media professional. Before the *Moked* interview,

Netanyahu had appeared numerous times on *Nightline* and *Meet the Press* in America and had countless TV confrontations as the official spokesman for Israel's policies.

"Do you plan to stand for election as the Likud candidate for prime minister?" Ronen asked. Netanyahu looked right into the camera and said, "Prime minister? Why would I do that? We already have an excellent prime minister, Yitzhak Shamir."

"Are you going to be a government minister if the Likud wins the next elections?"

"That's speculative. It is the prime minister on his own who determines the composition of his government and the ministers in it."

"Are you going to try to get elected to the Knesset on the Likud list?"

"Yes, I plan to get elected to a realistic place on the Likud list to Knesset."

Bibi was surprisingly informed on the political debate in Israel and attacked the political defeatism of the Labor party while presenting his own hawkish defense plan for the occupied territories. He went on to present his defense theories regarding the need for strategic control of the Judean and Samarian hills in the West Bank, which abut the most vulnerable parts of the country, along with his political platform.

His views were neither new nor exciting, but his presentation was both. The Israeli public had become used to leaders who were pompous and verbose, who spoke with a foreign accent, often Polish, and who displayed an old-fashioned thought process and a limited imagination. Here was a handsome young man with screen presence and a polished delivery—by all accounts a breath of fresh air. Even Prime Minister Shamir was pleased with Netanyahu's maiden interview on Israeli TV. Less delighted were the party "princes," and least thrilled of all was David Levy.

After the *Moked* interview, there was no doubt in the minds of the Israeli political establishment that a new star was among them. The success of Netanyahu's first appearance had exceeded even his expectations.

Bibi's next objective was to get the backing of the Likud branches scattered throughout the country. This was not as easy as a television appearance; he would need to roll up his sleeves and work hard. The aura that had attached to him during his years as ambassador to the United Nations was a good start. The Likud was riddled with power struggles and desperate for a new, charismatic leader. Bibi knew that anyone who was able to unite the various factions of the party would take control. He knew that the activists were looking for a genuine alternative to veteran leadership, and he believed he was the man for the job.

While he was still in New York, Bibi had devised a detailed plan for taking control of the Likud. Few knew of this plan, even fewer knew its details. Together with Eyal Arad, Netanyahu prepared his long climb to the top. He made frequent trips back to Israel and toured the country, visiting its regions and making friends with activists in the field. His model for success was derived from his army days—he built a small, intimate team, intelligent and faithful. Netanyahu had great respect for true believers. When he had to choose between brilliance, sophistication, and loyalty, he always chose the latter. He felt he could rely on his own intelligence and sophistication. It was loyalty he sought in those around him. Not that the loyalty was reciprocated—time after time, he dropped his former aides when he had no use for them.

He remembered Ya'akov Akset from one of his last visits to Israel before leaving the U.N. embassy. As soon as Bibi arrived in Israel, he called him and offered him a job in his campaign for a place on the Likud's list in the Knesset. Akset would manage the campaign headquarters which was located in the offices of a computer firm belonging to Bibi's friend, Yitzhak Fisher, in Ramat Gan. Akset did not hesitate. He took unpaid leave from his job and joined Bibi's election campaign. The team was joined by Odelia Carmon, Bibi's secretary from the United Nations, and Yaffa Motil.

Odelia Carmon was his American acquisition. She had replaced Eyal Arad as press secretary after Arad returned to Israel. Odelia agreed to join Bibi's team even though she was not a Likud supporter and did not share Bibi's political outlook. Blond and blue-eyed, Odelia attracted attention wherever she went. There were rumors of a romantic tryst between Odelia and Bibi, but those who saw them working together in the United Nations or in his campaign headquarters did not believe this was true.

Yaffa Motil had met Bibi several months before, when she was on a tour of the United States organized by members of the Jewish-American Committee. She was delighted to meet the young ambassador. Yaffa, a mother of four, was very taken by Bibi, and he by her. When Bibi returned to Israel, Yaffa phoned Eyal Arad and asked for a meeting with him. They agreed to meet for lunch, and Arad almost fell off his seat when Yaffa turned up accompanied by her four children. The next day, Yaffa was at the campaign headquarters, and that evening she told her husband, Motti, that she had decided to volunteer for Bibi's election campaign.

"Good," Motti responded. "How much are they paying?"

"Nothing," his wife said, "but I get my expenses back."

Motti raised no objections. He was also politically oriented, and soon joined the campaign himself.

Yaffa's job was to familiarize Bibi with the Likud enthusiasts around the country. A veteran Likud activist, she knew everyone, and the information she shared with Arad and the others was priceless in recruiting party workers in the field. Apart from Yaffa, whose expenses were paid, all the others in Bibi's campaign headquarters worked that year on a voluntary basis. Bibi did not have much money, yet he always told Arad that money was no object.

"How much money do we need?" he would ask Arad. "Just tell me how much you need and I'll get it. Even a million dollars."

But Arad did not need a million dollars. It was a modest campaign in the days when candidates did not need vast budgets to get elected to political office.

The biggest expense was the canteen near the headquarters. The arrangement was that anyone working on the campaign, especially volunteers, had free access to it. Arad remembers paying several thousand shekels to clear the bill.

Bibi's driver was paid a negligible salary, and the car itself was inexpensive. Eyal Arad was the only one with the right to sign checks. He figured that the entire campaign cost about $40,000. Expenses included renting halls and paying an enormous telephone bill. Bibi Netanyahu's political power was born in this modest fashion. To this day, the first people to join his camp consider themselves political pioneers.

Enthusiasm ran high. Everyone put in long hours of work. They believed in Bibi, believed that they were working not only for him but for a better future for the country and for the party. There was no clear-cut delegation of duty. Everyone did everything—answered telephones, filed papers, licked stamps, ran errands, proselytized, talked to other party members.

The results came quickly. Netanyahu's people found Likud branches desperate for new leadership. Within days the word had spread and Netanyahu's office was flooded with requests for visits and lectures. "We must not disappoint the people," Netanyahu told his supporters. "We will need them at the voting booth."

At first, Netanyahu did not have a car. He usually rode around with Arad, who drove a battered old Fiat. After a while Bibi was given a Peugeot 505 by Avi Taub, a diamond merchant and member of the Habad religious movement,* who became a personal friend. The car included Eli Biton, the driver.

Biton became very fond of Bibi, and a special relationship grew between the two men. Together, Netanyahu, Biton, Arad, and the others covered the country, driving from region to region, shaking thousands of hands, patting shoulders, smiling, explaining, promising. During those long hours on the road, a special atmosphere developed among the team, the kind of intimacy that grows among comrades in arms. Bibi always took the front passenger seat, next to the driver. Yaffa Motil and Ya'akov Akset sat in the back. Eli made sure that the car always had a supply of bagels. Yaffa kept them stocked with cold seltzer.

Arad did not travel with them, preferring his motorbike and red helmet. He did not look like a typical Likud supporter. He was swarthy, unshaven, his shirt undone to his potbelly, gold medallions hanging down a hairy chest and gold bracelets jangling on his wrist. Netanyahu often had to explain him away to other activists who did not know him. "Is he one of us?" they would ask, and Bibi would reply with a smile, "He is on the left but has right-wing opinions."

Netanyahu opened up in that car as he never had before. Normally a reticent and introverted man, Bibi spent the greater part of those long drives in heart-to-heart talks with his team. He told them about his father and the right-wing ideology he had learned from him. He described his grandparents and their impressive pedigree.

Once, on the way back from a tour of the country, Bibi invited Yaffa Motil to join him on a visit to his parents' home. Yaffa agreed gladly. She was awed by the beauty of the old colonial house in Jerusalem's Talbiyeh quarter, the rare mosaic in the garden, the old trees, and the playground.

---

*The Habad religious movement is based in Brooklyn, New York. It was founded as a Hassidic movement in Eastern Europe during the eighteenth century. Its members, who live all over the world, believe in the Messiah.

"This is where I spent my childhood," Netanyahu told her. "In this playground, Yoni and I used to play." He was noticeably moved.

Bibi's mother welcomed Yaffa and invited her to stay for dinner. Yaffa was no less impressed by the interior of the house—the elegant English furniture, the huge bookshelves with thousands of valuable books. The living room led to a study with a large desk. There was another large bookshelf behind the desk, and it was obvious that this was the room of a very special man.

Benzion Netanyahu, Bibi's father, came out of the study, ignored Yaffa, and called Bibi to join him. The two closeted themselves in the study. Yaffa heard the old man raise his voice at his son, but she could not make out what was being said. After a while Bibi came out ashen faced. He said good-bye to his mother, and he and Yaffa got into the car. He was silent for a long time. Yaffa did not know what to do. Bibi did not say a word to her, and she asked nothing. It was the first and last time she saw his parents' home. She never again mentioned the embarrassing incident.

14

Fleur, the Forgotten Wife

Bibi never tried to form any romantic attachment with Yaffa Motil or Odelia Carmon, but the two could see that his marriage to Fleur was in trouble.

"We felt that he belonged to us, the team, and not to anyone else," Yaffa recalls. Netanyahu felt at ease in the company of his close supporters. He was not embarrassed to ask the women to iron his shirts for him. Bibi has an obsession with clean ironed shirts and often changes them three or four times a day. In spite of his overwhelming schedule, the marathon tours and endless meetings and speeches, he always stayed fresh and well groomed, clean-shaven, giving off the scent of expensive aftershave lotions. Netanyahu's beard grows quickly, and he often has to shave twice a day. In order to maintain his fresh appearance, he kept a little electric shaver in the car. The ladies on the team tried to persuade him to loosen up a bit, to wear jeans and T-shirts instead of his conservative suits and starched cotton shirts. "It'll make you look younger," they said.

He would flash his boyish smile and ignore them. He had been brought up in America, where "clothes make the man." He rejected the sloppy, pseudo-casual look of many Israeli politicians. It was not for him.

Sometimes, on especially long journeys, Netanyahu considered putting his team up in a hotel, but then he would remember Yaffa Motil's promise to her husband and children that, no matter where she was during the day, she would always come home at night to Beit Horin, near Jerusalem.

Sometimes, they would arrive back so late that Netanyahu would have to sleep over in Ariel, at Ya'akov Akset's home.

On one of the journeys, Yaffa Motil told Bibi about her childhood and family background: "I come from a Moroccan family. We are observant Jews, right-wing but not extreme. I was brought up on Jewish tradition, love of Israel, to vote for the National Religious party. My mother told me about the good relationship she had with an Arab neighbor, who nursed me when my mother was sick. If this could happen in Morocco, why can't it happen here in Israel, between Jews and Palestinians?"

Netanyahu deliberated a while before replying: "One day it will happen here. But it won't be soon. It is a lengthy process. It will be years before we are able to break the circle of bloodshed and overcome terror. In order for this to happen, we must be strong. If we give the impression that we are weak, as the Labor party is doing, with helter-skelter concessions, we will create the next war instead of avoiding it. The Arabs know only force. If we are strong, they will come to talk to us. Sadat, the president of Egypt, recognized us only after the Yom Kippur War, when he reached the conclusion that he would never defeat us on the battlefield."

That small group, Bibi, Yaffa, Ya'akov Akset, and the driver, Eli Biton, gradually became a kind of family. "No one," Yaffa recalls, "knew Bibi as we did." They developed a mutual dependence, knew each other's weaknesses and secrets.

Yaffa, Ya'akov, and Eli were much more like Bibi's real family than his wife, Fleur, who was left in the apartment Bibi had been given by a wealthy friend, on Hayarkon Street near the Tel Aviv Hilton. The apartment had little furniture. In those days, Bibi's bank account was negligible, he had no checkbook or credit cards—nothing. Fleur would call and ask him, or Ya'akov Akset or Eyal Arad, to bring her food, or arrange a delivery. Once Bibi told her OK, but then discovered that the only money he had on him was a large wad of American dollars. He asked one of his colleagues to lend him some Israeli money. As usual, he forgot to pay back the loan.

Fleur was becoming more and more depressed. She had followed Bibi to Israel, but she didn't feel at home and was lonely during Bibi's campaign. People who knew her at the time said she was on the verge of a nervous breakdown. Finally, she decided to leave her husband and return to the United States, but she did not do so right away.

In the meantime, Bibi's small group of devotees darted from one place to another, energetically traversing the entire map of Israel. Bibi continued to capture the hearts and imaginations of hundreds of Likud members. Even then, however, Bibi displayed his inability to reach a firm decision and stand behind it. His tendency to waver, which ultimately could be his political downfall, was already apparent. It was especially obvious when his daily schedule was being planned. Almost every meeting or appointment he arranged was changed, postponed, or canceled altogether. His daily timetable was the most disorganized document imaginable.

As usual, he was late for all of his appointments. He would arrange for his people to pick him up at eight o'clock in the morning on the sidewalk at his home, and more often than not he would arrive at least half an hour late.

Bibi never raised his voice. When he began talking in a deep tone and balling his fist, it was clear to everyone that he was furious. He never outwardly demonstrated his anger, never shouted or humiliated anyone in public. He valued the devotion of his followers and was quick to forgive mistakes. On the other hand, he always demanded the best of everyone, one hundred percent efficiency, one hundred percent devotion, one hundred percent success. "We are doing our basic training right now," he would tell his people. "This is the stage in which we are learning, our baptism by fire. If we succeed in this, the whole road will be open to us."

"He treated us as if we were an inseparable part of him," Yaffa recalls. "He gave us a feeling of being partners to something great, something decisive in his life."

In the car, surrounded by the people who were closest to him, Netanyahu felt the intimacy of a close-knit family. The warmth and closeness was in contrast to his childhood in his father's house.

Yaffa Motil remembers, "It was a time of innocence, his and ours. It was before he had the need for the kind of know-how supplied to him later by people like Yvette Lieberman or Arthur Finkelstein."

Netanyahu loved his trips, especially his appearances before Likud members around the country. He had a rare, natural talent for getting his message across to an audience. Only minutes after the beginning of a speech, he would know if his audience was "his." Usually they were. A live audience, stormy and responsive, was something Netanyahu loved more than anything else. He thrived on the interplay with people. A good speech, to a good audience, put adrenaline into his veins and uplifted everyone listening. Netanyahu could create instant chemistry with his audience. Almost immediately, he was able to define the character of an audience and adapt to its needs. When he was addressing an audience of academics, he would come across as the brilliant MIT graduate. In development towns, he spoke like "one of the fellas," making use body language and a basic vocabulary. Ya'akov Akset would stand in the corner of the hall and look on in wonder.

Nevertheless, Bibi feared that these wonderful people who seemed to be falling under his spell would be unable to withstand the pressure of veteran Likud leaders and would desert him when it came to casting their votes. The tension increased as election day, May 29, 1986, drew near. Bibi's nerves were frayed to the limit, and he began to show signs of losing faith. According to all the analyses carried out by Eyal Arad and Ya'akov Akset, Bibi's victory in the Likud elections was a sure thing. Arad kept repeating to Bibi, "You're new blood. The voters have been waiting for you. You brought new dignity and honor to the country when you were ambassador to the U.N. You have hardly any opposition."

The Knesset—Israel's House of Representatives—generally holds elections every four years. Unlike voters in the United States, Israeli voters do not choose individuals to occupy seats in their country's main governing body. Rather, Israelis vote for a party. Any party that receives at least 1.5% of the vote is included in the Knesset. Beyond that minimum requirement, the number of Knesset seats bestowed upon a party is determined by the percentage of the vote that party receives. This system is known as "proportional representation."

As for the selection of the individual politicians who will occupy Knesset seats, that is determined entirely through each party's internal elections. In these elections, various committees within a party vote on the order in which candidates will appear on that party's list. When the votes in the general election are tallied and qualifying parties are awarded their proportional number of Knesset seats, the parties then refer back to the order of their lists. If, for example, a party receives a percentage of the vote that translates to twenty seats in the Knesset, then those twenty seats will be filled by the first twenty names on the party's list. The twenty-first on down are all equally out of luck.

Eyal Arad knew that in the internal election at hand, lack of opposition—and not popularity—represented the best chance for a high position on the Likud's list.

He also knew that Bibi had not yet managed to make any enemies within the Likud.

Not leaving anything to chance, Arad and Akset adopted efficient American methods of operation, which were unfamiliar to most of Bibi's opponents in the Likud. All the members of the Likud central committee were "marked" according to the camps they favored. Almost every one was approached, either by way of a telephone call from Netanyahu himself or from one of his senior aides. The special interests and needs of each committee member were recorded. Volunteers worked the telephones around the clock.

One evening, Bibi conducted a telephone operation that was unprecedented in Israel's political history. Ya'akov Akset supervised ten volunteers simultaneously, each on a separate line, calling up the voters. "Good evening, Bibi Netanyahu would like a word with you..." Bibi would hop from one phone to the other, say good evening, call the recipient by his or her name, which had been noted on a special data sheet, and introduce himself: "This is Bibi Netanyahu. How are you? I hope you won't forget me on election day...."

The effect of this phone drive was startling. Netanyahu seemed to gain an ally with every call. Arad's assessment that Bibi was unbeatable became stronger.

As usual, Netanyahu was not satisfied. He decided to send out personal letters to all 2,100 members of the Likud Center, the ruling members of the party. According to the system used at the time, candidates for the Knesset were elected by center members over two election sessions. The first elections determined the fifty candidates. This was followed by the "sevens," which determined the order of the candidates on the Likud's list.

Yaffa and Odelia prepared 2,100 printed letters with space at the bottom and top for a few personal words in Netanyahu's handwriting. He wrote "Dear" and ended with "Yours, Bibi."

The letters were carefully prepared over several days and nights. Akset and Eli, the driver, then set off and took the stamped envelopes to the local post office. Meanwhile, back at headquarters, Bibi burst into Odelia and Yaffa's room in a panic and insisted the letters be retrieved. Frantic phone calls were made. Couriers rushed off and intercepted Akset in the nick of time. The letters returned to headquarters.

"Throw all those letters into the garbage," Netanyahu said. "They have to be rewritten. There's a been a mistake."

The "mistake" consisted of one word—"yours"—which Bibi did not like. For him, one word was enough reason to rewrite a letter. His staff tried to persuade him that the original letter was fine, but he would not listen. With much extra effort, the letter was rewritten, retyped, resigned, resealed, restamped, and resent.

Of course, team Netanyahu would not stop at "personal" form letters. They decided to print special pamphlets and to hand them out to the members of the Likud Center. The timing had to be precise—between the first stage of the elections and the second. The pamphlet had to be printed immediately after the results of the first elections were published so that it would be available the following morning for distribution. Speed was critical. Arad and Akset were not convinced that their regular printer would be able to handle such an operation in one night. Bibi and his staff would decide on the content and composition at two o'clock in the morning, following publication of the results. The pamphlets had to be ready by six.

Bibi's solution was simple. He hired two printers simultaneously, so that if one were unable to handle the job, the other would complete it. He had learned this principle in the army: always have backup. There must always be an alternative in case the first option fails—even if it means extra financial outlay, as in this case it did. Netanyahu was willing to spend whatever he had to to achieve his goal.

Netanyahu's headquarters planned a big support rally two days before the elections. They estimated a turnout of several hundred Likud members. Arad and Akset ordered three hundred chairs, with a further three hundred on standby—once again, they had backup. The meeting was to take place in the prestigious Gan Oaring, a famous hall, in Exhibition Gardens north of Tel Aviv.

Two days before the designated date, Benny Begin landed in Israel after a long stay in America. Begin had just decided to enter politics; Netanyahu had been one of the people who persuaded him to do so. "The movement needs you," he had said in a telephone conversation. "The whole country needs you."

Begin, however, had done little to position himself for election. Being the son of Menachem Begin, Benny believed that his success in politics would be automatic. Yet he found himself back in Israel only a few days before the first-stage elections, with no volunteers and no campaign.

Arad suggested that Bibi invite Begin to be a guest at their fancy end-of-the-campaign party. Netanyahu agreed, and Begin was glad to accept. Word spread like wildfire: a grand Netanyahu party; Benny Begin, guest of honor. This first joining of forces between Benny and Bibi, successful and useful to both of them, would also be their last.

The function was planned for eight o'clock in the evening. At the entrance to the hall stood a supporter, ready to plunge roses into buttonholes. By seven, there were already some eight hundred people in the hall. The organizers scrambled to find more chairs. By eight there were fifteen hundred people. Arad and Akset had to close the doors to prevent an accident.

Bibi and Fleur waited in the management office. Fleur, who seemed detached from her husband's political campaign, knew that at times like this she should be at his side. It would be one of her last public appearances with Bibi. Fleur already knew that she had lost the campaign for her husband's heart, that he was married to his political ambition. Fleur had left a flourishing career behind her in New York, and was already harboring secret hopes of returning to the world of business.

But that night in Gan Oranim, she came, smiled, and shook hands. No one who spoke to her on that grand evening sensed her sadness and bitterness. Bibi's race to the top had pushed Fleur and her feelings to the sidelines.

The evening proved an enormous success. Bibi had been back in Israel only three months, and had been a candidate for the Knesset for only one month, when he took the microphone that night. A tremble passed over his body. He looked at the crowd and began to speak:

> I have decided to enter politics. I have decided to try to get
> elected to the Knesset. If I am elected, I will act to unite the Likud,
> to end the factions. We are one movement, one nation. Together, for
> the sake of Israel, we must unite and win.

The crowd went wild. The applause lasted for a long time. The people loved Bibi and felt that he loved them. Everyone in that hall was convinced: A new Likud leader had been born.

On the way home, Akset informed Bibi that David Levy had held a similar meeting that evening in the north of the country and only 150 people had attended. Moshe Katzav's meeting in the south drew even fewer people. Many more than half the Likud Center's members had attended Bibi's meeting. It was a tremendous show of support. Ya'akov Akset said to his friends that night, "Listen, he's going to be prime minister one day."

Akset's leave of absence from his regular employment was to end the next day. He prepared to have a farewell conversation with Netanyahu in the morning and then go back to work. During the night, however, Akset changed his mind. In the morning, instead of bidding Bibi farewell, he took him to his boss, Oded Shermeister, so that Bibi, master of persuasion, could try to convince Shermeister to extend Akset's leave of absence. Not surprisingly, Akset's leave was extended.

15

And the Winner Is...
Benjamin Netanyahu

The elections to the "panel"—the list of fifty candidates, from which candidates would be chosen in the next stage, the "sevens," had been set for May 29, 1988, at the Herzliya Country Club. The mayor of Herzliya, Eli Landau, had prepared the site with his usual efficiency. Each of the candidates was allotted a room in which he could rest or entertain guests. Netanyahu did not need Landau's room. His headquarters had already rented a comfortable apartment for him in Herzliya, in which he could rest during the arduous election day. In addition, he had a special mobile trailer, from which he could supervise his volunteers in the field.

Sara Akset joined her husband that day. Her job was very important and clearly defined. She was responsible for supplying Bibi with a clean, ironed shirt every few hours, just as he liked it. She did not know at first, that at the end of the scorchingly hot day, Bibi would be caught—probably for the first time in his career—without a clean shirt.

Bibi conducted his day from inside his trailer. Unlike the other candidates, he did hand out stickers, shake hands, sign posters, or distribute election buttons. On the day of the elections, his idea was to create an aura of mystery around himself, to make people wonder what he was up to.

Nahum Barnea, at that time editor of the weekly *Koteret Rashit*, described the afternoon of election day: "It was very crowded at the Herzliya Country Club. It was also very hot. Bibi Netanyahu was nowhere to be seen. Someone said that he was not walking around, on principle. Someone else said that she had seen him around midday, after he had changed his shirt for the third time. All his shirts are light blue. No one will ever catch Bibi Netanyahu perspiring. And you can be sure that if he does perspire, his perspiration will smell of the lavender that dreams are made of in America. Netanyahu, so it seems, is about to achieve everything he has ever wanted. And he wants a lot. They are saying, and he is not denying, that he wants to be prime minister. A rather difficult thought to digest. Not that he is any worse than the others, but he is much more persuasive."

In the meantime, the sun had set and the election committee had begun counting the votes. The candidates retired to their rooms. Many political destinies were about to be determined.

The large hall began filling up as announcement time drew near. Rumors that Netanyahu was leading filled the air. Bibi and Fleur entered the hall and were met with thunderous applause. They took their seats in the front row, opposite the podium. They were holding hands, but Bibi's fingers were fidgeting. This time the aides kept their distance. They did not want to disturb the couple's rare moment of intimacy.

The Likud election committee went onstage with a large white envelope. A tense silence filled the large hall. "These are the results of the election to the panel for the twelfth Knesset elections," the chairman announced. "Number one is Benjamin Netanyahu, with 1,408 votes. Second place, Moshe Katzav, third place, Moshe Arens, fourth place, Ariel Sharon...seventh place, David Levy."

A cold sweat mingled with the sticky heat and Bibi's shirt stuck to his body. He stood there, surrounded by supporters and fans. They poured champagne on him. Television cameras and press photographers took his picture. He went up on the stage. Someone handed him a huge bunch of red flowers. The crowd was ecstatic.

Bibi thanked the Likud members, the leadership, "the Likud's new winning team." He did not notice the animosity and shock on the faces of the Likud "princes"—David Levy, Roni Milo, Ehud Ulmert, and Dan Meridor. Bibi climbed down from the stage and went over to Fleur. He drew her close and kissed her on her mouth, her head, and her neck. Fleur enjoyed his sudden and unexpected show of affection. On his way back to the car, Bibi was stopped by a veteran Likud activist. "How old was Kennedy when he was elected president?" the man asked. "Don't get carried away" Bibi said, and smiled, and went on walking.

Bibi's landslide victory in the Likud's panel elections caused an earthquake. David Levy's camp declared war on the Shamir-Arens camp. "We have been betrayed," Levy said. "They made deals behind our backs. They said to the voters: 'Vote for anyone but David Levy, just make sure Levy's people are out.' We are not afraid. We shall fight. We'll meet in the sevens."

According to the "sevens" system, seven out of twenty-one candidates are chosen in each round of elections. Those who are not elected in the first round compete in subsequent rounds.

Levy did not know that his declaration of war, "We'll meet in the sevens," would become a Likud slogan. He meant every word of it. He sought revenge on Shamir, Arens, Netanyahu—anyone who had humiliated him and his people. Netanyahu was marked as the main enemy, and not only by Levy. Many in the Shamir-Arens camp were not happy about the meteoric rise of the new star. Bibi was seen as someone who was out to steal the party from its rightful owners.

Overnight, Netanyahu became the object of media curiosity. Commentators analyzed his tactics. Would he run for a place in the initial seven or the second? Adversaries followed his movements. Where was he appearing? When was he meeting with activists? What was he up to?

The euphoria of Bibi's first success dissipated as the next hurdle approached. This one, he knew, would be a battle for survival, and the first of many such struggles. Eyal Arad knew that things had changed, that Netanyahu now had many opponents. Now it was time to prove that he could really win.

In the "sevens," each candidate decides exactly which slot on the list he wants to compete to occupy. For example, five candidates can put their names in the fifth place of the first seven and only one can win. Bibi was faced with a dilemma. There were threats of a plan to bring down his votes as low as possible. He considered a tactical move—to place himself in the second seven, in order to alleviate some of the tension. But what he really wanted was to be elected to fifth place in the first seven. He consulted with political experts, and then made up his mind: "We're going for number five."

As the day drew near, Yaffa Motil was worried. Bibi was up against the Likud giants. Motil wondered if Bibi should aim for a lower place, since his victory in the panel assured him a Knesset seat anyway. "We have a good family friend, an important rabbi in Jerusalem, Rabbi Moshe Ben Tov," Yaffa told Bibi. "How about going to him to ask for his blessing?"

Netanyahu was less than enthusiastic. "Yaffa, are you out of your mind? I don't go to rabbis. You know how far I am from religion. In New York they drove me crazy because of my marriage to Fleur. I have no common language with rabbis."

Yaffa persisted until Bibi agreed to visit the distinguished rabbi. He took his daughter No'a with him. The rabbi told Bibi he would have a difficult time but he would succeed—and he gave him his blessing.

Today, Benjamin Netanyahu is a frequent and welcome guest at the courts of various Sephardic rabbis, especially the old and senile Rabbi Kaduri, one of the spiritual leaders of Jewish fundamentalism. Another favorite of Bibi's is Rabbi Ovadia Yosef, the Shas party leader, without whose blessing no government can convene in Israel. Rabbi Ovadia has said that Reform and Conservative Jews are not Jews and should be "cut out of the Jewish nation." He also told his followers that the Reform Jews "have straw in their heads."

Yaffa Motil's rabbi told Bibi that he would win, and he did. He got in at fifth place in the opening seven, just as he had hoped, just as he had planned.

"The internal elections are behind us," Bibi told his supporters. "Now begins the real battle, the Knesset elections." Following Bibi's victory, Nahum Barnea wrote in *Koteret Rashit*:

> What in fact is the secret of Bibi Netanyahu's charm? He does have charm, even charisma. It stems, seemingly, from a blend of good looks, a well-cultivated biological background and the speech style resembling Moshe Dayan. In fact, he speaks like a Moshe Dayan who has been sent for lengthy training in the United States....
>
> To the Likudniks, and not only to them, he looks more like a general than Sharon, although in many ways he is a new immigrant. He talks and acts more Israeli than David Levy.

Barnea continued:

He is obsessed with that antiaircraft rocket that can be packed into a briefcase, and never stops spouting the theory that as soon as we withdraw from the occupied territories, there will be a terrorist on every little hill overlooking Tel Aviv's Ben-Gurion airport, an open briefcase at his feet and a rocket pointing to the sky, ready to bring down every plane that takes off or is about to land. Just suppose that same terrorist with the suitcase positions himself in Dizengoff Center [one of the busiest shopping centers in the country]? This theory sounds better the more removed the listener is from matters of security. No wonder he has succeeded so well among the Jews of America and Likud activists.

16

Yes, Mr. Deputy Foreign Minister

B ibi and his team celebrated their huge success with a party attended
by hundreds of supporters. Ya'akov Akset did the organizing, Odelia
Karmon, Bibi's secretary, donated her parents' home, facing the sea, on a
hill overlooking Kibbutz Shefayim. Dozens of people, veteran supporters
and new ones who had joined the team after the victory, came to celebrate
beside the large swimming pool. Bibi arrived typically late, but atypically
accompanied by Fleur and his daughter No'a.

At the height of the festivities, when many of the participants were
drunk, Akset pulled Bibi, who had hardly drunk anything, toward the pool
and then, to the calls and whistles of the others, pushed him, fully dressed,
into the water. Yaffa Motil was thrown in after him, and so was Eyal Arad.
Bibi dived to the bottom of the pool and swam up at the other end,
soaking wet but wearing a huge smile. Fleur stood nearby with No'a. She
appeared distant and reserved, as if she had nothing to do with the victory.

Netanyahu soon became acclimated to his new life in Israel. He and
Arad combed the streets of Tel Aviv looking for a good Italian restaurant,
like the places he patronized in New York. They settled on Pronto, in the
city center. They then set about finding a place where they could get a
decent cup of coffee, like the espresso found in New York—an ultimately
unfulfilling search. To this day, Bibi hasn't gotten used to the espresso
served in Tel Aviv.

His long walks in New York were replaced by hikes from his Tel Aviv apartment on Hayarkon Street to Old Jaffa and back. He marched the length of the coast in long, swift strides with Arad barely managing to keep up alongside him.

The apartment on Hayarkon Street belonged to the Australian millionaire John Gendel, who put it at Bibi's disposal upon his return from New York. Arad had suggested that Bibi pay the Australian a token sum each month just so the apartment did not look like a gift. Bibi agreed, and probably saved himself embarrassment and trouble later on.

In the 1988 general elections, Bibi was given the responsibility of watching over his party's strategic polls. He took his job seriously and imported several American experts, one of whom, Frank Lunz, a junior researcher at the time, is now considered the world's foremost expert in the field of opinion polling. Eight years later, in the 1996 elections, Bibi would introduce Nathan Sharansky and his Russian immigrants party to Frank Lunz, who supplied the new party with professional advice regarding opinion polls.

Bibi set up a sophisticated computer system, the first of its kind in Israel. He did not rely on the country's opinion pollsters. His computer was able to supply him, through statistics, with a daily picture of the mood on the street. The computer system was located in Tel Aviv's Diplomat Hotel and managed by Eyal Arad.

Yitzhak Fisher, one of Netanyahu's first associates, was put in charge of finances. It was the first significant post he was given by Bibi. In time, Fisher became very rich as the partner of Ronald Lauder. He now sits in a large, fancy office in Manhattan and controls Netanyahu's American network of contacts and donors. Ya'akov Akset, another friend of Bibi's, was put in charge of organization. This troika constituted the nucleus of Bibi's team: Fisher handling finances, Akset running the organization, and Arad taking care of data, processing it and presenting it to the campaign heads.

Bibi based his system on American models. He put young associates in high positions and brought in American experts. He was confident that his system would supply the Likud with informational ammunition unavailable to their adversaries in the Labor party.

Bibi's campaign heads, however, thought otherwise. Moshe Arens, Bibi's erstwhile patron, was enthusiastic about Bibi's methods at first, but his mood soured when the first results started coming through. Roni Milo, head of publicity, was even more skeptical. Relatively early on in the campaign, Bibi's computers ceased to be taken seriously. Bibi was sending in detailed daily reports of a kind hitherto unknown in Israeli election campaigns, but they were thrown straight into the trash.

Moshe Arens was, nevertheless, impressed by Bibi's ability to raise money, and tried to draw him into the local fund-raising drive. Bibi spurned the request: "In America," he said to his friends, "someone gives you a hundred thousand dollars, but he doesn't think you owe him anything. Here, someone gives you ten thousand dollars, and you're beholden to him for the rest of your life."

On October 30, 1988, three days before the election, terrorists attacked an Israeli bus near Jericho. The bus went up in flames and a mother and her three children were burned to death. The attack gave the security-minded Likud a tiny majority, and the election. Yitzhak Shamir formed a national unity government. Shimon Peres, from Labor, was minister of finance and Yitzhak Rabin was minister of defense. Arens was appointed foreign minister. The three "princes," Milo, Meridor, and Ulmert, were all appointed ministers. Bibi Netanyahu, the biggest winner in the internal elections, remained on the outside.

Shamir did not appreciate Netanyahu's dazzling efforts to capture the leadership of the Likud. "What's eating him? He's still so young?" Shamir used to say.

Bibi asked for a personal meeting with Shamir. The prime minister was cold, as usual, and unwilling to commit. He never stopped reminding Bibi of how young he was and that he had his whole life before him. Actually, even before the elections Bibi had resigned himself to the fact that he would not be given a government post. In an interview with the *New York Times*, Shamir had said that none of the youngsters who had achieved a high position in the preliminary elections would be included in his next government because "it was too soon." Moshe Arens tried to help. He urged Shamir to offer Bibi a deputy ministership. "He'd be a great deputy foreign minister," he said. To his great surprise, Shamir agreed. And so did Bibi.

The waiting period before Bibi assumed his appointment was also the end of Fleur's days in Israel. She had tried to fit into Israeli society and to get a management job in an Israeli firm, but was unsuccessful. Bibi's friends at headquarters were not aware of Fleur's loneliness. Yaffa Motil admits that they wanted Bibi to themselves and were unwilling to share him. "We wanted to be with him, to be part of his fascinating political campaign. We didn't even think about Fleur," she said.

One evening Fleur told Bibi that she'd had enough and was leaving him and going back to New York. She wanted to say goodbye to Bibi's entourage and began with Yaffa Motil, whom she invited to lunch. She was very open with Yaffa, who was surprised. Until that moment Yaffa had been unaware of any trouble in Bibi's marriage.

She said, "I understood that it was final, that there was no going back. It just occurred to me that we, who were so close to Bibi, were so selfish as to completely ignore her feelings. I was ashamed that we had not thought enough about Fleur, who was alone in a strange country and a foreign culture."

Odelia Karmon, who knew Fleur from New York, tried to persuade her to stay, but Fleur had made up her mind. In March 1989, she left Israel. At that time there were rumors of Bibi's secret affairs, but his close associates insist that Fleur did not leave him because of another woman, that Bibi had no time for romance, that he was too concerned with getting to the top of the Israeli political ladder. Bibi and Fleur's parting was quiet. Fleur said she would not make any trouble for Bibi in the future and that she would refuse all interviews. Bibi promised to help her in any way he could. Not long after the separation, Fleur got a job with Ronald Lauder, the cosmetics manufacturer, a close associate of Bibi's. She still works there, and she still goes by the name Fleur Netanyahu, although she remarried a few years ago. She visits Israel from time to time, but has not kept in touch with Bibi, especially not since his marriage to Sara.

Arens, now the foreign minister, allowed his deputy to exercise a wide range of authority. One of the areas in which he was given free hand was that of propaganda. Bibi became responsible for presenting Israel's point of view, and on this issue he had full operative authority and did not require approval from Arens or Shamir. While Arens negotiated, Bibi was busy selling him to the media.

During the stormy days of the *intifada*, when Arabs protesting the occupation threw stones at Israeli soldiers, Netanyahu watched images of the violence in the occupied territories broadcast by the Jerusalem office of CNN. The commentaries were unfavorable to Israel. Bibi decided to change CNN's nightly portrayal of the eruptions. This was no easy matter. The TV star for whom all the American TV stations opened their doors was amazed to discover that he was unable to find a slot in the Israeli network. For this he blamed Robert Wind, head of the CNN office in Jerusalem. Bibi waited for the man to make a mistake that could be exploited. It happened soon enough.

One of the local dailies published an item claiming that Wind, a Jew, demanded the removal of a mezuzah which had been hung on the entrance to the building where CNN was located. Bibi pounced on the incident and waged a sharp attack, insinuating that anti-Semitism was rife in the CNN Jerusalem office.

It worked. Ted Turner, the network's owner, replaced Wind with a new team, which included people like Peter Arnett and Linda Scherzer. CNN took a new, more moderate line, and for the first time, pro-Israeli sentiment could be discerned. Bibi was satisfied.

He waged another campaign against the American administration's response to the war on terror. Again and again, terrorists struck at Israeli, American, and European targets all over the world, but in Washington, the response was tepid.

When the Shiite Hezbollah terrorists kidnapped and executed the American colonel William Higgins, head of the CIA office in Beirut, Bibi cried out for a sharp reprisal, which did occur. Israel kidnapped a senior Hezbollah leader, Sheik Obeid. The retaliatory kidnapping was also intended to press Moslem terrorists into releasing the Israeli navigator Ron Arad, captured by Amal, a Shiite Muslim group in southern Lebanon. Bibi praised the daring and dangerous Israeli act while continuing to hint at the weakness of the United States.

In May 1989, when two Israelis were murdered by terrorists in Jerusalem, Bibi waged a well-planned verbal attack on the United States and the entire world for believing in Yasser Arafat's peace initiatives while Arafat was sending out his men to murder innocent people.

One month later, an Israeli soldier was murdered in Nablus when a stone split his head open. Bibi personally led television crews to the site and sarcastically asked, "Where is Yasser Arafat's moderation? What is the man talking about?"

Terrorism peaked on July 6, 1989, when a Palestinian sent by Hamas took control of a bus on its way to Jerusalem and forced it into a wadi, or dry riverbed. Sixteen passengers were killed, and many more were wounded. The U.S. State Department avoided condemning the incident outright before the identities of the terrorist and the organization behind him were ascertained. A cartoon was published in America, blaming the Shamir government for terrorist activity: it depicted the Israeli prime minister driving a busload of passengers into an abyss.

Netanyahu was furious. He appeared on CNN, standing at the bedside of one of the wounded, an American woman who died shortly after. "Who do you believe," he asked the American viewers, "the victims of the attack who reported that it was a Palestinian terrorist, shouting 'Allahu akbar' as he grabbed the steering wheel, or Yasser Arafat's evasive tactics?"

The next day, Bibi ordered his press secretary to include in his daily press conference representatives of the families of the dead and wounded who were American citizens. This tactic worked well and quickly. Within two days the Bush administration admitted its mistake and published a condemnation.

Bibi once again became a familiar face to TV viewers, now all over the world, but in his personal life he was unhappy. He and Fleur had divorced quietly, without any public scandal. These were his first weeks without her. At the site of a terrorist attack in Nablus, Bibi said to Alon Liel, the Foreign Office spokesman, that he was lonely. "Since Fleur left me, I haven't been able to find a substitute. I need a woman next to me."

He would find one soon enough. In fact, he would find two.

Foreign Minister Arens gave Bibi responsibility for relations with the United States Congress and Bibi's strong relationship with Capitol Hill made it possible for him to take control of the Israeli lobby. Bibi was able to recommend Zalman Shuvel, an Israeli businessman, to Yitzhak Shamir and Moshe Arens, which later resulted in Shuvel's appointment as ambassador to Washington. Thus, the ties between Shuvel and Netanyahu were born, ties which would be strengthened in the future, up until Bibi's victory in the 1996 elections, when he chose Eliyahu Ben-Elissar, rather than Shuvel, as ambassador to Washington.

As deputy foreign minister, Bibi undertook several special projects. He led the negotiations with Norway over the heavy water affair, in which it was discovered that Israel had illegally obtained deuterium oxide, or heavy water—a vital ingredient in nuclear weaponry—from Norway. He also conducted negotiations with the Swiss, who were ordered to stop smuggling arms to Iraq, and he was responsible for stating Israel's policy toward a united Germany after the fall of the Berlin Wall.

Then came the retirement of Secretary of State George Shultz, a personal friend and associate of Bibi's. He was replaced by James Baker, and this meant an end to the excellent relations between Israel and the U.S. State Department. Baker was a new broom, not always supportive of Israel's positions, and not always easy on Israel. The diplomatic team also changed as new names sprung up, such as Dennis Ross, Aaron Miller, and Richard Hess.

Netanyahu waged a strenuous campaign in the U.S. Congress to halt the dialogue between the United States and the PLO, which was being conducted by Secretary of State Baker and the PLO's Abu Abbas. Bibi had no compunctions about using various embarrassment tactics to force the State Department's hand. He succeeded in ending the dialogue with the PLO but paid a high price for his victory. Baker never forgave him and broke off all relations with Netanyahu.

"I am not interested in having anything to do with this man," Baker said to his aides. "I have no interest in him, and I don't ever want to see or hear him again."

Bibi was surprised. He said, "I don't understand how a professional American diplomat can take such matters personally. It's nothing personal, and it's a pity that he had to bring it to such a level. Anyone would think I cheated him in a game of golf. All I did was force him into a change of policy, by applying a little diplomatic pressure. That's the name of the game and those are the rules. Aren't the Americans forever trying to pressure us into changing Shamir's policies? So what should we do, break off relations with them?"

After the Gulf War, Bibi hinted in private conversations that the Americans—especially Baker and two senior U.S. diplomats, Ross and Kerzer—had a hand in the breakup of the national unity government. Bibi claimed that the American team had conspired with Shimon Peres to bring down the government headed by Yitzhak Shamir, who was firmly and outspokenly opposed to Baker's peace initiative.

"In private conversations, they are even willing to admit it," Bibi said later. "So what? Are we supposed to feel insulted? To take revenge? To break up the coalition in the Gulf War? It's the name of the political game, after all." Baker came to Shamir with three difficult questions regarding the possibility of direct negotiations between Israel and the Palestinians. The dilemma was whether to reply yes or no. The Labor members of the government were in favor of saying yes. The Likud were divided. Most of the ministers, led by Arens, were in favor of yes. Ariel Sharon was firmly against it, as was Levy. Shamir was silent. After much debate and counter-debate among the Likud ministers, Shamir decided to refuse Baker's proposal. Shimon Peres threatened to topple the government. Shamir dismissed Peres, which broke up the national unity government. Israel's president then entrusted Peres with forming a new government. He tried and almost succeeded, but failed in the end.

17

Bibi's New Girlfriend

During this time, a rumor surfaced that Bibi was having an affair with an El Al stewardess. And it was true.

Bibi met Sara at a time when she had broken off relations with her husband, and Bibi's second wife had recently left him. Sara was working as a stewardess with El Al, Israel's national airline. In 1980, Bibi took a flight to Tel Aviv which made a stopover at the duty-free lounge in Amsterdam's Schiphol airport. There Bibi and Sara exchanged glances. She approached him and gave him her phone number, and he gave her his. From the very first moment, their relationship was extremely romantic. On the night of their first date Bibi took her to an orange grove near Hedera, north of Tel Aviv.

At first Bibi considered Sara no more than a temporary diversion. The pain was still fresh from his separation from Fleur. Sara had been watching the young politician, and her friends reported that she was looking for a husband, preferably someone wealthy or famous.

At a barbecue held at the home of Sami David, a Likud activist, Bibi arrived accompanied by a young woman with blond hair and blue eyes, wearing black jeans. Bibi introduced her to the others. Odelia Karmon was the first one to meet Sara, who shook hands briefly, smiled shyly, and barely said a word all evening.

Sara's first official introduction to Netanyahu's people took place several weeks later at a surprise fortieth birthday party arranged for Bibi by Ya'akov Akset and his wife. Bibi arrived late, as usual. The lights were off, and when they went on, Bibi wasn't the only one surprised. Nobody expected to see a young woman at his side, in her mid-twenties, her blond, well-coiffed hair stiff with spray, wearing an unflattering, old-fashioned dress. Bibi also brought another guest: Yvette Lieberman, who now headed Bibi's team.

Lieberman, uncomfortable with the surprised looks on the faces of the other guests, was quick to introduce the woman with the frightened blue eyes who was clutching Bibi's arm: "Meet Sara, Bibi's new girlfriend."

Of all those present, only Eyal Arad and Odelia Karmon had had any inkling of Bibi's secret romance with this El Al stewardess, but even they did not imagine that it would lead to marriage.

Sara never left Bibi's side that first evening. She spoke in whispers and only with Bibi and Lieberman. When she met the eyes of other guests, she lowered her gaze. Bibi introduced her to his people, and when he reached Yaffa Motil, he made a point of mentioning that Motil is a "mother of four," in order to head off any competitive or jealous feelings. Yaffa felt that Sara was examining her and Odelia. After Bibi blew out the candles on the huge cake, Odelia and Yaffa went to kiss him on the cheek, as they had done hundreds of times before. He held them off, and they returned, embarrassed, to their seats. Yaffa understood that their special relationship with Bibi was about to change. She guessed Odelia would be the first to be removed from the team.

Sara's first public appearance at Bibi's side took place at a reception in honor of the deputy foreign minister of Mexico, Rosenthal, who was visiting Netanyahu, Israel's deputy foreign minister. Sara was awkward and ungainly and had very little to say. Bibi seemed not to take her too seriously. When she tried to air an opinion on political issues, he would quickly change the subject or divert her attention.

Nobody knew it at the time, but Bibi was also having an affair with another woman, Ruth Bar. An image consultant at a public relations firm, Bar was hired to work closely with Netanyahu in the course of his political campaign. She was a beautiful, sensual, intelligent, and elegantly dressed woman, and would later become the center of a scandal.

Meanwhile, Sara began to accompany Bibi to see more places. The couple went on a double date with Eyal Arad and his wife, Heidi. Yitzhak Fisher invited them to a dinner party at his home. Bibi's friends gradually realized that Sara was homing in on him.

One day Sara told some of her friends a rather amazing story. As she was sitting in her apartment, studying for exams, she heard one of her neighbors calling out for help. "I couldn't concentrate," Sara complained, "so I had to move to another room, to get away from the noise." From then on, her friends gave her the nickname Mother Teresa.

Bibi's friends were decidedly not impressed by Sara, and she never succeeded in forming relationships with Bibi's associates or their wives.

One day, Bibi told some of his closer associates that his relationship with Sara was over. "I've solved the problem with Sara" was how he put it. And, indeed, Sara disappeared from sight. After a few months, they were surprised when Bibi informed them, "There's a problem. I'm marrying Sara."

Later they discovered that after he told her that he was ending their relationship, she asked to meet him "just one more time." Several weeks later, she told him she was pregnant.

Bibi realized that his options were limited. Twice divorced, father of one child from an earlier marriage, he could not afford another embarrassing revelation. He decided to marry Sara.

The wedding took place in March 1991 at Bibi's parents' home in Jerusalem. It was organized like a military operation. A few guests, close friends, and relatives were told that they were invited to celebrate Professor Benzion Netanyahu's birthday. The "birthday" was postponed three times. "Can't you guess?" said Cela Netanyahu, when she was asked why the event had to be so secret.

Later she explained that the secrecy was meant to keep the press away. The press, however, did arrive, and it did not take a sharp eye to discern that Sara Ben-Arzi was in an advanced stage of pregnancy.

Sara Netanyahu was born in 1960 in Kiryat Tivon, by Israeli standards a medium-sized town, northeast of Haifa. Sara was the child of her parents' old age, arriving after three older brothers. Sara's father taught the Bible. Her mother was a housewife.

The home in which Sara grew up was typically Mapai (Labor party). Her father admired the veteran Mapai leader David Ben-Gurion, whose knowledge and love of the Bible only made the Ben-Arzi family love him more. The Bible influenced the family's third son, Hagi, most heavily. Three years Sara's senior, Hagi was drawn to religion and subsequently became a "born-again" Jew. Today he is an ultranationalistic member of the Israeli extreme right wing and openly criticizes his brother-in-law for being too compromising and soft in his attitude toward the Palestinians. After Netanyahu signed the Hebron agreement, Hagi Ben-Arzi railed against him on public TV and then, in a symbolic move, went to live in Hebron.

Sara Netanyahu was a spoiled child. She was an above-average student at school, and when she finished her military service, she studied psychology at the Hebrew University of Jerusalem. At the age of twenty-two she married Doron Neuberger, a student and a member of Kibbutz Shefayim, near Tel Aviv. The two went to live on the kibbutz. Almost from the beginning, the marriage was unsuccessful. Doron Neuberger described Sara to the Israeli media as obsessive, with a tendency to violent outbreaks.

After seeing Sara on TV sitting next to the prime minister and looking over official documents, Neuberger insisted that the marriage took place to prevent a scandal. He announced his intention of writing a book describing his relationship with her, which caused an immediate rumpus in the prime minister's office. Sara Netanyahu is currently using legal means to try to prevent the publication of the book.

Sara has been a controversial figure. The Israeli press tended at first to treat her with kid gloves, despite stories that poured into the editorial offices about her unconventional behavior during Bibi's early days as prime minister. Then, in October 1996, the "nanny story" made headlines.

One morning Sara discovered that Tania Shaw, the nanny for the two little boys, Yair and Avner, had burned their soup. Sara became hysterical and fired the nanny on the spot. Then she looked through Tania's personal belongings to make sure nothing had been stolen, and ordered a security guard to do the same. When the nanny burst into tears, Sara ordered the guard to throw Tania and her belongings out on the street. He refused, so she did it herself.

The "nanny story" attracted international attention. In the English-language press, Sara was described in one place as the "first lady from Hell." The nanny has sued Sara Netanyahu and described her in court as being "obsessed by cleanliness," with a tendency toward extreme mood changes, including frequent outbursts of violence.

On December 12, 1997, *Yediot Ahronot* published the "Sara Netanyahu

File," subtitled, "To You, Mrs. Prime Minister," which included testimony by the veteran housekeeper of the prime minister's residence, as well as Mrs. Netanyahu's personal secretary and assistant. They described Sara's penchant for taking home gifts which were received in an official capacity, a breach of official protocol, which holds that official gifts are government property.

One day, Sara received an official gift of several rare bottles of wine. When the security services asked to check the wine, Sara volunteered her own method. She called for her personal secretary and told her to taste the wine to make sure it was not poisoned.

Then there was the time she threw eight pairs of shoes at her housekeeper, who, she said, had not polished them properly. For good measure, Sara told the housekeeper that the prime minister would cut her throat, and illustrated the threat with a finger-across-the-throat gesture.

As part of the Netanyahu family vacation in the north of Israel, Sara decided to take her family to see the house in Tivon where she grew up. The house had been sold when she went to live in Jerusalem. Her parents, wanting to help her with her young children, had moved to the capital.

On a Saturday afternoon, Sara, Bibi, and their substantial entourage arrived, unannounced and unexpected, at Sara's former childhood home. Sara barged into the house, followed by her embarrassed husband and about a dozen security men. She started touring the house, becoming more and more agitated at the sight of the changes made by the new owners. Then she lost control and screamed at the owners, claiming they had stolen her home and cheated her parents out of their property and that they had no right to make changes to it.

Bibi tried to calm her and managed to steer her out of the house and into the waiting car, her arms flailing. The new owners were still in shock fifteen minutes later when the prime minister called them on his car phone to apologize for his wife's outburst.

Sara does not restrict her outrageous behavior to Israel. On a recent Los Angeles visit, Sara went to an expensive department store to pick up a watch she had ordered for Bibi. When she learned the watch had not arrived, she had a tantrum. When her security guards tried to calm her down, she attacked them, in a most unregal manner.

While the prime minister's office has categorically denied all of this, the Israeli public believes the stories. True or not, Sara has never filed a libel suit.

In 1990, the national unity government was disbanded, and Rabin and Peres were sent into a political exile. Moshe Arens was appointed minister of defense. Bibi was faced with a dilemma: Should he join his patron and take the post of deputy defense minister, or should he remain in the foreign ministry, with which he was more familiar, and continue as deputy foreign minister under David Levy?

Yitzhak Shamir indicated that he preferred Netanyahu in the Foreign Office. Shamir never had much respect for David Levy and needed Netanyahu, a superb, polished spokesman, as backup for Levy, who did not speak English. Eyal Arad was also in favor of keeping Bibi in the Foreign Office with Levy. At the time, the animosity between Netanyahu and Levy was not yet strong.

It was Levy who helped Bibi make up his mind. He called him to his office and said, "I want you here with me. I have come to the conclusion that we can work together. You'll get all the responsibility you had before. We'll work as a team; we will complement each other."

"It is important for me to hear it from you," Bibi said. "I had to know that I am wanted here. Like you, I think that we can work together." "You'll be my deputy and close associate," Levy proposed. "I accept," Bibi responded.

The honeymoon lasted a few weeks. Things went very well at first. Dodi Appel, who was close to both Bibi and Levy, acted as their go-between, with great enthusiasm. The allocation of responsibility was clear. Bibi was in charge of correspondence with Washington; Eyal Arad was responsible for translating it. Aliza Goren and Uri Oren, Levy's aides, were to have nothing to do with these exchanges between Washington and Jerusalem.

But dark clouds were gathering. Levy was busy preparing for his first visit to the United States as foreign minister, unfamiliar territory for him. In these preparations Levy found Bibi's expertise invaluable. Suddenly a political storm broke out over the construction of Kiryat Sefer, a new settlement in the occupied territories. Levy had always been suspicious of Yitzhak Shamir and was convinced that the prime minister had created this crisis in order to strain Israel's relations with the United States, just in time to torpedo Levy's visit.

Bibi came to Levy's aid. He went to see Shamir and persuaded the prime minister to drop the Kiryat Sefer project. Levy, who meanwhile had suffered a slight heart attack, was recuperating at home. Bibi visited him every evening to update and advise him.

Levy set off for Washington. Bibi asked if he should come along. Bibi was hard to refuse, but Levy did not want him to go along. A star in the American media, Bibi was sure to steal the limelight. Levy was noncommittal. He sent his aide, Uri Oren, to Eyal Arad to explain why he was less than enthusiastic about Bibi joining him.

Bibi was peeved. "Okay, then. If he wants me to come, fine. If he doesn't, that's fine as well. I've already been to America."

The tension increased. Levy was being warned by his close aides that Bibi was undermining him. Bibi began to feel that Levy had declared war on him. This simmering feud was enhanced by rumors that Bibi had been acting behind Levy's back, taking advantage of his incapacitation from his heart attack, briefing ambassadors and issuing orders that contradicted Levy's initiatives.

During Levy's visit, Bibi, who did not end up accompanying Levy on the trip, received a call from the producer of *Nightline* asking him for a satellite interview from Israel, since Levy could not speak English.

Eyal Arad called Washington to get Uri Oren's permission to hold the interview. "Tell Oren," Bibi said to Arad, "that I think it might be useful, but it's up to Levy."

Arad spoke to Oren and the storm broke. "Bibi is trying to sabotage the visit," said Levy's associates. Oren continued to squirm and did not give Arad a straight reply. "We don't know. It might not look good. They ought to be more in synch."

"So let them get in synch," Arad said. "They can call each other and synchronize positions."

"We'll think about it," Oren said. "Okay, so he won't do the interview," Arad finally replied.

Bibi did not appear on *Nightline*, but damage had been done. Paranoia was now running wild.

Levy cursed the day he asked Bibi to be his deputy. Bibi felt persecuted. He believed that Levy was trying to ruin him politically, to neutralize him. Before the visit to Washington, Levy would hold a meeting every morning in his office. The atmosphere had been good.

When he returned, the frequency of these meetings dropped drastically. The last one took place on the eve of the Iraqi invasion of Kuwait. After that Bibi found himself ostracized, removed from all authority and denied information. All this in the office in which he had grown and flourished. Bibi was forced to go to the prime minister's office almost every morning in order to obtain classified information. Bibi wanted to remain informed, and Shamir permitted him to pore over classified files.

And then, on August 2, 1990, Saddam Hussein invaded Kuwait.

18

Interview in a Gas Mask

B ibi Netanyahu was one of the few people in Israel who were not surprised by Saddam Hussein's decision to attack Israel with Scud missiles. In interviews immediately following the Iraqi invasion of Kuwait, the deputy foreign minister reckoned that a military confrontation between the American coalition and Iraq was inevitable, and that the Iraqi leader would try to force Israel into the war in order to be able to depict the Iraqi invasion as a war of defense against American capitalism and Israeli Zionism.

On January 16, 1991, in the middle of the night, the United States attacked Iraq. Within twenty-four hours, American satellites, hovering high above Iraq, were able to make out Scud missiles headed for Israel. Within seconds, the Pentagon sent a message to the Defense Ministry in Tel Aviv, and the sound of sirens filled the air.

Netanyahu was in a CNN studio, being interviewed by Linda Shertzer, the network's Israel reporter when he heard the siren. The deputy foreign minister promptly put on his gas mask. He did not stop the interview. Millions of people all over the world watched as Benjamin Netanyahu continued the interview with a gas mask on his face and air-raid sirens wailing in the background. Forty-seven years after the Holocaust, when the Nazis put millions of Jews to death in gas chambers, an Israeli government deputy minister was warning his people of the dangers of poisonous gasses that Saddam Hussein was sending to Israel.

The dramatic interview proved enormously successful, and soon all the TV networks in the world wanted an exclusive interview with Netanyahu. Bibi's success troubled David Levy. His friends continued to warn him that Netanyahu was stealing the show and becoming an international media star. Levy became furious. He ordered Netanyahu to stay away from the media and stop giving interviews and briefings to reporters. His reason was that Netanyahu was acting without permission from the foreign minister and against his authority. The real reason was not mentioned: Levy feared Netanyahu's ambition.

Levy's decision came as a blow to Netanyahu. He knew that no one could do a better job with the media than he could. Nevertheless, he called the army spokesman, Nahman Shai, and told him he could not join him for a briefing with hundreds of reporters. He then called his friend, Ted Koppel, and told him he would not appear on *Nightline* that evening.

Yitzhak Shamir, who had also had reservations about Netanyahu's exposure, was swiftly changing his mind. He had become aware of Bibi's gift for articulating Israel's point of view. Throughout Bibi's four years as deputy minister, from 1988 to 1992, Shamir protected him and backed him up. With Shamir's encouragement, Bibi would become Israel's number-one spokesman during the Gulf War, despite Levy's opposition.

At the same time, Bibi kept busy developing his public image, making potential Likud voters even more aware of him. With the aid of Yvette Lieberman, he created a camp of his own.

Despite his success and the thousands of people who were taken by his charm, Bibi found himself with one very powerful enemy—the Israel media, for whom he was an easy target. His winning aura—the image of the young, successful, charismatic, ambitious politician—gradually disintegrated. Rumors were spreading. Many of the country's leading commentators viewed him as a pompous ass, a politician who would not survive.

Amnon Abramovitz, the political analyst for the Israeli newspaper *Ma'ariv*, wrote:

> One day Yitzhak Shamir will retire, Bibi Netanyahu will contest Benny Begin for leadership of the Likud. The balloon will burst. Nothing will remain of Bibi Netanyahu but Eyal Arad.

Arad was both amused and incensed. He called Abramovitz. "Suppose that Bibi is elected prime minister?" he asked. "What will you write then?"

"If Bibi Netanyahu gets to be prime minister, I will eat my hat," Abramovitz said.

On May 30, 1996, the morning Netanyahu became prime minister of Israel, Eyal Arad called Abramovitz once again. This time Arad was only amused.

"Well?" he asked.

"Believe me, I am eating my hat," Abramovitz laughed. "And it tastes terrible."

Bibi took all the criticism to heart. He would say, "What do they want from me? I have been successful in everything I have ever undertaken. I did a good job. What more do they want?"

When Sara started making headlines with her hysterical behavior, Bibi would exclaim, "What do they want from Sara? She only wants to help people. She's so good and clever."

As it turned out, all the bad press did wonders for Bibi's political image, as it caused his political enemies to underestimate him. Begin, Ulmert, Milo, and Meridor believed what they read in the papers and stopped taking him seriously.

But Bibi took himself seriously, and so did Yvette Lieberman. Far from the eyes of the press, Bibi's camp grew stronger and stronger. While the "princes" were laughing at his bad publicity, Bibi was building a power base they could not have imagined. "Don't worry, Boss," said Yvette, "Let them laugh, and we'll go on with our work."

While Yvette, Arad, and Bibi quietly continued their work, Meridor, Ulmert, Milo, and Begin slept on their watch. When they awoke, it was too late.

In the aftermath of the Gulf War, the atmosphere was ripe for peaceful negotiations between Israel and the Arab states. The U.S.-led coalition that defeated Iraq had included every Arab state except Jordan, which had remained neutral. For the first time, a common foe—Saddam Hussein—had temporarily aligned Israel with most of her historical enemies. Secretary of State Baker capitalized on this alliance of circumstance and managed to orchestrate a series of bilateral discussions between Israel and Syria, Lebanon, and Jordan. These momentous talks were held in Madrid beginning on October 30, 1991. The Madrid Conference marked the beginning of the U.S.-supervised peace process between Israel and the Arab states.

Yitzhak Shamir was virtually dragged to the conference, and decided not to have his foreign minister, Levy, accompany him. When Levy learned that the Israeli delegation would be led by the prime minister while all the other delegations were headed by foreign ministers, he was hurt and insulted. He announced that he would not attend the conference and forbade any of his people in the foreign ministry to help prepare for it.

Thus Levy was giving Bibi two valuable gifts which helped Bibi parlay the conference into genuine international stardom. First, Levy had cleared the way for Bibi, who was invited by Shamir to join him. Second, by forbidding the Foreign Office staff to help in preparing for the conference, he was allowing Bibi to hire his own experts, whom he recruited privately, to provide information to Shamir.

Bibi's success compelled Shamir to remove him from the foreign office and offer him the job of junior minister responsible for propaganda in the prime minister's office. Thus, Bibi was given an office four strides from the prime minister. A press conference was called. A cake was brought out and distributed among the smiling faces. Bibi had not been ostracized after all. His proximity to the prime minister was evidence of their ideological closeness.

Later, in November 1996, Shamir would say that in retrospect, it was a mistake to put so much faith in Bibi, who, according to Shamir, is an expert at getting elected but a poor leader. Shamir would add that Moshe Arens was actually the one mainly responsible for pushing Bibi forward.

Bibi was given a new driver, Eli, who drives for him to this day. Once forced to beg for overtime in order to make ends meet, Eli now drives an armored Cadillac and smiles all the way to the office.

The country was in a happy state of peace. In Washington, talks were taking place for the first time between Israel and the Arab states. New names were connected with the talks. Bibi was no longer a footnote.

Bibi started concentrating on internal affairs. The next general election was looming, and he had to get his camp in order. There was only one giant hurdle to overcome in solidifying his camp: the impending vote for a change in election procedure. The proposal called for the election of the prime minister by direct vote, and Bibi was much in favor of this idea. He felt a direct vote would make it much easier for him to become prime minister. Unfortunately, all the leading figures in his party opposed the proposal. Bibi decided to vote against his party when the issue was put to a vote in the Knesset.

Shamir, who was against the direct vote, called Bibi into his office. "You had a terrific future in the Likud," he said. "What a pity you have ruined it."

Arens, for his part, grabbed Eyal Arad in the Knesset and screamed at him, "Is this the kind of advice you give him? What kind of an adviser are you? Are you trying to bury him?"

Party pressure was accompanied by promises of dire consequences. At first there were hints; later, unequivocal threats. Bibi was made to realize that if he were to vote in favor of the direct election process, he was finished politically. Few believed that Bibi could withstand such pressure. Arad knew that Bibi would not bend. Two days before the vote, Bibi was called into Shamir's office. The two were joined by Arens, in a meeting which Bibi later described as being right out of the Mafia.

Arens has a different version. He remembers Bibi promising not to allow his vote to determine the issue. As it turned out, his vote did. The issue passed with fifty-six against and fifty-seven in favor.

Two days later, Bibi was traveling to Tel Aviv with Eyal Arad and Sara. "Well," Sara asked Arad, "how does it feel to be the one who has ruined Bibi's career?"

Arad did not reply. He had no regrets, and he knew Bibi felt the same way. Sara envied Arad's relationship with Bibi and would later make sure that Arad was removed from Bibi's inner circle.

Yitzhak Shamir did not hide his disappointment at the adoption of the direct vote. "This law does not suit the character of the Jewish people," Shamir said. "There is even proof of this in the Bible."

The internal Likud elections took place six weeks after the vote in the Knesset. Bibi used the same methods he had applied four years before. His camp was a well-oiled political machine, and he finished second in the elections to the panel, with only seventeen fewer votes than the first-place winner, Moshe Katzav, the Sephardic candidate from the southern town of Kiryat Malakhi, of which he was also mayor.

It was a dramatic achievement for Netanyahu. The "princes" were in shock. Not only was Bibi not "finished," he was a clear winner, and had demonstrated that he could stick to his guns and win. The elections for the sevens, several weeks later, confirmed the trend: in the Likud party, Bibi was in the lead.

19

Facing the "Princes" and David Levy

On June 23, 1992, the Likud party went to the polls, divided among its different camps. Netanyahu's job in the party's campaign was to bring in the immigrant vote, which was expected to go mostly to Rabin and the Labor party. Bibi was well aware that this would be the last election campaign for Shamir as head of the Likud. Next time, direct voting for prime minister would be in effect.

At ten o'clock in the evening, Chaim Yavin, Israel TV's anchorman, announced the results of the exit polls—an upset, and a change in the balance of power. Labor received forty-four seats, Likud dropped to thirty-one. Netanyahu was not troubled by his party's loss. He knew that a Likud victory would have meant a junior ministership for himself—at most. As far as Bibi was concerned, the worse the Likud fared in the elections, the better his own situation. Netanyahu hoped to anoint himself the leader of the Likud, but even he was not sure this was possible. Shamir's natural heir was Moshe Arens, and Bibi knew that Shamir would soon name Arens as his successor. Netanyahu would fall in line as number two—close, but not the leader.

What Bibi did not know was that Shamir had made a secret commitment to David Levy on the eve of the elections: if the Likud won, Levy would take second place after Shamir, notwithstanding the fact that

Arens and Sharon outscored Levy in the sevens. When Arens found out about the secret arrangement, he said that he would not accept the Likud's laws of the jungle.

A few days after the Likud's election defeat, Shamir announced his resignation from the Likud leadership. Bibi announced that he would support Moshe Arens as Shamir's heir. Then came the big surprise. Arens appeared on TV and announced that he was resigning from public life, a bombshell for which David Levy, Ariel Sharon, and Moshe Katzav, the three potential candidates for the Likud leadership, were unprepared. Bibi was the only one who did not fall off his chair. Conversations with Arens immediately after the Likud defeat led Bibi to understand that the older man did not deem himself fit to lead the Likud now that it had become the opposition party.

"At sixty-seven years of age," Arens told him, "I can't see myself as someone to put the Likud back on its feet and lead it for the next four years. In 1996 [when the next national election would be held] I will be seventy-one. I think that the leader of the Likud should be a younger man."

This was the moment for which Netanyahu had been waiting. On June 29, 1992, he went before the TV cameras to announce his candidacy for the Likud leadership. The first response came from David Levy, who laughed it off. He said that it was inconceivable that a man so young, so lacking in political experience, could consider leading the Likud. "Some waves wash over and some waves break up on the rocks," Levy said. "Likud members are not impressed by waves or stars. We've all seen these stars during the last election campaign, with their American marketing methods. And we know where it got us." Levy then proceeded to announce his own candidacy.

Not surprisingly, Bibi's candidacy was not supported by the Likud "princes." However, one new Knesset member, Tsahi Hanegbi, saw a bright future in Netanyahu. Hanegbi invited him to be guest of honor at a meeting to promote the adoption of primary elections for party leadership, rather than the panel and sevens system. Netanyahu was all for this change and agreed that the Likud was entering a new era.

Bibi knew that his bid for Likud leadership put him where he had been four years before, when he returned from America and took the movement by storm. He faced heavy opposition. He had enemies. Bibi formed a new support team, led by new people. Yvette Lieberman had become the man closest to Bibi and he made sure that no one else had access to "the boss."

Lieberman filled a void left by the departed Eyal Arad. Sara Netanyahu never trusted Arad and believed he was responsible for Bibi's affair with Ruth Bar. Sara saw to it that Arad was excluded from her husband's new team.

Lieberman suited Bibi like a glove, a tough leather glove. Bibi's 1992 campaign for the Likud leadership would not resemble the romantic story of the young politician who rode in from New York in 1988 and captured the heart of the Likud. This time, Bibi was going for the big prize, trying to put himself on the twelfth floor of Metzudat Ze'ev, the Likud headquarters, where Begin and Shamir sat before him.

Netanyahu gave Lieberman almost unlimited authority. Lieberman, an extreme right-winger, gave Netanyahu presence in the field, discretion, and a large reservoir of new voters among the Russian immigrant population. Lieberman turned Bibi's personal headquarters in Jerusalem into a closely guarded stronghold.

A new team of supporters surrounded Bibi. His circle of millionaire friends expanded to include Gabi Taman, Henry Kravitz, Sam Domb, Jack Nasser, George Meisner, Jay Meislis, Steven Schnaier, and others. Morad Zamir, the millionaire diamond dealer, became Bibi's closest confidant from this millionaire's club.

Bibi divided his time between the headquarters in Jerusalem and the apartment at Hayarkon Street 24.

Money flowed in. Some donors would fly to Israel for the weekend to leave money for Bibi. Accusations of illegal contributions were made, mainly by David Levy's people. Anonymous complaints were lodged with the state comptroller, but no proof was ever found.

Netanyahu decided to conduct an American-style election campaign. He presented himself as a Bill Clinton look-alike; pointing out, "We are both young and we both have white hair." Sara Netanyahu, too, patterned herself after Hillary Clinton, emulating the first lady's hairstyles and fashions. Campaign posters depicted Bibi and Sara as a young couple in love, with their young son, Yair, who was born shortly after their wedding. They held hands in public and were presented as the ideal family.

In his meeting with Likud voters, Bibi spoke like a TV star: "Take a look around you. It's all in ruins. The party must be rehabilitated, and the only man who can do it is one who is clean, who did not bring down the party from within. It needs me."

Bibi sought to change the Likud voting system. He wanted to bring in a primary system—no more panels, no more sevens, no more deals and conspiracy, no members excluded. The "princes" opposed the change and claimed that Netanyahu was a demagogue. Surprisingly, his archenemy, David Levy, was in favor of the change. Bibi asked the whole party to agree. In 1992, he said: "I want the widest possible primaries. I will force them to hold joint primaries for the party and for the party leadership. I will get a strong law through. The members of the Knesset will be elected through a direct vote." In 1996, when he realized that the primaries were no longer a foolproof way to get elected to a further term in office, he changed his stance on the issue and since then has been busy persuading and forcing Likud members to jettison the primary system and return things to their previous state.

In 1996, Joel Marcus, a reporter for *Ha'aretz*, wrote:

> People used to say about Moshe Dayan, who was a cunning politician, that he was capable of taking a man's socks off without removing his shoes and without the man feeling anything. Benjamin Netanyahu, no less cunning a politician than Dayan, is doing the same thing to the Likud heads: he is stealing the party away from them. While the Likud is down and still seeing stars from the blow it has suffered—Netanyahu is already in the middle of the race for the Likud leadership and the government.
>
> He is one of a rare breed of politicians; one can say of them that their appearance is electrifying. He speaks simply. He is not pompous like Levy, not frighteningly outspoken like Sharon. He lacks the original thought processes of Dayan, but his drive is a thousand times stronger than Dayan's. Moshe Dayan never tried to be a party leader or prime minister. Netanyahu's only objective is reaching the prime minister's office.

20

Adultery on Prime Time

Bibi's path to the Likud leadership appeared certain—until Wednesday, January 13, 1993. At six o'clock in the evening, the phone rang in the Netanyahu house. Bibi was out, and Sara picked up the receiver.

"Mrs. Netanyahu?" asked an unfamiliar voice.

"Yes, who is it?"

The man did not introduce himself. "I have some important information for you," he said. He seemed to be disguising his voice. Sara stiffened. The man told her that her husband was having an affair, that he had been routinely meeting a woman at an apartment in Petah Tikva. The anonymous caller continued: "We have a videotape of your husband with his lover. If, by tomorrow, your husband does not withdraw his candidacy for the Likud leadership, we will be obliged to release the tape, together with some very intimate details about your husband and his girlfriend. It's for his own good. If he makes an official announcement about the withdrawal of his candidacy, we won't publish a word. We'll destroy the tape and it will be as if this conversation never took place."

Sara Netanyahu was in shock. She became hysterical. "Who are you? Why are you doing this to me?" she screamed into the receiver. "You're ruining my life and my family!"

The stranger repeated, "It's all up to your husband. If he makes the announcement we want, nothing will happen. If not, he'll be responsible for the results."

Sara burst out crying. She was alone in the apartment with one-year-old

Yair. She decided not to call Bibi immediately. She had no doubt that the man was telling the truth. It had been a short conversation, but the stranger's information was convincing. Too many details seemed plausible. The man said that Bibi was meeting the woman in the afternoon, and Sara could remember too many recent occasions when she had tried to get hold of him in the afternoon and not one of his closest aides knew where he was. She now felt certain that her husband had a mistress.

Her first call was to her parents. After their talk, during which she wept and swore to divorce Bibi as soon as possible, she took a deep breath and called him.

"I know you are having an affair," she said to her flabbergasted husband. "I know everything."

Netanyahu canceled that evening's campaign meeting in Ma'ale Adumim and flew home. Sara was waiting for him, fuming, weeping, unwilling to forgive. "I never want to see you again. How could you do such a thing to me? How could you?"

Bibi was speechless. He tried to hold her, to appease her, but she pushed him away and wept hysterically. At first he tried to deny he was having an affair. Perhaps he feared a repeat of his disastrous admission of infidelity to his first wife, Micki, which ended their marriage.

He talked about an "attempt at political blackmail," about "an evil frame-up." "I will get to the bottom of this," he promised Sara, but she was not listening.

"You're a traitor," she said, over and over again.

Finally, Netanyahu broke and confessed: "Yes, there was another woman." Bibi even revealed her identity: Ruth Bar, his campaign public relations adviser.

Bibi was almost begging. "It only happened once, a passing fling which has been over for weeks." He swore to Sara that he loved her and their baby and asked her not to make a rash decision. But Sara did not want to listen or forgive. She asked him to pack his bags and get out of her life.

Bibi packed his belongings, kissed his sleeping son, and left the apartment in Rehavia. He went straight to his parents' home.

In the meantime, Sara, too, gathered a few of her belongings, and took Yair with her to her parents' home. She was determined never to see Benjamin Netanyahu again. She also had an account to settle with Eyal Arad. "I know Bibi has been unfaithful to me!" she yelled at him over the phone. "I know he is being unfaithful to me with Ruth Bar! It was you who introduced them! You're covering for him! You persuaded him to be unfaithful to me! You'd do anything to hurt me!"

Arad had not the faintest idea of what Sara was talking about. He answered her sharply, and the conversation ended in a mutual slamming of receivers.

In the meantime, Bibi called the all-powerful Lieberman to an urgent meeting. "I cannot wait for them to blackmail me," he said. "I plan to get in before them. I will go to the media. Attack is the best form of defense."

Lieberman liked the idea. While they were still talking, Lieberman's aide, Uri Aloni, walked in with a strange story to tell. It appeared that some stranger had made a similar phone call to Aloni's wife at their home in Rehovot, immediately after Sara's call.

"There's no doubt about it, this is political blackmail and we must take it to TV," Lieberman said. "We'll blow the whole thing up in their faces before they get a chance to release the tape and anything else they may have."

Lieberman and Bibi were not entirely surprised by the attempted blackmail. Several weeks before, Lieberman had demanded that Bibi put an end to his clandestine liaisons with Ruth Bar. Lieberman, who had built an efficient intelligence network with agents in all of the party branches, had come upon some information.

"Someone knows about your affair with Ruth Bar," he reported to Netanyahu. "Someone's putting together a file on you, collecting material. I believe they have evidence, maybe a videotape, perhaps some audio recordings."

Lieberman's source was Baruch Machluf, a young Likud activist from Lod and a member of the Levy camp. Machluf later admitted to being the anonymous caller, explaining that he was "young and foolish" and would never do such a thing again. Machluf has since changed his name and is a teacher in a development town.

According to Machluf, several Likud activists in the Levy camp were heard discussing Bibi's extramarital romance and its potential to ruin his career, going so far as to say that "Bibi's going to be a porn king and the whole country's going to know."

Ruth Bar is a very attractive woman, slim and sexy and always impeccably dressed. Bibi had met her five years before when, upon returning to Israel from New York, he ordered a small survey to be conducted from the Arielli publicity office, in which his cousin, Uri Mileikowsky, worked. Ruth Bar was given responsibility for the survey, which came on the heels of Bibi's announcement that he was entering Israeli politics. In the course of their work together, Bibi and Ruth became close. Later, when the 1988 municipal elections approached, Ruth was introduced to Eyal Arad, who was running Ruth's husband Zvi Bar's campaign for mayor of Ramat Gan. After the elections, Eyal officially introduced Ruth Bar to Bibi and discovered that they already knew each other. She had joined Bibi's team as special adviser for public relations. This was actually a few weeks before Bibi met Sara.

Bibi and Ruth kept their affair a close secret. Arad and other aides knew nothing about it. Yvette Lieberman did. Sara Netanyahu and Ruth Bar even attended several of the same social events and on occasion were photographed together.

Bibi reached Sara at her parents' home. He begged her forgiveness and asked for a chance to explain himself. But Sara wanted none of it. "It's over," she said. "Don't waste your time."

He told her of his intention to tell all on TV that evening as a preemptive strike against the blackmail. Sara was terrified of the thought of the entire nation getting a voyeuristic glance into her bedroom. Her family called Ya'akov Ne'eman, one of the country's leading attorneys.

On Thursday afternoon, Bibi called the TV news department of the Voice of Israel and promised them an exclusive for the evening broadcast. The Voice of Israel immediately started broadcasting preliminary details of the affair. At seven o'clock in the evening Eyal Arad picked Bibi up and they drove to the TV studios. Earlier, Arad had advised him against appearing on television. Bibi ignored his advice.

Bibi was charged and tense. Within a few moments everyone in Israel would know that he had been caught with his pants down. He went on the air. "I had intimate relations with another woman," he told the nation. "That ended a few months ago. If I owe anyone an explanation about this, it is my wife and my family. This is personal and it shall remain personal."

He then hinted that the perpetrator of the attempted blackmail was David Levy.

David Levy, watching at home, stared at his TV in disbelief. "I am talking about a senior member of the Likud," Bibi said, "surrounded by criminals."

Bibi's "honesty" made him a laughing stock in Israel. Israelis make very little of marital infidelity. Everyone knew about Moshe Dayan's and David Ben-Gurion's infidelities. Even Golda Meir was known to have had the odd fling. Everyone knew but no one cared. Bibi's behavior, however, made even his staunchest supporters question his judgment. Parodies of the "hot video," as it became known, filled TV screens for days, and many people thought that Bibi had really dug his political grave this time. Fortunately for him, the Israeli public has a short memory, and eventually the negative publicity subsided.

Things were not so easily forgotten by Sara, who was mortified. Eventually, though, she came around. Before their marriage, she and Bibi had signed a prenuptial agreement. After the "hot video" affair, they signed another agreement—a "peace in the home" compact. The agreement is secret in nature, but some of its details have been leaked. According to the agreement, Benjamin Netanyahu is committed to respect his wife and be utterly and completely faithful to her; to take her on all his trips, in and out of the country; to actively involve her in his daily schedule and in his social endeavors; to devote his weekends to his wife and children; and to make great efforts to end his work at an early hour each evening in order to join his family. One rumor has it that in the agreement, Sara is given the right to advise her husband on government appointments, including advisers, aides, and secretaries.

The media, which has a generally cynical attitude toward everything connected to the Netanyahu's married life, tends to attribute all exhibitions of warmth between the couple to their signed agreement.

Bibi came home from his parents' house, where he had stayed during the critical period with Sara. Bibi and Sara were together at home again, and soon thereafter, Sara was pregnant again.

Sara Netanyahu only joined her husband for a few campaign stops in the final stage of the primaries. In these appearances she waved to the Likud members and smiled coyly at the cameras, enjoying the warm hugs of her husband and the new text he included in his speeches: "On behalf of Sara, my wife, and myself, I ask that on March 24, you will not forget to vote for me in the primaries."

Bibi concluded the race in a giant assembly in Petah Tikva, under the auspices of the mayor, Giora Lev. Sara was at his side, as if there had never been a videotape scandal, as if Ruth Bar had never existed.

21

"Now It's Up to Him"

The Likud primaries took place on March 24, 1992. The next afternoon, the election committee convened to announce the official results. The Voice of Israel broadcast the event live from the Likud headquarters at Metzudat Ze'ev.

Bibi and his team spent the day in their suite at Tel Aviv's Sheraton Hotel. Bibi was certain he would win, but he was worried about his total percentage of the vote, and hoped he would get at least 50 percent. The results were announced. Bibi won, with 52 percent of the votes. After him, David Levy received 26 percent; in third place, Benny Begin got 16 percent; and Moshe Katzav, a senior member of the Likud, came in fourth with 6.5 percent.

Bibi raised his arms in victory.

David Levy, Benny Begin, and Moshe Katzav were all in shock. Begin was the first of the defeated to congratulate Bibi and talk about a united Likud. David Levy mentioned the possibility of election fraud and hinted that he was not accepting the results.

Netanyahu delivered his favorite kind of victory speech—statesmanlike and nationalistic. He appealed to his emotionally charged audience, which consisted mostly of his supporters. "From now on there will be no camps in the Likud," he said. "There is only one camp, the Likud camp. Together we will win and together we will return to power."

Shalom Kital and Hanan Kristal interviewed him live for Israel TV.

"Congratulations on your victory." Kital said. "Thanks. It was hard, but we did it." Bibi replied. "You made the prophecy of seven years ago come true," Kital said. "You predicted you'd be challenging Ehud Barak for prime minister in 1996. Now all you have to do is help Chief of Staff Barak get elected chairman of the Labor party."

"I've done my part. Now it's up to Ehud to do his," Bibi said.

That evening, Bibi's supporters held an impromptu victory rally in Ramat Gan. People poured in from all over the country to see Netanyahu, to touch him, to bear him on their shoulders. He was their new leader, from a new generation of Likudniks, who promised to bring the Likud back to power.

When Netanyahu arrived at the rally, leading his wife by the hand, the ecstatic crowd burst into song: "Bibi, King of Israel." He opened his speech with a sentence which he would repeat countless times in the next few years: "I would like to begin by thanking my wife, Sara, who has been by my side all the way."

Netanyahu promised the crowd, "We'll aim to topple [Yitzhak Rabin's Labor] government, even before the 1996 elections." He called on David Levy, Benny Begin, and Moshe Katzav to lay aside their differences and unite for this cause.

Netanyahu knew that he had a lot of work to do, and he wasted no time. The very evening of his victory, he called the Likud general manager and asked him to prepare the chairman's office for his arrival the following morning.

First thing the next morning, Bibi visited the retiring chairman of the party, former Prime Minister Yitzhak Shamir, to receive his blessing and to accept the key to Metzudat Ze'ev. From that day on, for three years, Bibi and Shamir had a regular weekly lunch date which Bibi eagerly attended. They two ate together in private, and Bibi refused to take any telephone calls during the meal. During those years, Bibi showed Shamir a great deal of respect. (The minute Bibi was elected prime minister in 1996, however, his respect for Shamir evaporated.)

The morning he arrived at Metzudat Ze'ev as the new party chairman, Bibi discovered that the Likud was in shambles. His new stately palace looked more like a deserted railway station. One of the two elevators had been disconnected. The second screeched and faltered all the way to the twelfth floor, where the chairman's office is located. Netanyahu made a brief tour of the building, entering the rooms, and everywhere he found broken furniture and disconnected telephones. His meeting with the party treasurer was not encouraging, but at least it explained things a bit. The man told Bibi about the miserable financial situation of the Likud, the party which had governed the country only a few months before. The kitty was empty. Millions of dollars in debts had piled up. Bailiffs were knocking on the doors, holding up orders signed by the "previous owners" for goods that had not been paid for. No court had actually decreed it, but the Likud party was, in fact, bankrupt. Bibi was surprised to discover that the party continued to employ dozens of management workers. Salaries were being paid with bank loans which had no guarantees.

His first job was to appoint a new general manager. He knew just the man—Yvette Lieberman. The appointment met some opposition, but Bibi did not care. He needed a reliable right-hand man who would carry out his boss's orders. Lieberman had always stood firmly at Bibi's side in absolute, unquestioning devotion. (As this book was being translated, Yvette Lieberman had just handed in his resignation, after yet another scandal.)

Bibi ordered Yvette to fire all unnecessary staff. Dozens of letters were prepared, although neither of the two had the faintest idea where they would get the money for severance pay. Bibi found the resurrection of Likud a boring job, and was especially grateful for Lieberman's devotion and energy. Lieberman set about sweeping out the deadwood and putting the place back on its feet. A search turned up some land owned by the Likud. The land was promptly put on the market to raise money to pay debts.

Bibi, master fund-raiser, went abroad and returned with about $1.5 million for the bankrupt party.

Netanyahu's major contact in New York is Yitzhak Fisher, who was among Bibi's first supporters when he arrived in Israel in 1988. At that time, Fisher had little more than burning ambition. Nowadays, he occupies the forty-third story of an elegant office on Fifth Avenue, opposite the Plaza Hotel. A communications and TV expert, Fisher had suggested to Ronald Lauder that he enter the communications business in Eastern Europe, which was just opening up to the West. "You'll supply the money," he said to Lauder, "and I'll supply the knowledge." Lauder agreed. Today, Fisher is Lauder's partner in many TV stations throughout

Eastern Europe. As previously mentioned, Bibi's second wife, Fleur, works for them. Fisher is considered one of Bibi's closest associates in America.

Ronald Lauder, of Estée Lauder fame, worked in the Pentagon at the time of Bibi's service in Washington. At that time their acquaintance was only superficial. Lauder was later appointed American ambassador to Austria. Bibi, as Israel's ambassador to the United Nations, was leading a campaign against the Austrian president, Kurt Waldheim. In Vienna, Lauder helped Bibi expose Waldheim's Nazi past. Bibi held Waldheim responsible for some of the more extreme decisions against Israel during Waldheim's term as United Nations secretary general.

Lauder returned to New York toward the end of Bibi's term as U.N. ambassador. They became fast friends. Bibi was a well known personality in New York, and Lauder was a wealthy Jew and a Republican. They suited each other.

Lauder became an honorable member in the list of contributors to the Likud. His donations reduced a peak during the 1996 election campaign, when Lauder transferred over $1 million to Bibi's campaign coffers.

Another member of Bibi's millionaires club is Marvin Idelson, who was once married to Barbara Walters. He is also the owner of the farm in Aspen where the Netanyahu family planned to spend a holiday until the press got wind of it. Also in the club are Tim Willinger, Morad Zamir, Joe Marmelstein, Sandy Eisenstein, Henry Kravitz, and Sheldon Idelson.

Idelson's name was first prominently mentioned in Israel in 1991 when he was married at the Knesset in Jerusalem. One of the guests of honor at the strange wedding was then Deputy Foreign Minister Benjamin Netanyahu. He is said to have been the one responsible for allowing Idelson to be married in Israel's house of government. Netanyahu denies this claim. Idelson, a gambling magnate whose wealth is valued at over $1 billion, has never denied his financial aid to Netanyahu. "I support him because I believe he is good for the State of Israel," he has often said.

And there are others: Sam Domb, an ex-Israeli who has made a fortune in New York; Larry Reinhardt, a school friend; Hart Heiston, a banker from Indianapolis; Marvin Josephson, a major film, theatrical, and literary agent and the head of International Creative Management; George Klein, a veteran Republican; George Meisner, an attorney and one of the Likud heads in the U.S.

(*Above*) Bibi and
Odelia Carmon, his
secretary, during his
political campaign in
May, 1986. *Govern-*
ment Press Office

(*Right*) Netanyahu
with his second wife,
Fleur, while cam-
paigning. *Govern-*
ment Press Office

Bibi with his close political assistants. From right to left: Bibi, Yaffa Motil, Eyal Arad, and Odelia Carmon (seated). *Government Press Office*

Bibi (left, rear) in the pool after his victory in the 1986 Likud election. *Government Press Office*

Netanyahu (center) as Deputy Foreign Minister, 1991. *Government Press Office*

Bibi meets with Russia's Gorbachev, who is shaking hands with Prime Minister Yitzhak Shamir. *Government Press Office*

(*Left*) Bibi with his son Yair. *Government Press Office*

(*Below*) Netanyahu addresses a political rally in Jerusalem. *Government Press Office, Moshe Milner*

Bibi (right) listens to Dani Naveh, the government press secretary. *Government Press Office*

Netanyahu (right) and Elyakim Rubinstein, Israel's Attorney General. *Government Press Office*

Bibi with his wife, Sara, and two of his children: Yair (right) and Avner (left). *Government Press Office*

The night of victory. The new prime minister, Bibi Netanyahu, with David Levy (center) and Yitzchak Mordechai (right). *Government Press Office, Moshe Milner*

(*Above*) Netanyahu
meets with Yasser
Arafat.
*Government Press
Office*

(*Left*) Netanyahu
and Jordan's King
Hussein (left) in
Jerusalem.
*Government Press
Office*

Bibi and Bill Clinton at the White House. *Government Press Office*

Similar, shorter lists exist in other countries. Gabi Taman, for example, is considered one of Bibi's greatest supporters in Europe; also John Gendel, the Australian millionaire. Media tycoon Rupert Murdoch is a close friend of Netanyahu's and shares his political opinions.

Some of these donors contribute funds to Bibi's causes, while others help him by connecting him to the right people.

Before he became prime minister, Netanyahu made a habit of staying in hotels all over the world at the expense of his friends. At that time, he did not have an open expense account, the Likud coffers were empty, and his personal resources were limited. Many of his frequent trips abroad were paid for by his donors, who would pick up his hotel bills, supply him with transport, invite him to restaurants, and pay for his plane tickets.

Netanyahu conducted his affairs through the use of foundations. Everything was done in secret. The foundation system is essential where contributions are concerned, due to the clear-cut tax laws in both Israel and the United States. Bibi's foundations were intended to blur the connection between the recipients of the moneys and the sources from where they came. An example is the Shalem Center, founded for Bibi by Ronald Lauder, located in Jerusalem and headed by Dr. Yoram Hazoni. The chairman of the board is Lauder himself. Steven Shnaier is on the institute's payroll, as are other Benjamin Netanyahu activists. The Shalem Center is defined as an "institute for national policy." It operates as a semiacademic research institute with a right-wing bent. Recently, there have been rumors that the institute serves as a tool for transferring funds for various purposes from the United States to Israel. These rumors have been vehemently denied.

Tania Shaw, the nanny who was fired by Sara Netanyahu for burning a pot of soup, told the Israeli daily *Ma'ariv* that she often came across checks lying around the house. These checks were mostly from American banks and were written and signed in English. The sums were often in thousands of dollars and even tens of thousands.

In mid-1993, such eyebrow-raising over Bibi's fund-raising had not yet occurred. He had not yet been elected prime minister; he was only the leader of an opposition party whose financial situation could not have been worse. He was at the top of a pyramid that threatened to crumble at any moment.

One of the first things Bibi did when he took up occupancy in the

Likud headquarters on King George Street in Tel Aviv was call Benny Begin, Dan Meridor, Roni Milo, and Moshe Katzav for a working meeting. He did not invite David Levy.

Netanyahu wanted to create a new young leadership force for the Likud, to turn it into a vibrant party which would carry the country's younger generation. His first step in this direction was to attempt to obtain the cooperation of his colleagues. However, he knew that his chances of getting the "princes" on board were slim.

Indeed, Benny Begin, Dan Meridor, and Moshe Katzav rejected his invitation. They still saw him as an outsider, a passing fantasy that would soon go away. On the other hand, Roni Milo surprisingly indicated he might cooperate. Milo was minister of internal security in the government of Yitzhak Shamir from 1988 to 1992. The next year he was elected mayor of Tel Aviv.

Limor Livnat and Eyal Arad pressured Milo for his full support. "Bibi is our future. He is the leader who can take us back into power. There is no point in opposing and ignoring him now that he has taken over the movement." Milo agreed. (In November 1997, Milo, Livnat and Begin, together with Ehud Ulmert, the Jerusalem mayor, and Dan Meridor, would lead the ministers' revolt against Netanyahu for his attempted reversal of the primary system of voting. The system had helped Bibi unseat others and gain power, and now he wants to make sure it does not enable anyone to unseat him.)

In 1993, Milo was essential to Bibi. The Likud was supposed to convene on May 18, and Bibi wanted to pass a resolution that would give the Likud chairman wider authority. However, a month after becoming chairman of the party, Bibi still could not gain the support of his colleagues in the leadership. He finally understood that he was not going to get the cooperation he had hoped for. At best he would be able to form a wavering coalition, most of whose members would be sitting on the fence waiting for the first opportunity to jump to the other side.

At this point, Netanyahu began to demonstrate early signs of paranoia, which would grow stronger in time, reaching a peak after he was elected prime minister. "Either you're with me," he said to the "princes," "or you are against me."

He declared that anyone who remained on the fence would be considered an enemy. He would not tolerate a gradual process of acclimatization. He wanted it all—now. On the eve of the party conference, he suddenly found himself surrounded by people without the faintest understanding of how the party worked, or of the sensitivities and relationships within the party. Those who stood squarely on Bibi's side of the fence were raw rookies in everything connected with the conference and the party. Thus, at that time, Roni Milo's support became crucial for Bibi.

The following deal was arranged with Milo: he would be chairman of the conference, and Limor Livnat would serve as his deputy and manage the event. Milo kept his side of the bargain to the letter. He controlled the conference, helped Netanyahu pass any resolution he wanted, including the adoption of a new constitution, and turned himself into the most likely contender for the position of next-in-command to Netanyahu.

The party's new constitution was formulated by Netanyahu's friend and confidant Tsahi Hanegbi, a young man well known for using strong-arm methods to reach his goals. Officially, Moshe Nissim was chairman of the constitution committee, but it was Hanegbi who made decisions. Nissim's protests were meaningless; Hanegbi could bring down the iron fist of his boss and get his way.

Netanyahu wanted a new constitution and he got it. Afraid of making fools of themselves, David Levy and Ariel Sharon withdrew their objections at the last moment. The vote was open. Levy had demanded a secret ballot, but Bibi said, "For a constitution we vote openly, not like thieves in the night."

An interesting proposal was put forward at the conference by Ariel Sharon, Benny Begin, and Tsahi Hanegbi: "The Likud will not recognize any agreements signed by the Rabin government with the enemies of Israel; these agreements contradict the Likud platform."

Bibi, Dan Meridor, and Roni Milo opposed the proposal, and it was narrowly rejected. Thus, the Likud party decided that if and when it returned to power, it would honor the pacts made by the Labor government.

22

A Bombshell From Oslo

During the early months of 1993, talks took place in Oslo under the auspices of the Norwegian government and its foreign minister, Johan Jorgen Holst, between representatives of Israel's Labor government, under the leadership of Yitzhak Rabin, and members of the Palestinian leadership. The negotiations were exhausting. Both sides were unwilling to give in, but both also knew that without peace there was no hope for the future of the Middle East. For seven years the region had been in the throes of the Palestinian *intifada* being waged in the territories occupied by Israel since the 1967 Six Day War. On both sides, the feeling was that it was time for mutual recognition and peace.

The negotiations culminated in what became known as the Oslo accord, which was signed by Israel and the PLO in September 1993. Israelis were overjoyed—Benjamin Netanyahu was caught off guard. He and his men had been busy preparing a powerful campaign. A budget had been set, a publicity staff hired, slogans written. The country was to be flooded with banners calling for "Elections Now."

The polls were favorable to Netanyahu. He had a plan to topple the government within a few months by aggravating tensions between Labor and the ultra-Orthodox Sephardic Shas party. This would clear the way for a landslide Likud victory in the forthcoming municipal elections, which would carry over to a general election.

And then, on the very same day Bibi's banners were hung all over the country, the Oslo accord was announced. Bibi was in Europe on a fund-raising trip and returned home immediately. Eyal Arad was waiting for him at the airport, and they had a panic-stricken conversation at a nearby gas station. They could see one of their banners—"Elections Now"—flying in the breeze before them. They both knew that if the country were to go to the polls at that moment, Yitzhak Rabin would have a resounding victory.

Once the initial shock wore off, Netanyahu quickly regained his composure, as usual. "It's not over yet," he told his supporters. He believed that the Oslo accord would still have to overcome many obstacles. "There'll be terrorism, there'll be trouble," he said. "It's not so simple."

Netanyahu now faced a grim future. After taking over the Likud; after surviving the debacle of the "hot video"; after putting the party back on its feet financially; after changing the party constitution and establishing himself as the opposition leader; just when it seemed that he was ready to fight for the prime ministership—Shimon Peres and Yitzhak Rabin had hurled him back to square one.

Bibi was uncharacteristically speechless. The media was dominated by images from Oslo of the accord that held the promise of peace. Most Israelis were ecstatic. They watched Prime Minister Rabin and Foreign Minister Peres, President Clinton, PLO Chairman Arafat, and other world leaders hugging, kissing, shaking hands, talking about peace, and making amends. Public opinion polls showed wide support for peace with the Palestinians. Even the stock exchange rose in response to the accord.

Shimon Peres spoke of a "new Middle East." International investors started pouring money into Israel. Peace was coming and everyone wanted to get on the bandwagon.

The leaders of the right and the Likud were seen as "yesterday's news." No one had patience for their prophecies of doom. Bibi became a popular media punching bag. It was getting increasingly difficult to get him on TV. Any expression of opposition to the peace process came under heavy fire. The Likud's agenda began to seem like a lost cause.

Bibi, the main object of media criticism, adopted a new strategy. He would personally respond only to issues on which the Likud stance was not too unpopular. Other issues that might draw fire from the media and the government would be addressed through an official Likud statement.

Nonetheless, Bibi felt he was on his own. A massive wave of euphoria swept the nation in the wake of the Oslo accord, which Bibi opposed. His break with David Levy was absolute. Ariel Sharon had distanced himself from Bibi. The "princes" had not yet recovered from Bibi's victory in the primaries.

The first opponents of the Oslo accord to take to the streets were representatives of the settlers in the occupied territories. Jewish settlement in Judea and Samaria, the area commonly known as the West Bank, and the Gaza Strip, had begun several months after the Six Day War, in June 1967. Israel's Labor government, under the leadership of Levi Eshkol, had allowed hundreds of enthusiastic Israelis to settle in the newly occupied territories.

Over the years, these hundreds turned into thousands, and the few settlements which dotted the territories turned into many dozens. Towns were built in the West Bank, the largest being Ariel, Alfei Menashe, and Imanuel. The majority of the settlers in the West Bank were, and remain, religious right-wing nationalists and ardent Zionists. Most of these settlers believe that the territories belong to Israel—historically—and that not one inch of land should be returned to the Arabs.

The first demonstration against the accord was organized by the Judea and Samaria Regional Council. It took place on October 5, 1994, in front of the Knesset and the prime minister's office. It was a massive turnout, with about thirty-five thousand participants. Bibi was surprised at the number of people who did not support Oslo.

But peace stayed in the headlines. Every day, whole sections of newspapers were devoted to stories and anecdotes surrounding the peace process. One headline declared that within two weeks all the Arab states would be establishing diplomatic relations with Israel. Another newspaper reported that Israelis would soon be able to eat hummus in Mecca. An unprecedented economic breakthrough was expected. Economists foresaw a sharp increase in the GNP, and predicted that the Tel Aviv financial district would become the Geneva of the Middle East.

Events strengthened the feeling that peace was on its way. Prime Minister Rabin visited Morocco, Indonesia, and the Arab principality of Oman. Israeli representatives went to Qatar. The public seemed to feel that the impossible was about to become reality. King Hussein of Jordan did not deny that Rabin had made secret visits to his palace in Amman and his summer house in Aqaba as preliminary steps toward establishing diplomatic relations with Israel.

At Benjamin Netanyahu's personal headquarters in Tel Aviv, there was confusion. The feeling was that their vision of a greater Israel had died. Apart from the extreme right, no one seemed to believe in the possibility of peace and security without the return of territories. Bibi convened his closest associates, brought out maps, and spread them on a desk. He held a ruler and measured out each of the government's proposals to see if enough land would remain for the safety of the State of Israel.

Dr. Yoram Hazoni proposed dividing the West Bank between areas occupied by Arabs and those of Jewish settlement. This marked the first time in the history of the Likud that a discussion was taking place over the possibility of territorial compromise in the West Bank and the Golan Heights.

Most of the participants at that meeting agreed that the Likud had no choice but to recognize the Oslo accord and produce an alternative plan of its own that would include autonomy for the Palestinian population. Bibi carefully examined every suggestion.

Suddenly, he waved his hand defiantly. "Absolutely not. I will never agree to a map like this one. It's not for this that I am trying to get elected prime minister."

An embarrassed silence filled the room. Up to that moment, Bibi had never so concretely expressed the notion that the only chance the Likud had of surviving was to stick to its own political program. "I'm sorry," Bibi said, "but it is against my principles and my conscience. It is now January 1994. At this point, Oslo seems promising to everyone. Let's wait and see how things look in January 1996. I have a gut feeling the whole process will turn upside down."

Shortly after the signing of the Oslo accord, Bibi was faced with the municipal elections, planned for early November 1993. He believed victory in these elections was supremely important for the Likud, and ultimately for himself. He had three reasons:

One, morale: The Likud was in desperate need of a victory of any kind.

Two, money: The Likud was still in deep financial trouble. Bibi and his adviser, Yvette Lieberman, had fired hundreds of people in order to cut the payroll, and they knew that unemployment could produce pockets of dissent in the party. A sweeping success in the municipal elections would enable Netanyahu to bring hundreds, even thousands, of Likud activists back to salaried positions, and when the time was right, they would become his soldiers.

Three, politics: Surveys had shown that municipal elections had a decisive effect on general elections. Data showed that a town governed by a Likud council would be more likely to vote Likud in a national election. "When the mayor of a town belongs to your camp," Bibi said, "you have a carrier." Eyal Arad figured that was worth several thousand votes at the polls.

Bibi's agenda for the municipal elections was to build new leadership in the Likud and complete the changing of the guard. He had already been disappointed by the attitude of the "princes" and was determined to show them who the real boss was. He was ready to take matters into his own hands.

Bibi recruited the support of second-tier Knesset members Limor Livnat and Tsahi Hanegbi, who were ready to back him all the way.*

They were joined by Yehoshua Matza, Shaul Amor, the late Chaim Kaufman, and others. It turned out that most of those who helped him at this time were later given positions in Netanyahu's government.

Bibi poured all his energy into his election campaign. He formed a central headquarters, headed by Ovadia Ali, created a polling system backed by Gallup, and set about personally raising funds for various candidates all over the country. He directed many donors and large sums of money to Roni Milo's campaign in Tel Aviv, Ehud Ulmert's in Jerusalem, and Zvi Bar's in Ramat Gan. They were all, of course, Netanyahu supporters.

He was involved in each and every local campaign throughout the country, closely monitoring all of them and intervening freely in the local primary elections. When he foresaw victory for a candidate he found unsuitable he would cancel the primaries and appoint a new candidate. He was determined to achieve an overall victory, no matter what. He was already racing for the prime minister's office.

During the campaign, Netanyahu put a dramatic and unequivocal halt

---

*As previously mentioned, Limor Livnat would eventually help lead a Knesset "revolt" against Prime Minister Netanyahu. "He is not reliable," Livnat and others said. "You cannot believe a word he says." Later still, Livnat would decide to give Bibi another chance.

to the payment of Likud debts. "Stop paying our creditors," he ordered his team. "As far as I'm concerned, they can bring in the collectors. From now and until further notice, every penny we have is to be spent on the campaign."

Yvette Lieberman was in charge of organization. Netanyahu adopted Eyal Arad's brilliant idea and established an advertising office for the Likud. The office prepared "publicity packages" for the various towns. This greatly reduced costs because all the posters, letters, and other materials could be mass-produced, identical except for the name of the candidate in each town or city.

The Likud's victory in the municipal elections was overwhelming. Milo won in Tel Aviv, Ulmert in Jerusalem, Zvi Bar in Ramat Gan. The Likud managed to "protect" the wavering towns, to "save" Giora Lev in Petah Tikva, Nehemia Lahav in Hedera, and Yitzhak Rager in Be'er Sheva. In addition, the Likud managed to win over towns such as Eilat, Bet Shemesh, Bat-Yam, and Kiryat Motzkin. The loss of Holon and Netanya was significant, but the other successes more than compensated.

The Likud, an opposition party, had managed to capture most of the local elections throughout the country. For the first time, the media treated Netanyahu as a real, legitimate, leader. Netanyahu was now convinced that the stage was set for him to climb the next rung on the ladder to prime ministership.

With less than three years to go before the next Knesset elections— scheduled for October 1996—Netanyahu decided to complete his takeover of the Likud. The objective was to push out the Arens-Shamir camp and pump new blood into the party's central committee, specifically Netanyahu supporters.

Bibi had mixed feelings about Yitzhak Shamir. He never forgot how Shamir had excluded him from his government in 1988, instead choosing Dan Meridor, Roni Milo, and Ehud Ulmert. He also remembered that Shamir had refused to give him a significant job in the 1992 election campaign. Much later, Shamir would complain about the treatment he received from Netanyahu: "From the moment Netanyahu was elected prime minister, all cooperation ceased between us. I was active in the Likud up to the elections, and from time to time, he would consult with me. From the moment he was elected, it was as if I no longer existed. He behaves in a patronizing and arrogant manner toward other people. It is not typical of leaders who have grown up in the Likud. It contradicts the character of the Likud as a political party. It is very typical of Netanyahu. I stepped back and took to watching things from a distance. I saw the way he formed the government and humiliated the senior members of the Likud. It's a different generation. A different kind of leadership."

Netanyahu's relationship with Arens remained good—officially. In reality, however, Bibi chose not to reciprocate the good will of the older man who had been responsible for bringing him to Washington and supporting him in his early days in politics.

Netanyahu decided to break up the biggest camp in the Likud to make way for his own supporters. In early 1994, he proposed adding 243 new members to the Likud's central committee. David Levy and Ariel Sharon were firmly against this plan, aware that under such circumstances they would lose much of their clout. Netanyahu called a special meeting of the Central Committee on March 10 to discuss his proposal and try to get it approved. David Levy threatened to sabotage the meeting. Netanyahu appealed to David and his brother Maxim, mayor of Lod and chairman of the Likud Central Committee, to join him. He believed the Levy brothers had come to realize that their chances of rebuilding their large faction and creating an alternative to Netanyahu leadership were minimal.

A couple of months later, Ariel Sharon announced: "I am not satisfied with the party. The current leadership has failed in navigating the opposition against the government's decisions. The real leaders are the settlers. The Likud is not being heard. The Likud has failed miserably. The party needs a leader who can really lead the struggle [against Labor's peace initiative]. We have a problem, a real problem. There has to be an alternative to the leadership, which has failed."

Sharon did not name a possible replacement for Netanyahu, but the hint was clear: himself. It had been Sharon's idea to form the Likud in 1973, and he continued to believe that only he was capable of leading the party and fulfilling its political objectives.

Sharon planned to take over the Likud leadership by the end of the 1980s. He could not have anticipated that when the time came, Netanyahu would be the one in that position. This is probably why he never really joined forces with Bibi.

Sharon never understood the secret of Netanyahu's political charisma, and never respected him as a political leader. But in all his political maneuvers against Netanyahu, Sharon never overcame Bibi's three decisive advantages: his youth, his winning image, and his rare talent for captivating an audience, especially on television.

The new Likud created by Netanyahu was different from the old Likud, which was ideologically torn between Jabotinsky's "both sides of the Jordan" credo and Menachem Begin's pragmatism. The new Likud was built in the image of its leaders—but with no real underlying ideology. Pragmatic like its predecessor, the new Likud was, however, intolerant of other political opinions, including those of its own dissenting members such as David Levy, Benny Begin, Ariel Sharon, and David Magna.

From the moment Benjamin Netanyahu took over the Likud Central Committee, he turned it into a warm place—for himself. It became a safe haven. The culture of debate, which had in the past defined the Likud as a party of the people, disappeared almost completely under Netanyahu. The Likud has now become a party of a single opinion, unable to listen to other voices. Even at the height of the ideological wars between Shamir, Levy, and Sharon, the word *traitor* was never uttered toward political adversaries the way it is toward Benny Begin and other political enemies of Bibi's.

After the Oslo accord became reality, Netanyahu began a series of discussions within the Likud. Roni Milo and Meir Shitrit, who abstained at the Knesset vote, signaled the beginning of a more moderate camp within the Likud. Some members were convinced that there was no chance of stopping the tide of history and that the Likud should change with the times.

Netanyahu realized this trend and prepared for it. He began to formulate an alternative political program. Later, when Zalman Shazar returned from Washington after being replaced as Israel's ambassador to the United States, he published a political program of his own. In it, many saw a reflection of Bibi's views.

Netanyahu supported, in principle, a program based on "cantonizing" the Palestinians. He drafted his program on napkins in restaurants and coffee houses, which is where he would present it to listeners. Interestingly Netanyahu's "cantons" plan turned out to be very similar to the second Oslo accord, which was signed much later. The difference is that Netanyahu saw his plan as the final stage in the agreement, while Rabin and Peres saw the second Oslo accord as only an intermediary step toward a permanent arrangement. Under the second Oslo agreement, Israel would withdraw from Hebron and the Israel Defense Force would redeploy in the West Bank, beyond the area where the Palestinian population was concentrated.

Netanyahu wanted to rid Israel of authority over as large an Arab population as possible, at the lowest possible cost. In impromptu political meetings in various coffee houses, he would state: "My objective is to let eighty percent of the Arabs have widespread autonomy, while Israel reserves for herself authority only in external and security issues."

At that time, Netanyahu tried to conduct a dialogue with Prime Minister Rabin in order to reach a common formulation. Two meetings were arranged through the offices of Avner Regev, but when they were leaked to the media, Rabin rid himself of the entire business.

Bibi tried to gain support for his program in the Likud. Ariel Sharon, Benny Begin, and Moshe Katzav were against it. Dan Meridor, as usual, said nothing, and Roni Milo supported it. Bibi considered forming a small committee that would present several proposals, out of which the party could adopt one. He faced serious opposition. The dissident group was joined by Yitzhak Shamir, who still maintained considerable influence in the party.

Proposals were made for a possible joining of the Likud with the Labor party to form a national unity government. The logic was simple: if the Likud supported autonomy for 80 percent of the Arab population and almost entirely independent Palestinian cantons, there was no reason it should not enter a national unity government and achieve national consensus. Many in Bibi's camp were in favor of this idea. After some consideration, however, Bibi decided against it. "I want to reach a national consensus with Rabin," he said, "but I don't want to join the government. It would only blur the differences between us. We'll turn into an offshoot of the Labor party."

As time passed, Bibi became more and more determined to take over the government, believing that if Israel stayed its current course, "There'll be terrorist attacks, the whole business will wobble, and in the end it will topple over."

He had drawn a few far-reaching conclusions, which he kept to himself. Only his closest confidants knew that he said: "I have no doubt that the

PLO has become Israel's partner and this situation is irreversible. That's the way things are. But we must not admit this outwardly. We'll speak with Arafat, but only after the elections, and we'll charge a very high price, politically, for doing so. We must not accept Arafat right now, and save that card for later."

Bibi reconciled himself to the reality of Arafat long before the elections, though he refused to admit it openly. In an interview, he said that if it became necessary to speak with Arafat, he would send his foreign minister to do so. As he confided to his associates, "The foreign minister will almost certainly be Shimon Peres. If we win the elections, there will most likely be a national unity government. So let Peres speak with Arafat."

And if he did not form a national unity government?" In that case," Bibi explained, "I will appoint Dan Meridor foreign minister. And then it would also not be a problem for me if Meridor goes to speak with Arafat."

Shortly before the signing of the Oslo accords, Benjamin Netanyahu, the Likud leader, had already realized that Israeli politics had undergone a historic change. He knew that the PLO had become Israel's partner in peace; that the dream of a greater Israel was clinically dead; that talks with Arafat were unavoidable, and that the only solution to the Israeli-Palestinian problem was territorial compromise.

Benjamin Netanyahu was aware that everything he had learned at his father's knee, all the ideology with which he was raised was no longer relevant. He believed nonetheless that he would be able to reduce as much as possible the amount of land Israel would have to relinquish in that necessary territorial compromise, but until the election was won, he would keep those thoughts to himself. When Yvette Lieberman suggested that the Likud recognize the PLO, Bibi rejected the suggestion.

It was at the beginning of 1994 that Bibi first formulated his concept of "mutuality," which he has consistently reiterated to this day. "We must honor agreements," he insisted, "on the condition that the other side also honors them to the letter." The media tended to believe that only the second part of his dictum was possible. They had little faith that Bibi would ever be capable of adopting the Oslo accords.

Bibi decided that there was no need for the Likud to form any clear-cut policy so early in the process. "We must use a holding defense tactic and constantly criticize the accord. It is not necessary to offer an alternative," he said. "We have no way of knowing what the situation will be in three years. Oslo in an ongoing process. We'll just wait and see."

Netanyahu was surprised to discover a rather embarrassing dearth of Likud supporters—"soldiers"—in the field. At the huge protest rally held on October 5, 1994, in front of the Knesset, it had been the West Bank settlers, perfectly organized and disciplined, who filled the arena. From that day on, Netanyahu knew that when it came to public protest against the Oslo accords, he could only rely on the settlers. From that moment on, Bibi started moving to the right.

It was a tactical move. A master of circumspection and circumvention, Bibi was attacking the Oslo accords in order to appease the settlers, and win their enthusiastic support. Bibi appointed himself spearhead of the settlers' protest. He stopped raising money for the Likud and turned most of his financial energies toward the territories.

No Likud candidate ever had a more efficient and devoted group of activists than Bibi's settlers. Eighty branch offices were set up in the larger towns and main settlements, and activists were sent everywhere possible. They took over the country's main road junctions, organized events and advertising campaigns, and produced reams of propaganda. Bibi was satisfied, but he had paid a high price. His name became inextricably linked with extreme right-wing elements, like the fanatic Elyakim Ha'etzni and Rabbi Meir Kahane's murderous Kach movement.

Netanyahu's political love affair with the settlers wouldn't last forever. Just before the assassination of Yitzhak Rabin, Netanyahu led some of the fiercest rallies in the country's history, against the prime minister. Later, faced with Rabin's murdered body, Netanyahu tried to disown the mark of Cain which clung to him. In November 1997, history seemed to repeat itself. Then pictures of Netanyahu, his head wrapped in an Arab kaffiyeh, were plastered by settlers on walls all over the country, accompanied by the captions "Liar!" and "Netanyahu does not have a mandate to give in to Arafat!" Under intense American pressure, Bibi had tried to make some progress in the dying peace process, and the settlers, whose support had been instrumental in getting him elected, felt betrayed.

23

Secret Channels to Jordan

In March 1989, the American secretary of state James Baker delivered a speech to a conference held by the American Israel Public Affairs Committee (AIPAC), Israel's lobby in Washington. Netanyahu, then Israel's deputy foreign minister, did not have a friendly relationship with Baker—to put it mildly. In order to study the political ramifications of the secretary of state's speech, Netanyahu called on Dr. Dore Gold, a young researcher at Tel Aviv University's Jaffe Center for Strategic Studies. It was their first meeting. Gold analyzed the speech for Netanyahu, and since Bibi remembered by heart the speech of his friend, Secretary of State George Shultz, a year before, Gold was able to compare the two speeches and analyze their trends.

Around the same time, Gold refused to sign a report on a special research project conducted by the Jaffe Center under the title: "Support for a Palestinian State." Since he was a member of the institute's staff, Gold's refusal to sign the report received wide media attention. It also caught the attention of Bibi and the rest of the Likud leadership.

Following their first meeting, Bibi started calling on Gold from time to time for consultations which sometimes even included Ambassador Moshe Arens. Bibi found that Gold's politics were very much in synch with his own. He decided to take Gold with him to the Madrid conference as his special political adviser.

Bibi continued to make use of Gold's services. When he was booked for a televised debate the with Palestinian spokeswoman, Hanan Ashrawi, Netanyahu sent Gold in his stead so as not to raise Ashrawi's importance. She held no official office in the Palestinian administration at the time. Gold's appearance on TV, in English, proved most impressive.

On the day of the Knesset vote on the Oslo accords, Gold visited Chaim Assad, Yitzhak Rabin's strategic adviser. According to Gold, Assad tried to find out if he, Gold, would be interested in joining Rabin's advisory team, if only as an external observer. Assad explained that Rabin felt Peres was drifting to the left, and he wanted to "compensate" with someone from the right. The delicate balance between Rabin and Peres, which had been upset by the accords, could possibly be restored by adding Gold to Rabin's team. In the middle of the meeting, Assad received a phone call from Fuad Ben-Eliezer, who told Assad that the Likud was on the verge of disintegrating, and that in a little while the party would no longer exist.

Gold went home troubled by what he had heard. His phone rang at eleven o'clock that night. "Dore? It's Bibi. Can you come over at once?"

Gold made his way quickly to Netanyahu's home. There he found Bibi and his advisers busy preparing alternative political programs. Gold joined in. He realized then that Bibi had no intention of letting the Likud disintegrate.

No alternative to the Oslo accords was ever published, but Bibi's attempt to formulate one was a good example of his unwavering spirit. Even in the most difficult times, he does not allow himself to feel undue pressure. He simply looks around for a way to recover and goes on.

Dore Gold had a large network of contacts in the Arab world. Since 1991 he had been searching for a common denominator by participating in an independent program produced by a group of Americans who arranged meetings between Israelis and Arabs in various places around the world. This program differed from the various European initiatives, which mainly included Israeli and Palestinian intellectuals. "We are conducting meetings with people from the entire Arab world, not only Palestinians," Gold said. "People from Oman, Saudi Arabia, Kuwait, Jordan, even Syria."

Immediately following Oslo in 1994, Gold recognized "the great Jordanian opportunity." Jordan was hurt and worried following Israel's recognition of the PLO. The agreements made with the PLO caused King Hussein and his people to fear that the Labor party was abandoning its historic covenant with the Jordanian royal family, in favor of Yasser Arafat. Hussein felt that for Israel, the Jordanian option had been replaced by the Palestinian option. He felt threatened and isolated, especially when he took into account Israel's residual animosity from his support of Iraq during the Gulf crisis.

Gold knew that Bibi and the Likud could squeeze themselves into the void left by the rift between Amman and Jerusalem. Thus began an exchange of letters between King Hussein of Jordan and Israeli opposition leader Benjamin Netanyahu, under the auspices of Dr. Dore Gold.

Bibi's first meeting with Crown Price Hassan of Jordan took place in May 1994. Bibi and Gold secretly flew to London, where they met Hassan at the home of a member of the royal Hashemite family. Rabin knew nothing about the trip and when he learned about it, he was stunned.

Shortly after the meeting, gestures were made toward a peace agreement between Israel and Jordan under the auspices of Elyakim Rubinstein, general secretary in Rabin's cabinet, and the deputy Mossad head, Ephraim Levy. But Bibi and the Likud maintained contact with the Jordanians. "The cooperation was fruitful, and based on trust," Gold says of that period, "The Jordanians were keen to know what we thought and wanted to maintain our option. They took into consideration that Bibi might one day be prime minister."

Meetings followed meetings, and at one of them, Prince Hassan presented a draft of a peace agreement. Bibi read the agreement. "All in all, I have no problem with it," he told Prince Hassan. "I should be able to get the Likud to accept it." And, indeed, when the agreement was brought to a vote in the Knesset, most of the Likud voted in favor of it.

Netanyahu was pleased. The Jordanian leaders had reached the conclusion that he was a potential leader of Israel, and they demonstrated this belief forcefully at a meeting in London, where Jordan requested Bibi's approval in advance of signing an agreement with Rabin.

Gold denies charges that Bibi also sent messages to Syria in order to prevent Syrian President Hafez el-Assad from arriving at an agreement with Rabin and later Peres. But he does not deny having made connections with Syria. A meeting Gold attended in 1993 in Oslo part of the "common denominator" program, was also attended by Dr. Aziz Shukri, dean of the law school at the University of Damascus. Before long, Gold found a common denominator between himself and Dr. Shukri—

they were the two people at the meeting who lashed out against the Oslo accords. Though each had his own reason for disapproving of the accords, their general agreement made for a pleasant acquaintance.

Later, Gold wrote an article in the *Jerusalem Post* in which he exposed Shimon Peres's strategy of isolating Syria by engineering a pact between Israel and Turkey. Gold was well aware that his article would be read in Damascus. Gold published another article in the *Middle East Insight*, the Washington journal edited by George Nader, which dealt with potential security arrangements between Israel and Syria.

Later, Nader would act as a secret liaison between Gold and Netanyahu and the Syrian president.

Gold, of course, denies that he sent messages to Syria. However, sources close to Bibi reject Gold's denials outright: "Clear messages were passed on by various means from Bibi to Assad, long before the elections," a source says. "According to these messages, it was hinted to Assad that it would be worth his while to wait for Netanyahu, and that if he signed any agreement with Rabin or Peres, he would be causing himself harm."

The Syrians were under pressure. After Rabin's assassination, Shimon Peres was determined to reach election day with a signed peace agreement with Syria in his pocket—or at least a declaration of intent. But Syria heeded the countermessages they were receiving from Netanyahu and put a stop to the peace negotiations, which were on the very brink of success.

Bibi was convinced that he could reach an agreement with the Syrians. His theory was simple: "The Syrians don't want real peace with Israel, anyway. Witness the fact that they did not want to sign an agreement with Rabin, although he was willing to give them back the entire Golan Heights. They are not prepared to pay the cost of such a peace. Assad cannot stomach the thought of Israeli tourists eating hummus on the streets of Damascus. Israel holds a similar outlook. We too, are not willing to pay the cost of peace with Syria by giving back the Golan Heights."

Netanyahu saw not a problem but a potential solution in Israel and Syria's mutual unwillingness to make a concrete trade: "Instead of selling the goods, we'll rent them out. In place of a peace agreement, we'll make do with a nonbelligerence agreement. Rather than returning the Golan Heights, the IDF will withdraw and redeploy at the foothills, and the Syrian army will withdraw toward Damascus. A huge no-man's land will divide the two countries. There will be no embassies, no blue-and-white flag will be flown in Assad's face. We don't need embassies; we need only to be free of the Syrian army hovering above us on the Golan Heights with their rockets.

"And what will the Syrians receive in return? They will be removed from the list of countries who support terror and we will ensure that they receive generous financial support from the United States. Assad will be free to stabilize his administration and Israel will have some peace and quiet."

This was Netanyahu's plan for an agreement between Israel and Syria.

Prime Minister Yitzhak Rabin often blamed the Likud and their leader for passing on secret messages to Damascus promising that "Bibi will give them more." Through a senior source in the United States administration, presumably Warren Christopher, now secretary of state, Rabin received information from the Syrians. Every time he urged Syria to be more flexible toward Israel in the negotiations—warning that "if you don't let up, a Likud government won't give you anything"—the Syrians would counter by hinting that they received conciliatory messages from the Likud.

At this time, Bibi was forming an efficient intelligence system that constantly supplied him with valuable political information. On many occasions, he was privy in advance to important developments related to the Labor government's peace negotiations. Bibi maintained excellent connections in Washington to ensure a constant flow of valuable intelligence. He also maintained good sources in the Foreign Office, where general manager Uri Savir succeeded in stopping some of the information leaks, but couldn't catch all of them.

During this time, senior Palestinian officials were reaching out to Netanyahu. Bibi refused to respond. He felt that until the elections he had to keep a safe distance from the Palestinians.

Just to be on the safe side, however, preparations were made for a possible meeting between Bibi and Abu Mazen, Yasser Arafat's deputy, before the elections. But the need for such a meeting never arose. Bibi would remain "untouched" by the Palestinians before going to the polls.

The year 1994 brought the resolution of many of the upheavals in Bibi's life. His relationship with Sara had improved; she had apparently forgiven him for the "hot video." She was often seen holding Bibi's hand, and he made a point of keeping his distance from other women.

The Netanyahus had a new baby. King Hussein personally called Netanyahu to congratulate him on the birth of his son, Avner. Bibi saw this telephone call as a genuine gesture, and not just a "thank you" to Bibi for having voted in favor of the peace agreement with Jordan. He told Hussein, "I promise you that peace will reign between our nations, not only between our governments."

Netanyahu had no problem with Israel's peace agreement with Jordan. The agreement included no significant territorial concessions, except for a few minor amendments to the southern border, and was as acceptable to the Likud as it was to Rabin's government. Rabin shook Netanyahu's hand and thanked him for his support. It was a rare moment of peace and gentlemanly behavior between two contenders for the prime minister's office.

In August 1994, Netanyahu hired a new press secretary, Shai Bazak, to replace Danny Naveh and Zvika Hauser, who were resigning to return to the more lucrative private sector. Of all the people on Bibi's team, Shai Bazak, a young political reporter with the Itim news agency, soon became Bibi's closest adviser. He went everywhere with his boss. In time he became known as the national denier, because of the constant need for him to deny Bibi's or Sara's slips of the tongue and other mishaps.

Two months after his appointment, Shai Bazak accompanied Bibi on a trip abroad. Bibi was amused to learn that it was Bazak's first time out of the country. They flew to London for a meeting with Crown Prince Hassan of Jordan. Dr. Dore Gold, who arranged the meeting, would also attend. In London, Bibi and Bazak stayed at a particularly shabby hotel. The Likud budget was still tight, and Bibi tried his best to keep down expenses on occasions when his millionaire friends were not picking up his hotel bill.

The meeting was a deep and guarded secret. Bazak did not want the Rabin government to sabotage it, so he informed only the Israeli reporters in London and asked them to keep it under their hats. Even the Israeli Embassy was not informed of the meeting in advance. Netanyahu made a point of keeping the Israeli embassies uninformed of his political meetings as a safeguard against information leaks to the prime minister and foreign minister, who might make things difficult for him.

After meeting with Hassan at the London home of the Jordanian ambassador to England, Bibi and Bazak met Knesset member Sylvan

Shalom and his wife, Judy. They went for a dinner at a Japanese restaurant and lost track of the time.

At one point, Bazak drew Bibi's attention to the fact that they were going to be late for the airport. Bibi gave his usual reply: "It'll be okay."

Fifteen minutes later, Bazak reminded him again, "Bibi, we're in London. There are procedures we have to go through. We should have been at the airport an hour ago."

Bibi replied, "There's still time, don't worry."

When they finally got into the taxi to head to the airport, Bibi understood they were in trouble. The gates to their flight were already closed. Bibi, who was accustomed to Israel's Ben-Gurion Airport, where he received the respect due to the leader of the opposition, realized that if he missed his flight he would be helplessly stuck in London. Using a portable phone, he called British Airways on the way to the airport, and tried to explain his importance as the opposition leader in Israel. This did not impress the British security officer. The man who would be elected prime minister of Israel in just over a year's time was obliged to go through the same security procedures as everyone else. When they arrived at the airport, Netanyahu stood with his arms out and was frisked for weapons like a common passenger.

Shai Bazak befriended the local political reporters in Israel. At first he took to heart every negative word written about his boss but he soon got used to all the critical remarks. Bazak reported to Bibi that his newspaper colleagues advised him against becoming Bibi's press secretary—Bibi's a dead horse, they told him. Bibi laughed upon hearing this. "This dead horse," he told Bazak, "is going to give everyone a run for their money."

Bazak and Netanyahu grew closer. Bazak's responsibilities extended far beyond the parameters of the job. It was he who made sure Bibi had a constant supply of clean shirts, a portable electric razor, a makeup set. Netanyahu is very conscious of his appearance, especially on TV. Bazak soon learned to quickly apply makeup to Bibi's face for any passing TV camera.

When Bibi started gaining weight, Shai Bazak put him on a diet. He made sure to keep fattening foods well out of Bibi's reach. He instructed all hosts to serve only nonfattening meals, fruit, and diet drinks. Under Bazak's influence, Bibi has become accustomed to drinking only seltzer or unsweetened grapefruit juice with his meals (he has recently taken to drinking iced tea, imported from the United States).

Bazak learned to rely on Bibi's gut feeling. Every time he raised an issue for discussion among his advisers, Bibi would state his own opinion authoritatively. When asked how he could be so sure, his reply was always, "My gut feeling."

Bibi's confidence in his instincts became well-known among his advisers. Especially when it came to forecasting the public mood, Bibi invariably declared, "You'll see, in the end my gut is right." Then he would laugh, but Bazak knew he was dead serious.

Every Friday, Bibi met with his senior advisers. The group included Eyal Arad, Yvette Lieberman, Shai Bazak, Shai Reuveni from Gallup (later replaced by Ya'akov Levy), and Oded Levanter. There were others, too, like the popular psychologist Yair Hamburger, who later disappeared from the scene.

The Friday meetings were always kept secret and rarely reached the press and public. They lasted for hours on end, during which the participants ate, drank, analyzed data, and exchanged ideas.

The Oslo accords and the Cairo agreement, which determined the agenda for the IDF's deployment in the occupied territories, gave Rabin great prestige and left Netanyahu way behind in public opinion.

Then a series of horrific attacks perpetrated by Hamas terrorists trying to put an end to Rabin's peace program somewhat restored the political balance between Rabin and Netanyahu. The attacks occurred in Jerusalem, Afula, and Hedera, and reached a crescendo in October 1994, when a suicide terrorist blew himself up on a number 5 Tel Aviv bus in Dizengoff Circus in the very heart of Tel Aviv. Nineteen people were killed, dozens were wounded, busses and cars were burned out. Horrific pictures of the dead and wounded appeared on Israeli and international TV.

Netanyahu blamed Rabin's government. He demanded that Rabin withdraw from the Oslo agreements. The wave of violence made it hard for Rabin and Peres and the Labor government to defend the agreements. Shimon Peres's "new Middle East" began to look like a dangerous illusion.

At the end of October 1994, President Clinton arrived in Israel. His state visit was a clear demonstration of American support for the peace process and Israel in the face of the Hamas suicide terrorists.

Opposition leader Netanyahu did not take comfort in the obvious affinity between the president and Israel's prime minister. Bibi feared that his recent rise in the polls would stop unless he, too, found a way to meet with the president.

After many hints and much pressure, the long awaited telephone call arrived from the embassy, and Bibi was invited to meet Clinton. It was a short meeting. Bibi wanted to be photographed with the president in order to counter the many pictures of Rabin alongside the American leader. Before Clinton left, Bibi told him, "We'll meet again."

A week later, Netanyahu was surprised by a telephone call from the office of Jordanian Prince Hassan, inviting him to visit Karameh to inaugurate a memorial to the soldiers of the Jordanian army. On March 21, 1968, Israel's armed forces had attacked terrorist camps in that Jordanian village. Netanyahu was pleased by the invitation, and he accepted. Twenty years after taking part in the battle at Karameh as a young soldier in his first military operation, Netanyahu was entering Jordan via the Allenby Bridge. He was met on the other side by an official car belonging to the royal Hashemite family. Netanyahu was driven past stretches of desert which had once been the main camp of the PLO.

The entire royal family was waiting for Bibi at Karameh. King Hussein had arrived in a Royal Jordanian Air Force helicopter, with his attractive wife Nur. The king flew the helicopter himself and waved to his Israeli guests from the cockpit. Crown Prince Hassan gave Netanyahu a warm welcome.

Netanyahu told the king and the crown prince, "I fought on this very spot twenty-six years ago. I was a young man of nineteen. I can still remember the bullets whistling over my head.

Prince Hassan smiled. "I was here, too," he told a surprised Netanyahu. "I was twenty-one years old, a young officer in the Jordanian army. We were at war with each other and now we sit down as friends and talk about the old days."

Netanyahu laid a wreath in memory of the eighty-four Jordanian soldiers who fell in the battle. Then Bibi thanked the king for his invitation. "We will continue the peace with you," Bibi said, "and we will make it even stronger after we win the elections and I am elected prime minister." He caught the king's surprised expression and added, "That is what will happen. I'm going to be elected prime minister."

Hussein responded diplomatically, "I wish you good health and success."

Prince Hassan personally drove Netanyahu to the border checkpoint at the Allenby Bridge. "On this visit I entered Jordan in daylight for the first time," Bibi said to him as they parted. "Up until now it has always been in the dark. It is much nicer to cross the border on the Allenby Bridge."

Netanyahu returned to Jerusalem, still excited by the honor he had been given. He believed that King Hussein, like Clinton, was reading the polls in Israel. At the end of December 1994, those polls showed that Netanyahu had a 2 percent lead over Prime Minister Rabin.

24

"Death to Rabin!"

At the beginning of January 1995, the right wing started its campaign against Prime Minister Rabin. A plan for protest was concocted by the joint headquarters of the Likud and the right-wing parties. No one could have predicted how this campaign would end on November 4, 1995.

A special headquarters had been set up for the sole purpose of organizing protests against the prime minister. Netanyahu's representative in the headquarters was Tsahi Hanegbi, the young Knesset member with a history of promoting violence. Hanegbi gave Uri Aloni responsibility for organizing the Likud's young supporters. The headquarters also had representatives from the Judea and Samaria regional council and the fanatic Moledet movement. Subsequently, the activities were joined, uninvited, by members of the extreme right movements Kahane Lives and Kach.

The first demonstration took place in response to an attack near the Bet-El settlement, in which a woman was killed. Thousands of angry demonstrators were bussed into Jerusalem, where they squatted in front of the prime minister's official residence. Protestors also congregated in Tel Aviv, in front of Rabin's private home. For the first time, the chant "Rabin is a traitor" was heard.

A worse attack took place only a few days later, on January 22, early on a Sunday morning, when two suicide terrorists blew themselves up at the Bet Lid junction, where hundreds of soldiers wait for rides back to their army bases. Dozens were killed or wounded, and the entire peace process seemed to be blown into one of those two categories.

Three terrorists, members of the Islamic Jihad movement, turned up at the junction dressed in IDF uniforms. The first one set off the explosives attached to his body, killing himself and four soldiers standing nearby and wounding dozens of other soldiers. As the second terrorist anticipated, hundreds of people rushed over to help the wounded. That was when the second terrorist detonated his own explosives, killing himself and a large number of Israeli soldiers. The third terrorist apparently got cold feet and ran away instead of blowing himself up.

After this attack, Netanyahu was more outspoken in his outrage than anyone else. He held Rabin personally responsible for the death of dozens of soldiers. "If you put an end to this false peace process and make a decision to combat terrorism," Netanyahu told Rabin, "I will stand beside you all the way. If you continue, I will continue to fight against you and your government and this peace process which is leading to a Palestinian state."

Public opinion polls showed a drastic drop in Rabin's popularity. Netanyahu's rating, at the bottom of the polls when the peace process began, was gradually rising. He began to believe that the public would help him topple the Rabin government long before the designated election date of October 1996.

Rabin's advisers suggested waging a personal offensive against Netanyahu. At the end of February, when Rabin rose to speak at a Knesset debate, the jeers and catcalls from the opposition made it impossible to hear a word he was saying. Loudest of all was Netanyahu's baritone voice. Rabin waited a few moments and then shouted to Bibi, "You just shut up. When Menachem Begin made the decision to withdraw from the Sinai peninsula, you weren't even here. You have never in your life filled any kind of position involving responsibility for security."

Bibi was stunned. All he managed to get out of his mouth was a weak, "Oh, ho."

That evening Rabin was asked if he had decided to change his tactics against Netanyahu: "Who is he anyway? He's the one to talk? I had respect for Menachem Begin and Sharon. Those were men who made important decisions. Who is this Netanyahu? When did he ever have to make a decision? All he is is a hero in an American soap opera. He spent seventeen of his forty-seven years in the United States and now this emigrant wants to be prime minister of Israel. We should check to see if that name he gave himself in America, Ben Nitai, is not a sign that he intended to settle and make a life for himself there."

Rabin told his friends at that same gathering how Netanyahu asked the Shabak, the general security services, to supply him with a bodyguard. "The Shabak head asked me what I thought and I said to him, do whatever you see fit. Now they're thrilled to bits in the Likud. Bibi's got his own bodyguard. He's swaggering around as if he's prime minister."

Before this outburst, Rabin had created the impression, in public at least, that he respected Netanyahu. The truth was rather different. Rabin loathed Bibi and had absolutely no respect for him as a political adversary. In the three and a half years that Rabin was in office, he had no more than three or four private conversations with Netanyahu. He saw Bibi as an emigrant, a man who had spent most of his adult life away from the country.

After Rabin's outburst in the Knesset, Bibi became convinced that he would be the political target in Labor's next election campaign. Up to the moment when Rabin openly insulted him at the Knesset, Bibi had generally behaved respectfully toward the older man. In his speeches he attacked the government, not the prime minister. He never forgot Rabin's sensitivity toward the Netanyahu family after his brother Yonatan fell in Entebbe. It was Rabin who decided to change the name from Operation Entebbe to Operation Yonatan.

Only those really close to Netanyahu knew how much Rabin's insult before the Knesset hurt him. "Starting today," Bibi declared, "we are opening a new chapter with Rabin. From now on I will relate to him differently. I always saw him as a symbol. Now I will prove that he has held one job too many."

Just as the Likud was recovering in the polls, it was drawn into another political storm when David Levy demanded that 40 percent of his people be included on the next Knesset list and in the party offices. Netanyahu adamantly refused, believing that Levy was capable of switching to Rabin's camp after the elections. The most Bibi was willing to concede to Levy was 20 percent.

Things soon got out of hand. Levy offered an ultimatum: Either you support my request, or I will resign from the Likud—and I will take my followers with me.

All attempts of Likud functionaries to reach a compromise failed. Bibi was adamant: Let him leave if that's what he wants. Bibi did not respond to Levy's last warning. He simply packed up and took Sara and Yair for a private vacation in Italy. Had Bibi wanted Levy to remain in the Likud, he would have found a way to keep him. However, he had come to the conclusion that separation was preferable, taking into account the short-term political price he would have to pay.

On June 5, the Likud held its conference. Bibi spent the entire morning beforehand preparing his speech. He planned every word, leaving very little room for improvisation, as he always did in his speeches.

That Likud conference was one of the most dramatic in the party's history. Levy boycotted it. The stage was completely free for Bibi. Sixty-nine percent of those present were in favor of holding primaries with no fixed rankings, a position that Netanyahu supported and Levy opposed. Two weeks later, Levy responded by gathering his supporters at a conference at the Renaissance Halls in Tel Aviv. There Levy announced his resignation from the Likud and the formation of a new political party called Gesher (Bridge).

Opinion polls indicated minimal damage to Bibi and the Likud: Two or three seats at most would go to Levy's new party. Only later, as the election drew near, did Netanyahu understand that the real danger was not in the number of Knesset seats taken by Gesher, but in the percentage of votes Levy would get for prime minister. Once Bibi understood this danger, he was willing to pay any price for Levy's withdrawal from the race.

In the middle of January 1995, Bibi's situation had markedly improved. The polls showed that he was ahead of Rabin. The public's trust in the peace process had been dealt several heavy blows by the terrorist attacks. Bibi was convinced he had won.

At the beginning of July 1995, a large rally took place in Kfar Saba, where Bibi headed a "funeral procession" in which Rabin's coffin and a hangman's noose were borne on high. Cries of "Death to Rabin!" could be heard. (Later Bibi claimed to have had no knowledge of this.) Netanyahu took the stage a few minutes before eight o'clock in the evening, just in time for the prime-time television news broadcast of the day.

Earlier that day, two Israeli soldiers had been killed in Lebanon. Bibi called for a moment of silence and then went straight to work: "Terrorists who come from Kalkilya to Kfar Saba—and I covered that distance today in five minutes on foot—will come in and murder Jews. Rabin is taking Israel back to the 1967 borders and is preparing towns of refuge for the terrorists. Who is going to protect us? Rabin? Shahal [the minister of police]? No one is going to protect us."

For the first time, the slogan "Through blood and fire, Rabin shall expire" was heard. Shortly after the rally, Carmi Gilon, the head of Shabak, asked for a meeting with Netanyahu. Gilon briefed him on intelligence he had received about a plot to assassinate Rabin. He asked Bibi to tone down his remarks against the prime minister. Gilon explained that incendiary comments attacking Rabin might very well lead to an attempt on Rabin's life.

Bibi discussed the Gilon meeting with several members of the Likud, including Ariel Sharon, who had recently announced that he was not opposing Bibi for party leadership. Sharon was most displeased by Gilon's message. "It's a Stalin-like conspiracy on the part of the government," he said.

After Rabin was assassinated, Netanyahu said that the message delivered by Gilon was not unequivocal and did not refer specifically to the extreme right and the Likud. It was a general briefing and dealt only with the possibility of a political assassination initiated by extreme elements in the country.

Bibi did nothing to tone down the protests following his meeting with Gilon. On the contrary, he was convinced that the right's attacks were weakening Rabin's determination, and he ordered his young henchman, Uri Aloni, to step up the protests.

At least one member of Bibi's inner circle, Dr. Yair Hamburger, resigned when the wave of vehement attacks against the Rabin government began. Today Hamburger refuses to explain why he resigned, but his friends say it was because he opposed the approach taken by the Likud.

There were those in Bibi's inner circle who believed that in order to get

Bibi elected, all means were kosher. When various protest activities were discussed, many in the group supported the more extreme proposals. Uri Aloni felt he had a free hand to go to any extreme he saw fit. The strategy was clearly defined: to demonstrate whenever and wherever Rabin was making a public appearance. "Every time I see Rabin's face go red when he sees a small group of our people, I enjoy myself," Aloni said in an interview at the time. In that same interview, Uri Aloni said that Netanyahu was not always aware of the protest activity: "Only when we are planning something really extreme do we go to him and put him in the picture."

25

They've Shot the Prime Minister

The campaign against Yitzhak Rabin reached its peak in October 1995. Huge banners calling Rabin a traitor and a murderer appeared along the main highways. The country's crossroads were taken over by groups of right-wing protesters who called out hysterically, "Through blood and fire, Rabin will expire." In other places, Israelis were setting fire to tires—just like the West Bank Palestinian demonstrators had done in the *intifada*.

A mass rally was held in Ra'anana, and opposition leader Benjamin Netanyahu played an active role. A parade was led by a number of unruly protesters bearing a coffin draped with a black cloth. "We are burying Prime Minister Rabin," they said proudly. Netanyahu shook hands with them warmly but refrained from making any mention of the "funeral." At that rally, Benjamin Netanyahu gave carte blanche—a stamp of kashruth—for a future attack on Rabin's life.

Indeed, an attack was already being concocted in the warped minds of a small group of right-wing fanatics. This group was led by Yigal Amir, a slightly built, dark-skinned young man with a black skullcap on his head. A West Bank settler, Amir was seduced by the subversive, rabble-rousing speeches of right-wing rabbis who preached that Rabin was a dangerous traitor who was selling off the State of Israel to the Arabs, and that for this sin there was only one punishment—death.

Rabin's assassination was the culmination of a thoroughly calculated plan. The extremist rabbis had issued a *din rodef*, which in Halakhic terms means that Yitzhak Rabin was sentenced to death. The leader of the opposition in Israel's Knesset knew about this and did nothing to prevent it. On the contrary, says Leah Rabin, Yitzhak Rabin's widow, "Netanyahu was the one who supplied the inspiration to the group of subversives planning the execution, and to the assassin himself." According to Mrs. Rabin, Netanyahu did not believe he could beat Rabin at the polls, and so his rise to power would have to come through the streets.

When nine rabbis published a Halakhic decree prohibiting evacuation of settlements in the Land of Israel, Netanyahu did indicate that there was no intention of violating the law or disobeying orders. He did not, however, speak out against the extremist rabbis. Nor did he discourage dozens of his supporters from standing outside the prime minister's home in Tel Aviv every Friday afternoon, chanting, "Rabin is a traitor! Rabin is a murderer!"

In October, when the Knesset voted in favor of the second Oslo accord, all of Israel's right-wing movements joined forces in a mass rally in Jerusalem's Zion Square. More than one hundred thousand people crammed into the area, creating a wall-to-wall, right-wing coalition ranging from Likud supporters to those from the Kahane Lives movement. On the balcony overlooking Zion Square stood Israel's entire right-wing leadership, with Bibi in front. In the crowd, huge simulated photographs of Rabin in a Nazi SS uniform were raised high. "Rabin is a murderer!" and "Rabin is a traitor!" were among the more moderate chants emanating from the hysterical crowd. Crazed demonstrators set fire to Rabin's picture. The scene became more and more reminiscent of the *intifada*. Onstage, looking over the crowd, Netanyahu realized that he was being carried further and further to the right. As he gazed around him, Bibi noticed that Dan Meridor was nowhere in sight, nor was Roni Milo, nor Benny Begin. David Levy had been on the balcony, but the jeering crowds sent him away for being too moderate. Cameras captured Bibi Netanyahu speaking to the masses, his hands stroking the huge red letters on the poster which called for "Death to Rabin" in Hebrew—and, for good measure, in English.

Among those who witnessed the demonstration in Zion Square that evening was a French businessman, Jean Friedman. A Nazi hunter and a fervent opponent of racism, Friedman was shocked. For older members of Israeli society, survivors of the Holocaust, this sight brought back memories of *Kristallnacht* in Nazi Germany. This kind of protest, with pictures of the prime minister of Israel dressed in a Nazi uniform bandied around a public square, was unprecedented in Israeli politics.

That evening, Friedman, a close friend of Shimon Peres, spoke with Shlomo Lahat, a former mayor of Tel Aviv, and told him that he was prepared to finance a mass rally in support of the peace process. A few days later, Lahat and Friedman met Rabin in his Knesset office and convinced him of the importance of holding a counterdemonstration in Tel Aviv in support of the prime minister and the peace process. Rabin was reserved at first, but finally agreed. The three decided upon a date for the demonstration—November 4, 1996.

Bibi was uneasy on the morning of Rabin's rally. Given the volatile political circumstances, it would not take much to ignite a full-scale battle on the streets of Tel Aviv between the right and the left, the supporters and the opponents of the peace process. He consulted with Shai Bazak, and together they decided to publish a "tranquilizing announcement," which Bibi composed. In it he called on his supporters not to disturb the demonstration. He feared that right-wing demonstrators would attempt to seriously disrupt the demonstration, and this would reflect poorly on Netanyahu in the media. "They must be allowed to demonstrate in peace," Bibi said.

Bibi stayed at home in Jerusalem while the demonstration took place. Not far from Netanyahu, Shai Bazak, following the proceedings on TV, was pleased. It was a quiet gathering, with no untoward incidents. Danny Naveh also sat out the demonstration at his home in Jerusalem.

As the rally drew to a close, Bazak switched the TV over to cable channel 1, which broadcasts an IDF audio program over a collection of visuals from various other channels. He went about his business, listening with one ear to the radio report of the rally. Suddenly, Bazak heard the IDF reporter say, "Just a minute, just a minute, what's that noise? I can hear shots." Moments later, the report came—"There's a rumor that the prime minister has been shot. There were sounds of gunfire in the square." Bazak trembled. "It can't be," he said to himself.

Bazak picked up the phone and called Bibi. "What's going on?" Netanyahu asked.

"They're saying on the radio that someone shot Rabin at the rally," Bazak said. "So far it's only a rumor."

"Get over here!" Bibi ordered Bazak. "Right away!"

Bazak heard tremendous fear in Netanyahu's voice. He ran down the stairs, jumped into his car, and sped over to Bibi's house at Sokolov 7. On the way, he heard a radio report confirm that Rabin had indeed been shot. It was still unclear how badly he was hurt.

Bazak arrived at Netanyahu's home in minutes. Bibi was in his small study, listening to the radio. Sara, pale and tense, was wandering worriedly around the house. The children, Avner and Yair, were in their room asleep.

Bazak immediately set out to compose a statement denouncing the "attempted assassination." He was already passing his message on to the press when the telephone rang. Bibi picked it up, had a brief conversation in English, and put down the receiver. Bazak glanced at Bibi's face. He was deathly pale.

"Oy, vavoy," Bibi said.

"What's happened? asked Bazak.

"He's dead. They've killed him," Bibi replied.

Bazak was incredulous. "It can't be," he said to Bibi. "It's final," Netanyahu said. "I've just received confirmation from the hospital."

The man who had called Bibi was Martin Indyk, the U.S. ambassador in Israel. Like many others, he believed that the assassination was part of a plan by the extreme right to take control of the Israeli government by force. Indyk wanted reassurance that Benjamin Netanyahu was not party to such a plan. He had phoned from the basement of Ichilov Hospital, where Rabin's family had congregated with his close friends and government ministers to await the outcome of the doctors' struggle to save Rabin's life.

Indyk learned that Rabin was dead moments after the doctors announced it. He was inconsolable. "What's going to happen now?" he asked Bibi. "How does your system work? Who takes over?"

Netanyahu tried to explain to Indyk what could be expected. "It's a democracy," Bibi said in a reassuring tone. "The administration will be handed over in an orderly fashion."

Netanyahu had already decided not to take advantage of the prime minister's death by making any kind of attempt to grab power. The following morning he would advise the president of Israel to appoint Shimon Peres prime minister and to entrust Peres with the job of forming a new government.

It was up to Martin Indyk to inform Washington of what had happened. He could never have imagined that one day he would face the grim task of reporting to President Bill Clinton that his friend, the prime minister of Israel, had been assassinated.

The telephone in the Netanyahu residence rang nonstop. Israeli TV had broadcast live an emotional announcement of the assassination by Eitan Haber, Rabin's chief secretary, "The government of Israel is in deep shock..." the distraught Haber forcefully told the cameras. Bibi watched the television screen and let out a sigh from deep in his heart. Shai Bazak had never heard a sigh quite like it. "Oy vavoy, oy vavoy. That something like this should happen to our country, to Israel," Bibi said. Danny Naveh arrived and began answering the many phone calls.

Minutes after the announcement of Rabin's death, TV stations were broadcasting scenes of demonstrators bearing signs calling Bibi a murderer. Netanyahu was in shock. A cold sweat covered his forehead.

"Here it comes," he murmured. His hand was shaking. On the TV screen in front of him, the Labor party spokeswoman was accusing him of the incitement that led to the assassination. Netanyahu watched in a daze. "Here it comes," he said over and over.

Sara grew increasingly nervous about the media's accusations. "Where's it going to lead?" she asked in a panic. No one paid any attention to her.

Throughout the night, the media put heavy pressure on Netanyahu to go on television and face the nation. When it became obvious that some kind of response was necessary and unavoidable, Bazak informed ITV channels 1 and 2 and CNN that Netanyahu was prepared to make a brief announcement to the press. Within seconds, reporters had congregated on the staircase of his apartment building. Bibi descended the stairs and issued a short statement:

> I am shocked by the murder of Rabin. It is a cowardly murder, carried out by a loathsome man. In my name and in the name of the Likud, I condemn this murder. I denounce the perpetrators of this crime and participate in the sorrow and mourning of the Rabin family and the people of Israel.

He refused to reply to any questions. The media was somewhat satisfied as Netanyahu's response was broadcast throughout the world. Still, the pressure was far from over.

Rami Sadan, one of Netanyahu's associates and Sara's press officer, arrived at the Netanyahu household. Like everyone else, Sadan was shaken. "We've lost any chance we ever had of taking over the administration in the next fifteen years," he said. "It's all over."

Bibi did not respond.

The commander of the bodyguard unit from the general security services arrived and told Netanyahu not to leave the house and not to make a move without first informing them. "The situation is still very delicate," he said.

Netanyahu promised to remain in the house. Within thirty minutes the house was surrounded by dozens of policemen, security guards, and reinforcements. Netanyahu's neighborhood had suddenly become one of the safest places in the country. Bibi began making a round of telephone calls to the Likud heads, informing them of his decision: they were not to attempt a political coup; they were going to recommend that the president appoint Peres to form a new government. "In Israel, we don't use a gun to topple the administration," Bibi said over and over again.

Most of his colleagues agreed. The Likud was still in shock. Within a few weeks, many of its members would break their close working ties with Netanyahu. Many made a point of not being seen in his company. Netanyahu feared that his name had been indelibly besmirched by his role in inciting the murder of Rabin. He couldn't help recalling scenes from the demonstrations he had led: the horrible things his supporters had said, the vile slogans, the pictures of Rabin in an SS uniform, the way he stood by without condemning the mock funeral.

Bibi knew that he had not intended to incite murder, but that was no help to him now. He would have to find a way to rid himself of the stigma, to prevent it from sticking to him.

He analyzed his situation. The big question was: Would Peres announce an immediate general election? Bibi's assessment was simple. If Peres went to the polls, Bibi and the Likud were finished; an election was a waste of time. "If he's got any sense at all, he'll announce a general election immediately," Bibi said, "and then it's all over for us."

And if he didn't? Bibi was convinced that if Peres decided to stick to the original election date, almost a year away, then anything was possible. After long talks with Yvette Lieberman and Eyal Arad, a general consensus emerged that early elections would indeed result in Bibi's downfall. However, not everyone in Bibi's braintrust thought that Peres would choose this option. They prayed in their hearts that Peres would make a mistake, that he would want to first work the peace process through, to prove himself and not get elected over Rabin's dead body.

At three o'clock in the morning, Bibi's associates began dispersing. As he was leaving, Shai Bazak said to Bibi, "What a shitty situation this is. Instead of mourning our murdered prime minister, we have to work. We didn't even have time to weep."

Bibi didn't sleep that night. Neither did Naveh and Bazak. They both felt that it was a lost cause, that the bullets Yigal Amir had fired into Yitzhak Rabin had also killed their patron's political career. Bibi thought otherwise. The following morning he called Eyal Arad: "It looks bad. The assassination has changed everything. I can't believe something like this could have happened in Israel. I'm in shock. But we have to go on. It's not over yet. Nothing's changed as far as the basic issues are concerned. There's no reason to give up."

For weeks after the assassination, people crossed to the other side of the road when they saw Netanyahu approaching. Leah Rabin refused to accept his condolences. Only his most ardent supporters, like Shai Bazak and Arad, continued to stand by him. Bibi's telephone stopped ringing. The invitations stopped pouring in. Netanyahu found himself ostracized in political circles where he had been warmly received just a short time before.

Never for a moment, however, did he consider giving up. It never occurred to him to pass the torch to Dan Meridor, a well thought-of Likud leader, and allow the untainted Meridor to run against Shimon Peres, who was not being borne along on the waves of national mourning. Bibi never thought to capitulate. From the depths of his emotional and political exile, he stubbornly continued to plan his climb to the prime minister's office.

26

Seeking Allies Among
the Orthodox

In December 1995, one month after Rabin's assassination, the atmosphere at the meeting of the Likud's propaganda team was one of
utter dejection. Ya'akov Levy presented the latest poll results: Peres was
leading by 29 percent.

Bibi listened grimly. He thought that as time passed after the
assassination, the public would recover. But it wasn't happening. Six
months passed between that gloomy meeting and the next Knesset
elections. In those six months Netanyahu managed to climb out of his
political abyss and reclaim Likud leadership. He had never lost faith.

During the difficult days after the assassination, Bibi put together a
group of people who met for coffee every morning at seven o'clock at the
Angel Coffee House in Jerusalem. While Bibi drank espresso and ate a
croissant, the group, which consisted of Yitzhak Molcho, Danny Naveh,
Shai Bazak, Rami Sadan, and Yvette Lieberman, worked out their strategy
for the day. Sometimes Eyal Arad would drive up from Tel Aviv. The
coffeehouse near the gas station served as an improvised headquarters for
Bibi. His people sat together, poring over the daily newspapers, discussing
burning issues, and trying to put together a formula for resurrecting the
Likud's campaign. These powwows became the model for what is now
known in the prime minister's office as a team meeting.

Bibi became very close to Danny Neveh, who was called in to join the team about two months before the elections. Neveh took unpaid leave from his job with one of Israel's sick funds. Alongside Lieberman, who was responsible for operations, and Arad, who was chief strategist, Naveh found his place as a top confidante.

Although Bibi believed he would succeed, he found it hard to convince others. Everywhere he looked, confidence was shattered. Still, he persuaded his supporters that anything was possible if they pulled together and worked hard.

"It was not us who assassinated Rabin," he said, "It was a terrible thing, but it does not change our differences in philosophy and the historic decision that the nation is going to have to make."

The famous "spirit of Bibi" was exemplified by Netanyahu's ability to inspire people to follow him. He recruited Ariel Sharon, who put his heart and soul into the campaign. During a drive from Jerusalem to Tel Aviv, he had a long conversation with Dan Meridor. Bibi put on the pressure, and soon Meridor announced that he was joining the team and would give his full support.

On one of those difficult days, when Peres was well in the lead, Bibi bumped into Danny Naveh in the Knesset. "Don't pay any attention to those opinion polls," he said. "I am going to win the election."

Bibi had already seen a detailed analysis of the polls, which was supplied by Arthur Finkelstein, his American campaign strategist. Finkelstein required a large amount of information for his expert analysis. Numerous and varied opinion polls were sent to him in America, along with an accurate cross section of the independent voters—who they voted for in the past, their general political outlook, occupations, and so forth. The Gallup organization supplied the information. Finkelstein then did his analysis, after which he told Bibi, "You're in the picture. You can win the election."

Bibi was heartened. He knew that if he avoided mistakes, he could win. "Peres will make his share of mistakes," he told his friends. "We will just have to be there when he does."

Arthur Finkelstein began supplying exact election results, as he saw them. He would check the day's polls, put pencil to paper, and within five minutes declare the winner.

Bibi was optimistic, though most of his team members did not share his view. He was aware that the Likud needed a boost, and that if a famous personality joined the ranks, it would raise the general morale and combat the sense of inevitable defeat. Thus, he used all of his persuasive powers to convince retired general Yossi Peled, former Mossad leader Gideon Ezra, and Gen. Yitzhak "Itzik" Mordechai, all to join him. Bibi knew that these three men from the military establishment, all highly respected and decorated, would breathe new life into the Likud.

The most vital addition was General Mordechai, the recently retired chief of the Northern Command. He was known as a brave soldier and an excellent commander, having taken part in Israel's wars as well as its special operations. Of Iraqi origin, Mordechai retired from the IDF in 1994 after being skipped over for the post of deputy chief of staff, a position which he felt would have crowned his military career. He is relatively moderate in his political views—so much so that he considered joining the Labor party. However, Shimon Peres, who was certain he would win the forthcoming elections, refused to promise Mordechai a position in his government. Mordechai went to Netanyahu, who offered him a better deal.

The winning of Mordechai has been recognized as a stroke of brilliance on Netanyahu's part. Less than twenty-four hours after he stormed out of Shimon Peres's office bitterly disappointed, the general was ensconced in a comfortable armchair facing Netanyahu. Everything Mordechai was denied by Peres he got from Netanyahu, and more, including a promise to be named minister of defense, if and when Bibi won the election.

The meeting with Mordechai took place on the last Sunday of January 1996. The evening before, Itzik Mordechai consulted with a group of close friends. He told them about his disappointing meeting with Peres. "If that's the case," a friend said, "go to Bibi. He'll give you more." Mordechai's other friends concurred.

At a later meeting at Mordechai's home near Jerusalem, Moshe Katzav attended to serve as a witness to Bibi's promises. "In any government I form, you will be minister of defense," Bibi vowed. "I have not intention of being both prime minister and minister of defense."

Unlike Peres, Bibi did not make the job contingent on Mordechai's success in the primaries. He also hinted that he would like to see the general in the role of the Likud's campaign chairman.

In choosing the campaign chairman, Bibi was torn between Itzik

Mordechai and Ariel Sharon. Though Sharon was better known and more experienced politically, Bibi chose Mordechai. In appointing the general, Bibi demonstrated the Likud's willingness to bring in new blood, and proved that even after the assassination of Rabin, the Likud was still able to attract big names from the military establishment.

In appointing Mordechai, Bibi had to firmly instruct Yvette Lieberman to give the general sufficient freedom of movement. Bibi did everything he could to ensure that Mordechai received all the respect he deserved, and Itzik paid him back with compound interest. In the course of the campaign, he would reveal himself as one of the Likud's greatest electoral assets.

At the beginning of December, however, the mood was gloomy at the meeting of Bibi's braintrust at the coffeehouse near the gas station. Ya'akov Levy, the Gallup CEO, attended. The polls were most discouraging, but Levy tried to cheer Bibi up: "It's still early to eulogize you. Peres is going to make a whole series of mistakes. It's part of his personality." The current polls, Levy explained, were a reflection of the nation's emotional response to Rabin's assassination, as evidenced by the thousands of memorial candles in Rabin Square in Tel Aviv, where the late prime minister was killed. Levy reckoned that if Peres were to bring the elections forward and hold them within sixty to ninety days, he would win by a large margin. If Peres decided to defer the elections to a later date, there was still hope for Bibi.

Levy spoke of the thought processes of the Israeli voter. He called it the "law of sixty-sixty." 60 percent of the nation wanted peace; 60 percent did not want to give up the Golan Heights. If Bibi could satisfy those two conflicting desires, he'd win the elections. Levy explained to Netanyahu that Rabin won the 1992 elections because he spoke to the Likud voters in their own language—peace *and* security. "All we need is time," Levy said. "Everyday that Peres chooses not to bring forward the elections works in our favor."

Bibi gave Zvi Hauser a secret mission: to build a bridge to the left. Hauser was instructed to find left-wing voters who could identify with Bibi and his political outlook. "It is very important," said Bibi, "that I publicize the stories of people who supported Rabin in 1992 and are now disappointed with Labor and want me instead."

This part of the campaign was only marginally successful. Hauser managed to find a few frustrated left-wingers who were disappointed with

Labor and willing to sign a petition in favor of Netanyahu. This, however, had no real impact on the voting trend of the left wing.

What did change the shape of the elections was Bibi's bid for the support of the ultra-Orthodox Jewish community. Bibi has never been an observant Jew and has always enjoyed a secular lifestyle. Nonetheless, he knew that in order to win the election he would have to connect with religious voters.

Bibi embarked on a mission to capture the religious vote. He kissed Torah scrolls, visited synagogues, stood at the graves of the righteous, met with rabbis and sages. All the while, he dispensed benevolent promises to people of faith. The plan worked. The Sephardic rabbi Ovadia Yosef instructed all his followers to vote Shas* for the Knesset and Netanyahu for prime minister. Ultimately, Bibi's widely publicized visits to the wise men and his friendships forged among the ultra-religious Habad community translated into massive support—both monetary and moral—from the religious sector. A few days before the elections a new bumper sticker appeared on cars all over Israel: "Bibi is good for the Jews."

But unforeseen hurdles awaited.

---

*The Shas party is an ultra-Orthodox Sephardic party whose spiritual leader is Yosef, the former Sephardic chief rabbi of Israel. It is a political party of the working classes and draws much of its electoral strength from the poorer sections of society. The party's political leader, Rabbi Ariye Der'i, has been facing trial for several years for various forms of corruption and misappropriation of public funds. Shas holds a political grudge against the Labor party for not having prevented Der'i's case from going to trial. The trial forced Der'i to resign as minister of interior.

27

"You All Answer to Arthur"

In the beginning of December 1995, with election day drawing near and Peres still comfortably in the lead, Bibi decided he needed some additional reinforcement. His intimate advisers had carried him through the early stages of his plan—victory in the primaries and control of the Likud. But Bibi knew that in order to go all the way, he needed something more. He decided to bring on someone from the outside. He consulted his friend Ronald Lauder, the business tycoon, and Lauder found Bibi his man—Arthur J. Finkelstein.

An American Jew of Russian origin, Finkelstein was already a mythical figure in American politics. He was considered a computer genius, having pioneered the programming of computerized sample election polls.

In 1980, Finkelstein had orchestrated the stunning upset victory of a little-known politician, Al D'Amato, over a formidable and revered U.S. senator from New York, Jacob Javits. In *Boston Magazine*, Stephen Rodrick quoted D'Amato's account of an exchange with Arthur: "I trailed 64 to 7," D'Amato recalled. "Arthur said, 'That's the good news. The real truth is that only one percent really knows you. You're terrible looking, you dress funny, and you have a terrible Brooklyn accent.'"

Nevertheless, Finkelstein ran a brutal campaign against Javits, who was vulnerable on two scores—many Republicans were unaware of Jacob Javits's liberal voting record, and many were also unaware that the senator suffered from the fatal Lou Gerhig's disease. D'Amato attacked him on

both counts. He repeatedly ran a commercial written and produced by
Finkelstein that ended with a narrator saying, "Now, at age 76 and in
failing health, Jacob Javits wants six more years."

Al D'Amato has become one of the most powerful senators in the
United States and is the chairman of the National Republican Senatorial
Committee, which is involved in every campaign for the Senate.
Finkelstein remains D'Amato's chief political adviser.

Arthur was also widely credited with having single-handedly
engineered George Pataki's defeat of Mario Cuomo in New York's
gubernatorial election in 1994. A brilliant and tenacious campaign
strategist, Finkelstein was famous for his "go for the jugular" approach to
defeating the opposition. He organized election campaigns according to
his own unique understanding of politics, and rarely listened to others, no
matter the sense or logic of their words.

The first meeting between Bibi and Arthur took place in New York at
the end of December, and caused a rift between Bibi and Moshe Arens,
the man to whom Bibi owes his political career. On December 27, 1995
Arens threw a party in Jerusalem to celebrate his seventieth birthday. Bibi
did not show up. Arens was deeply hurt because there was no apparent
reason for Bibi's absence.

The truth was that Bibi had decided to keep his interest in Finkelstein a
complete secret. Not even his closest advisers had the vaguest notion that
on the night of Arens's party, Bibi flew to New York for a meeting with
Finkelstein. The trip would last only twelve hours. Upon returning, Bibi
was unable to explain to Arens why he missed his birthday party. He lost a
friend but gained a powerful political adviser.

At that first meeting Finkelstein made a smashing impression. Bibi was
convinced that he had found the perfect man to lead his campaign. Then
Finkelstein mentioned his fee: $1,000 an hour, excluding expenses. The
astronomical salary was rather off-putting for Bibi, but Lauder had made
it quite clear that he would pay whatever Finkelstein demanded—and he
has been doing so ever since. To this day, every time Bibi makes a mistake,
Finkelstein is consulted.

Finkelstein had been preceded by Dick Worseline, one of the world's
foremost experts on opinion polls, a Mormon from Utah with a family of
eight. Bibi met Worseline during his Rim days, and later promised him
the world if he would come work for him. Worseline accepted a position

as adviser and arrived in Israel before Rabin's assassination. He analyzed the opinion polls and reached the conclusion that Bibi should base his campaign not on political issues but on family values. Bibi's team found that advice somewhat ridiculous as Bibi is hardly a model of family values. After several futile weeks, during which he received no salary, only expenses, Worseline left the country in high dudgeon.

Arthur Finkelstein's hiring came as a complete surprise to Bibi's Israeli team. First to learn the secret were Limor Livnat and Eyal Arad. Bibi revealed, "Arthur Finkelstein is now in charge of campaign strategy. He is the leading campaign adviser in the United States, and exactly the man we need to win these elections. Our success will depend on out ability to keep Finkelstein's presence a complete secret." To ensure secrecy, Finkelstein checked into the King David Hotel in Jerusalem—under the name Eyal Arad. When the real Eyal Arad met Finkelstein, Arad was extremely impressed. So was Motty Moral, another senior member of Bibi's team. A Jew in his late sixties, balding, smiling, easygoing, Moral had no problem ceding control to Finkelstein. "If he's such a genius," Moral said, "it's worth learning from him. If we want to win this election, we should accept any help we can."

It was important to Bibi that Arad, Moral, and the rest of the team accept Arthur as someone who had come for only one reason—to win. From the moment Arthur Finkelstein arrived in Israel, he assumed sole control of Netanyahu's campaign. In accordance with his arrangement with Bibi, Finkelstein was the boss. He promptly canceled all previous campaign programs devised by the Likud advisers and instituted three key concepts in their stead: Peres was going to divide Jerusalem; under Peres Israel would withdraw from the Golan Heights, which would compromise security; Benjamin Netanyahu stood for a secure peace.

The promotional films Finkelstein produced with director Ron Asulin were short, straightforward, and not especially artistic, but they would prove effective. The films aggressively attacked Peres, presenting him as Arafat's partner, a man who was willing to entrust Israel's well-being to terrorists. Netanyahu, of course, was portrayed as the answer to Israel's prayers. He was the man who would bring peace, security, and prosperity to this troubled land. Finkelstein depicted Netanyahu as a born leader, and filmed him in an office specially designed to give the impression of stately authority. Most important of all was Finkelstein's emphasis on media saturation. Art was sacrificed for volume, as the films' simple message was relentlessly hammered into the consciousness of the Israeli public.

Finkelstein's greatest contribution of all was his preparation of Bibi for the televised debate with Shimon Peres. Finkelstein instructed Bibi to attack Peres where he was most vulnerable, right from the start, by raising the issue of terrorism and security. Finkelstein stressed: Even if the coordinator of the debate, veteran Israeli journalist Dan Margalit, asks you about your personal life and the "hot video," just keep attacking Peres. And that is exactly how it happened. The debate was a dazzling victory for Bibi; some even argue that it was the source of the momentum that would keep building until Peres was finally overtaken in the polls.

According to *Boston Magazine*, Arthur Finkelstein is gay and lives with his partner in a huge castlelike home in Ipswich, Massachusetts. He and his partner are bringing up two children, one of whom bears the name Finkelstein and the other the name of his partner. Senators Jesse Helms (North Carolina), Bob Smith (New Hampshire), and Don Nickles (Oklahoma), who are all known to disapprove of homosexuality, have at one time or another set aside their hostilities in order to avail themselves of Finkelstein's strategic genius.

Bibi's team was unaware that Shimon Peres had also attempted to procure outside help for his campaign, and that Chaim Ramon, Labor's campaign manager, had torpedoed the appointments of two foreign experts who had come to Israel to help Shimon Peres win the elections. The first expert was the French elections strategist, Jacques Segala, who was responsible for the victory of President François Mitterand. Segala had been brought to Israel by Jean Friedman, Peres's close friend. The second was Doug Shone, who had been on President Clinton's advisory team. Ramon sent Segala packing, but kept Shone out of the respect for Clinton and proceeded to totally ignore all of Shone's suggestions.

Midway through Bibi's campaign, Finkelstein had to leave, albeit only physically. He expressed regret that prior commitments prevented him from staying with Bibi and his staff, and he promised to make numerous short visits to Israel throughout the campaign. His hectic schedule kept him in the air more than he was on land. He had not been in his New York home base for weeks and had not even managed to meet his new secretary. Finkelstein appointed his assistant, Alan Rot, as his and Bibi's go-between. Finkelstein and Bibi agreed to stay in constant telephone contact and to exchange information through coded fax messages. They parted with a warm handshake, and the American adviser, wearing a long coat and a wide-brimmed hat, made his way to Ben-Gurion Airport.

The secret of Arthur Finkelstein would not have been leaked were it not for an unexpected occurrence at campaign headquarters. Before Finkelstein's arrival, Knesset member Meir Shitrit was chosen to appear in the campaign TV clips as a presenter/narrator. Bibi had approved the selection and Shitrit had begun rehearsals.

Finkelstein saw the clips featuring Shitrit and rejected them all. "The clips speak for themselves," he said. "No presenter is necessary." A Likud team member explained to Shitrit that he would not appear in the clips because Arthur had rejected them.

"Arthur? Who the hell is Arthur?" Shitrit shouted. *Yediot Ahronot*'s political correspondent, Bina Barzel, got wind of the spat and gleefully exposed the secret adviser of the Netanyahu campaign.

The impact Arthur Finkelstein had on the campaign was tremendous. Bibi depended completely on the American adviser and still does to this day.

Just about everything Bibi did during his campaign for prime ministership was dictated by Arthur. Bibi's restrained, almost regal response to the latest terrorist attacks had Arthur's stamp all over it. Bibi was steered clear of impetuous blunders like the one he had made after the attack on Dizengoff Street in Tel Aviv, when he rushed to the site, stationed himself firmly among the blood and rubble and loudly blamed the government for the murder of innocent civilians. Finkelstein did not permit any such hot-headed reactions.

Arthur was pleased with the film clips to be shown on TV, particularly the ones focusing on the Jerusalem issue. "It's powerful. It'll work. It goes straight to the head and the heart," he told the production team. "Great job. But you're going to have to make sure that no clip runs more than thirty seconds." Someone on the team protested: "What can we show in thirty seconds?" Arthur replied: "Plenty. Thirty second spots that are repeated every evening will sink deeper into the viewers' brains. Every evening we're going to knock our message into their heads. Every night we're going to show Peres with Arafat, Peres dividing Jerusalem in two, Peres giving back the Golan Heights. We're going to show how Bibi will bring peace but also security. Over and over again. Like Chinese water torture."

Arthur called this tactic the "hammer method." He explained to the team that it was the way things were done in modern elections. A short, sharp, incessantly repeated, easily absorbed message. Nothing complicated. No unnecessary sophistication. "This isn't a soap opera," Arthur would say. "We don't need long episodes." Finkelstein's approach saved time and money. The Likud's creative team finished work relatively early each evening, while Chaim Ramon and his team labored late into the night in producing their intricate and artful broadcasts.

Eventually, Arthur Finkelstein insisted that Bibi appear every evening in the Likud television clips. Ron Asulin, the director, created a "prime minister's office," which he modeled after the oval office in the White House. It had mahogany bookshelves, a national flag, and it had Bibi, with heavy makeup and his gray hair whitened to make him appear older, more distinguished and more statesmanlike. And Bibi played the role like a professional. Eyal Arad wrote the texts. Almost overnight, Netanyahu shed the image of the screaming opposition leader and became a dignified, rational, and serious candidate.

Bibi's new persona proved so successful that a large portion of the public completely forgot his past ranting and his frantic arrivals at the scenes of terrorist attacks. Most important of all, Finkelstein had clouded the public's memory of the not-so-distant days when Bibi led the horrific demonstrations in which his supporters accused Rabin of treason, held a "funeral" procession with Rabin's coffin and a hangman's noose borne on high, and burned effigies of Rabin dressed in a Nazi SS uniform.

The public seemed to forget all these incidents, and the Labor party inexplicably failed to remind them. Throughout the campaign, Labor never once made use of all the available film footage showing that until his recent transformation, Bibi was a rabble-rousing demagogue.

Another Finkelstein rule was that Bibi's campaign would not respond to Labor's comments or charges. "Let them attack as much as they want," he told Bibi. "You are not going to be drawn in. You are not going to respond. You just do your own thing. Every evening, your clips will run thirty seconds each time, over and over again." Limor Livnat was worried. "And what if they start talking about the 'hot video?'" "Let them," Arthur replied. "Just ignore it."

Bibi settled the issue. "We're doing it the Arthur way."

At a meeting of the senior advisers, Arthur told the team, "Labor's clips are going to be fancier, and the press is going to favor them, but when the campaign is over, voters will only remember our simple film."

Livnat suggested producing some clips showing people who had voted for Rabin in 1992, but were disappointed with Labor and were now supporting Bibi. Arthur agreed, but on the condition that his golden rule be followed: no clip could last longer than thirty seconds. Not a second more.

28

Netanyahu vs. Peres:
The Television Debate

The campaign was running smoothly when an unanticipated hitch occurred. Sara Netanyahu insisted on making her own personal TV clip.

None of Bibi's confidants wanted to be the one to break the news to the prospective first lady that there was no room in the campaign for her clip. Everyone had experienced her hysterical outbursts when she did not get her way.

As always, Arthur Finkelstein saved the day. "Do the clip," he told Bibi's staff, with a glint in his eye. Sara beamed with pleasure when she was invited to shoot the film. She didn't mind that the director wanted to reshoot the clip repeatedly, in fact, she rather liked it. She would arrive at the set happy to be made up, dressed, and coiffed, each time anew. The production dragged on, just the way Finkelstein wanted it. Time passed.

Every time the clip seemed ready, someone on the team remembered that it needed "touching up." And so it went, until it was too late. The elections came and the spot had never been broadcast.

Sara had to turn her fury on another target—Limor Livnat. Sara enjoyed watching the TV satire *Spitting Image*. At that time, the show made a habit of hinting at a possible affair between Bibi and Livnat, his attractive adviser. This infuriated Sara, and she gradually began to believe that it was true, that her husband was romantically involved with Livnat. Sara demanded an explanation from Bibi and began to get hysterical.

Bibi, who also watched the TV show, prayed in vain that it would lay off the topic. He was finally forced to call Arthur Finkelstein and ask him to calm Sara down and convince her that there was no truth to the rumor that he was having an affair with Livnat. Finkelstein apparently succeeded, and Sara cooled off, at least for a while.

The TV debate between Shimon Peres and Benjamin Netanyahu was eagerly anticipated by Bibi's team. Labor campaign manager Chaim Ramon, on the other hand, did not hide the fact that he feared this event more than anything else. "I would run from this confrontation as if it were fire, if I only could," Ramon said. "Bibi's a professional on TV. He'll tear Peres to pieces."

Ramon knew that Bibi had built his political career on his star turns on TV. Peres, a master of political polemic with a tendency to long-windedness, was a giant as a leader but a show-biz amateur.

From the moment Ramon undertook to manage Peres's campaign, the thought of a televised confrontation made him lose sleep. At one stage, Peres suggested holding the debate at the beginning of the campaign to get it over with. "God forbid," Ramon replied. "It must be left to the very end."

Ramon believed that a debate at the beginning of the campaign would supply the Likud with enough ammunition to last until election day, so he did nothing to initiate one. He simply waited for the call from Likud campaign head Limor Livnat.

Eyal Arad and Limor Livnat discussed the debate with Arthur Finkelstein. "Confrontations of the question-answer type are obsolete," Finkelstein told them. "Nowadays there is the Ping-Pong system, a direct dialogue between two contenders. Let them go on together. Bibi'll kill him."

After negotiations with Ramon as to the time, place, date, and host, the debate was set for Sunday, May 26, 1996, at eleven o'clock in the morning, at a Tel Aviv TV studio. Ramon did not realize that the conditions which Eyal and Livnat had manipulated him into accepting favored Bibi in every way. They were confident he would destroy Peres.

Bibi was worried nonetheless. On the morning of the debate he went for a haircut and told his barber to take special care—he could afford no mistakes on this day. Then he put on a new suit, rented especially for the occasion.

Bibi sat with Sara, Danny Neveh, and a bodyguard as Eli drove them to the debate. Bibi was wound up like a spring. He sorted his prompt cards, which contained ideas, replies, questions, and sharp one-liners. Over and over in the car, Bibi went over the phrase, "You don't need to be photographed with children, Mr. Peres, you need only protect them." This was one of the jabs he threw at Peres for which the prime minister had no reply. The line belonged to Tsahi Hanegbi, who came over to the King David Hotel from time to time to supply the team with rhetorical ammunition.

As the debate approached, Arthur had asked that Bibi be surrounded by as few advisers as possible. He suggested that Naveh, who was especially calm and low key, accompany Bibi, and no one else.

In the dressing room, minutes before the debate, Shai Bazak showed up. Bibi asked Bazak which tie to wear. Bazak, who chose the colors and styles of all Bibi's clothes, picked out the darker tie. Bibi asked him to tie it for him. To this day, Bibi does not know how to knot a tie. Bazak, usually so composed, felt his hand shake.

It was time. Bibi smiled and strode out of the dressing room toward the studio.

Bibi did not know that before the official broadcast began, he was being watched on a TV monitor in the adjoining room. Bibi was nervous. He kept arranging and rearranging his cards on the lectern before him. Then he asked for a glass of water, then asked for some Scotch tape, then started taping the cards along the edges of his lectern.

In the adjoining room, the press reporters watched all of this with amusement. Most of them, convinced that Peres would prevail, openly denigrated Netanyahu. Shai Bazak, on the other hand, remained quiet. He knew that no matter how nervous Bibi appeared up to the last moment, as soon as the red light went on above the camera, Bibi himself would light up. Eyal Arad also believed that his boss would eat Peres for breakfast.

And then Peres walked in. The prime minister appeared tired and older than his seventy-three years. Bazak smiled to himself. When Peres began his opening speech, Bazak's smile grew wider. Peres had opened with the issue of Jerusalem. The future of Jerusalem had become the most critical issue of the election campaign. Bibi and the Likud's claim that Peres would divide Jerusalem) had caused irreparable damage to the Labor campaign.

"Good God," Bazak whispered, "who told him to start with Jerusalem? Don't they do any polling surveys? Don't they knew that Jerusalem is the most dangerous issue for them? Why is he playing into our hands?"

Bibi's team had feared that Peres would talk about himself, about his experience and his record, comparing all his accomplishments to Bibi's. But Peres persisted in talking about Jerusalem, and back at Likud campaign headquarters, Netanyahu's friends rubbed their hands and smiled.

The second the debate ended, Bazak, who had quietly tolerated the reporters' jibes before it began, jumped up and shouted for all to hear, "It's a knockout! We won!"

Bibi and his associates marched victoriously out of the building and went for coffee. Bibi called Sara and reported that it went "okay." When Danny Naveh asked Bibi for his assessment of the debate, Bibi replied, "I won."

29

The Ultra-Orthodox
to the Rescue

Around the time of the fateful televised debate, a covenant was being formed that would deal Shimon Peres's government its fatal blow. The fanatic, messianic, ultra-Orthodox Habad movement was joining the political battle on Netanyahu's side. the connection between the outspokenly secular Benjamin Netanyahu and the movement of the Habad Hassidim had actually been many years in the making. On the evening of the Feast of the Tabernacles in New York, in October 1984, Bibi, who had recently taken up his post as Israeli ambassador to the United Nations, came to the court of the rabbi from Lubavitch in order to receive a New Year blessing. The embassy made a point of informing many Habadniks of the pending visit in advance. Netanyahu arrived with several embassy staff members. Wearing a blue suit (his favorite color) and a white and gold skullcap, Bibi waited among the large crowd for his turn.

When someone whispered to the rabbi that the ambassador had arrived, Bibi was called out of turn for an introduction. Bibi was honored and touched.

The rabbi placed his hand on Bibi's head, looked at his young face, and said to him, "Never apologize." The meeting went on for nearly five minutes. When they parted, the rabbi wished Bibi a long life and success.

It was the first meeting between the two. Bibi has since made a habit of visiting the old man frequently.

Four years later, before his return to Israel, Bibi came to receive the rabbi's blessing once again. This time he was joined by two close friends— Shmaryahu Harel, a soldier from his army days, and Avi Taub, a Habad activist and a wealthy diamond merchant from Natanya.

Shmaryahu proudly told the rabbi that Bibi had been his commanding officer: "He is one of us, a believer in a greater Israel. He will protect the country from the gentiles and the Arabs. One day, he will be prime minister of Israel."

The rabbi nodded his head and wished Bibi success in his new political path.

After his victory in the Likud's internal elections, Bibi returned to New York and, together with Harel and Taub, paid another visit to the rabbi's court. The Habad Hassidim were very excited about this visit. Word had spread of Bibi's success. The rabbi placed his hand on Bibi's shoulder and murmured, "You are going to have to struggle against one hundred nineteen people. You surely will not be hindered by this. God is with you."

The Habad Hassidim listening in on the conversation had no idea what the rabbi was talking about. Only in 1996, after Netanyahu had been elected prime minister, did they understand what the rabbi had prophesied in 1988—that Netanyahu would be prime minister, and that his job would require that he stand firmly against the 119 members of the Israeli Knesset.

Before he left, the rabbi told Bibi's friends Harel, Taub, and David Nahshon that they must "help Netanyahu from now on and forever, unless he changes his skin."

In 1991, when Bibi's first son, Yair, was born, the rabbi sent him a personal letter of congratulations. The rabbi added a line in his own hand to the typewritten letter: "May his luck be lit up" (a play on the name Yair—"will light"). The rabbi's disciples knew that this handwritten note represented a rare compliment and was proof of the rabbi's special feeling for Netanyahu.

In response, Bibi wrote to him that since their first meeting, the rabbi's image had been following him, and his success was proof of the rabbi's blessing.

Two weeks before the election, Ariel Sharon saw an ad in *Ha'aretz* in the name of Habad, calling on all believers to vote for the candidate who would ensure that Israel remained undivided. No mention was made of Netanyahu.

Concerned about Bibi's campaign and well aware of the power of the movement of Habad Hassidim, Sharon called Rabbi Yitzhak Aharanov, the Habad chairman in Israel and the organization's strongman, immediately. "Let's meet," Sharon said.

Aharanov was interested. "What about?"

The elections," Sharon replied.

Rabbi Aharonov said, "Okay, and let us also invite some more rabbis from Habad."

The "summit meeting" with the Habad rabbis took place thirteen days before the elections. Both sides wanted it kept secret, so it was held at a school in Kfar Habad, the headquarters of the movement, located south of Tel Aviv. Sharon arrived with two of his assistants. The Habadniks turned out in full force—with the exception of Rabbi Maidanchik, who is affiliated with the Labor party.

On the table were bottles of soft drinks and pistachio nuts. Sharon arrived at ten o'clock and spoke to the rabbis: "What are you interested in?" he asked.

They replied that their only interest was that Israel remain undivided.

Sharon gave them the proforma promises, but knew those would not suffice. That is why he had arranged, as only he and Rabbi Aharonov knew, for the Likud candidate himself to appear.

When Sharon arranged the meeting, he planned to attend it alone. Aharanov made it clear that it would not be so simple. "We want the candidate, the one who is going to be prime minister," Aharanov said unequivocally. "This time we are going to demand promises that can withstand the test of reality. Yitzhak Shamir also made all sorts of promises to us and nothing came of them. We are not so gullible now."

Sharon called Bibi and stressed the importance of attending the meeting. "This movement has two hundred ten branches all over the country," Sharon said. "If they want to, they can bring thousands of activists out into the streets. They can give us the push we need."

Bibi needed no further convincing. "I'll be glad to come," he said.

Bibi showed up at eleven o'clock—late, as usual. He arrived in a Volvo with a driver and a bodyguard. Understanding the need to maintain secrecy, he came without his assistants, advisers, and hangers-on. The secrecy was somewhat broken by the many security men and Shabak vehicles which flooded Kfar Habad in advance of Bibi's arrival, but this was unavoidable. In those days, security around him was very tight and he could scarcely make a move without attracting a whole troop of guards.

One of Sharon's assistants met Bibi outside the meeting room and brought him up to speed on the situation inside. Bibi placed a skullcap on his head and went in. The rabbis explained their stance to Netanyahu. They were interested in a "whole," not a partitioned, Israel, because of the sanctity of the land. Netanyahu immediately started making promises. He preached his theories on the "wholeness" of Israel and told the rabbis that Shimon Peres was going to divide Jerusalem and withdraw from the Golan Heights. The sticking point, however, was the Oslo agreement. The rabbis asked him if he planned to honor it. Bibi stuttered. "I have already announced that I plan to honor Israel's agreements," he said, "but I will make sure that the other side also honors its side of the agreement. I will insist on mutuality," he said.

"And what about the Orient House?" they asked. The building known as Orient House is the center of Palestinian activity in East Jerusalem.

"I will close it down," Bibi said. "Believe me. If they don't keep their side of the bargain, we won't keep ours."

"Don't worry, they won't," the rabbis said.

"Then we won't either," Bibi responded.

The rabbis seemed to be satisfied, but Sharon doubted this was so. As Netanyahu was speaking, Sharon passed a note to his assistants. "Look at their eyes," he wrote. "They don't believe him. They suspect him."

Sharon was one hundred percent behind Netanyahu's campaign, but that did not mean he respected the candidate for whom he was working. Behind his back, Sharon continued to talk about Netanyahu's failings, his low credibility rating, his opportunism, his henchmen (referred to by some as the "KGB").

Whenever he made promises to the rabbis in Netanyahu's name, Sharon always added a promise of his own: "Don't worry, I'll be there, too. It's not only one man. There will be a leadership team, and I will be one of the three people leading the government. I am giving you my word. All the promises will be fulfilled." Contrary to Sharon's misgivings at that first meeting, the Habad Hassidic movement placed its considerable weight behind Netanyahu's election campaign. They came out in force, taking over the country's streets and road junctions, putting up huge banners along hedges, and handing out stickers. Their best slogan, the one with which they inundated the country, was unveiled just three days before the election: "Netanyahu Is Good for the Jews."

It was a simple slogan, but it struck a chord with many undecided voters, especially among the ultra-Orthodox. Fifty years after the birth of the Israeli nation, four years before the turn of the millennium, five words—"Netanyahu Is Good for the Jews"—would tip the political scales and anoint a new prime minister by the narrowest of margins.

30

To Bed With Peres,
Waking Up With Netanyahu

On November 29, 1996, Israel held a general election using a completely new and untested system: direct election of the prime minister. The Direct Election for Prime Minister Law was passed by the Knesset in 1992 by a two-vote majority—61 to 59. The swing vote belonged to Benjamin Netanyahu, who voted with Labor and the left, in favor of changing the old election law. Even then, Netanyahu was primarily concerned with his own career, and was willing to cross party lines to vote for a law that would improve his chances for the prime ministership.

The law was implemented in time for the 1996 elections. The thesis put forward by the law professors from Tel Aviv University who formulated the law held that the new system would reinforce the larger parties. This proved wrong. Many voters opted for the smaller parties, and Labor lost ten seats, dropping from forty-four to thirty-four. The Likud—together with its offshoot parties, Gesher (David Levy), and Tsomet (Rafael Eitan)—also lost ten seats and ended up with thirty-two.

Shas, the ultra-Orthodox Sephardic party, went from six to ten Knesset seats. The National Religious party increased its power from five to ten seats. Israel be-Aliya, led by Russian immigrant Natan Sharansky, took seven seats and caused a sensation. The Third Way, led by Labor party dropout Avigdor Kahalani, earned four seats with the platform, "The

Golan Heights are ours." The other ultra-Orthodox (Ashkenazi) party took four seats. Meretz, the left-wing party, increased its representation at the expense of Labor and took nine seats. The Arabs and the Communists together took six Knesset seats.

On the morning of May 30, 1996, Israel woke up to a new reality. Most of the population had gone to bed believing that Shimon Peres had just barely managed to win and retain his prime ministership. They awoke to the news that they had a new leader, Benjamin Netanyahu. He had received 50.6 percent of the votes to Peres's 49.4 percent. Among the Jews, Bibi received 11 percent more votes than Peres. In turn, Peres received 90 percent of the Arab vote.

Netanyahu spent that day on a cloud of euphoria. It was hard for him to comprehend what he had achieved. He had made it. He was prime minister. Sara was the first lady.

Now came the formalities. Bibi had to be officially appointed by the president to form a government. This was the time for Bibi to pay off his debts and fulfill his promises, to reward his supporters with government appointments. He had promised the nation that his would be a government of experts, of excellence. In reality, however, he had to form a government from the material available, which meant choosing his ministers from the parties which made up his coalition and to which he was beholden—the National Religious party, the ultra-Orthodox Ashkenazi, the ultra-Orthodox Sephardi, the extreme right. They all wanted a piece of the pie, and Bibi had made promises to all of them.

Before he could even roll up his sleeves, his cellular phone rang. It was the defeated prime minister, Shimon Peres. He was sitting in his Jerusalem office with a heavy heart, trying his best to downplay his disappointment. He knew that the "loser" stigma would be hard to shed.

His two grandsons sat on his lap, his daughter Zicki sat opposite him. At such difficult times, Peres preferred the company of his family to anyone else. When it became obvious that the final count of the soldiers' vote was not going to save him, Peres asked his secretary to get Benjamin Netanyahu on the line.

"The prime minister wants to speak with Mr. Netanyahu," the secretary told Shai Bazak. Bazak handed the telephone to Netanyahu.

"Yes," Bibi said.

Peres took the phone. "Good day to you, Mr. Prime Minister."

"Good day to you, Mr. Prime Minister," Bibi replied.

"Congratulations on your victory," Peres said. "I would like to congratulate you and tell you that I shall do my best to help you take over the post. We shall hand over everything in an orderly manner. You have nothing to worry about."

"Thank you," Bibi replied. "I really appreciate it."

It was a short conversation, two minutes at most. Netanyahu was unable to suppress a broad smile. On the other end of the line, Peres was not smiling.

The guiding principle for Bibi and his people was simple: Now that they had the country in their hands, they would change the method and style of administration in the State of Israel. Bibi had learned a cautionary lesson from observing the way Menachem Begin governed the state when the Likud beat Labor in 1977.

According to Netanyahu's thinking, Begin won the elections but did not take control of the government. Once in office, he did not lay a finger on the administrative elite. He left all the institutions as they were and kept the government clerks, especially those in the ministries of law, finance, and foreign affairs. According to Netanyahu and his friends, Begin became a prime minister with no real power—a puppet.

Bibi was determined not to repeat that scenario. He felt empowered by the new system. He had won a direct election and along with it the right to surround himself with a loyal team which would govern the country the way he wanted. His aim was to replace as many people holding high government positions as possible. "All the people holding top positions are left-wing sympathizers," Bibi's advisers told him. "If we do not replace them, we will never truly take over the administration."

Bibi's first objective, therefore, was to replace the attorney general, appoint a minister of justice, replace as many high-ranking government clerks as possible, neutralize the foreign minister's office, David Levy's domain, attach as many government bodies to the prime minister's office as possible, and create an Israeli "White House." This was all to be done as quickly as possible.

In other words, what Bibi wanted as prime minister was to establish a "presidency" in Israel similar to that of the United States. (Israel has a president, but it is basically a figurehead position.)

Danny Naveh, who had been appointed government clerk, favored the appointment of experts, and not politicians, to form a cabinet suitable for the twenty-first century. However, Netanyahu the candidate had maneuvered himself into a complex web of promises which now became serious hurdles for Netanyahu the prime minister.

Yvette Lieberman was firmly against the appointment of Dan Meridor to any government position. Lieberman had sworn to destroy Meridor, especially after the feeble attempt at a coup a few months before the elections, though Meridor had not conspired against Netanyahu.

Sara Netanyahu, for her part, had placed an irreversible veto on Limor Livnat, whom she hated. Sara's veto presented a conflict for Bibi in his attempt to form a government. Bibi had great respect for Livnat, who had played an active role in his successful campaign. However, the last thing he needed at this point in his life was a major quarrel with his wife. He also had to contend with his commitment to Ariel Sharon. During the campaign, Bibi had promised to appoint Sharon to one of the top government positions. Sharon took this to mean that he would be made minister of either defense or finance. Though he had already accumulated some bitter experience with Bibi's promises, Sharon believed him this time. However, Netanyahu did not really want Sharon in the government. He was familiar with Sharon's opinion of him and kept abreast of comments Sharon made behind his back. Neither was Yvette Lieberman overjoyed at the thought of having Sharon in the government. He feared the possibility of a Sharon-Levy-Meridor coalition developing, which could weaken Netanyahu's position in the Likud.

Netanyahu and Lieberman did not want Meridor in the Justice Office, preferring attorney Ya'akov Ne'eman, a close friend of Netanyahu's who was the first person Sara sought out when news broke of the "hot video." Rather than Sharon, Bibi would have preferred Itzik Mordechai in the Defense Ministry. Bibi planned to appoint Benny Begin, a geologist by profession, minister of science in the hope that he would opt out and choose to be chairman of the Knesset's foreign affairs and security committee. He wanted Ya'akov Frankel, director of the Bank of Israel, in the position of minister of finance.

At the same time, Netanyahu continued to make promises. He promised Dr. Yossi Ulmert that he would be the next ambassador to the U.N., and promised Sylvan Shalom a government ministership. When

Shalom found out that his name was not on the government list, Netanyahu told him not to worry, "There'll be lots of changes yet."

He made promises to Sharon, Mordechai, Shaul Amor, Frankel, and Ne'eman. Hundreds of people were walking the Knesset corridors, convinced that they were about to be given top government positions. Most of them soon discovered that Netanyahu's promises were of little value.

The most complicated problem by far concerned Limor Livnat, Bibi's attractive adviser, and Sara Netanyahu, his wife.

The conflict began several months earlier when the election campaign was just beginning. Livnat, who had been put in charge of Likud publicity, worked very closely with Netanyahu. At that time they were consumed with the task of overcoming Peres's clear advantage in the polls.

Early one Friday evening, Netanyahu called Livnat and asked her to clear something up with Roni Milo immediately and to call him back as soon as this was done. Livnat did as she was told and then called Netanyahu at his home. The phone was picked up by Sara, who over the past few weeks had developed a pathological hatred for Livnat. Particularly paranoid in the wake of the video incident, Sara began to believe that there was something going on between her husband and Limor. The fact that the two politicians spent a great deal of time together only served to fuel her suspicion.

"This is Limor," Livnat said to Sara. "Is Bibi there?"

"Bibi is here, but he's not going to talk to you," Sara replied.

"Excuse me?" Livnat said.

"It is Friday night and I would much appreciate it if you would not call him up at such hours," Sara said sharply. "Bibi is with the children."

"He asked me to check on something and to get back to him. It is important," Livnat explained.

"You are always calling here at such hours. It is very inconvenient," Sara responded.

"That is not true," Livnat said. "I hardly ever call you on Friday evenings, only when it is really urgent. He asked me to call."

"Look," Sara snapped. "I have already told Yvette to tell you not to call here again. You've been told this over and over again. I don't understand why you are so insistent."

For a moment, Livnat was speechless. She had heard the stories about Sara's unpredictable behavior but had never actually experienced it herself. However, unlike many in Bibi's close circle, Livnat is no shrinking violet, not the servile and acquiescent type.

Sara's behavior brought the blood rushing to Livnat's head. "Just tell me, how do you think you are behaving?" she said to the wife of the Likud leader. "Can you hear yourself? You are talking a whole load of garbage, concerned about something that never happened. You are hindering us in our work. I suggest you apologize nicely and let me speak to Bibi."

Sara raised her voice. Livnat raised hers even louder. The two women went into a loud shouting match.

Sara Netanyahu erred in a way no experienced politician would have— she came within firing range of Limor Livnat's mouth. "You are completely insane," Livnat told her. "Now I believe everything I've ever heard about you."

Furious, Sara slammed down the receiver.

The two women have not spoken a word to each other since. Sara Netanyahu made an oath to ruin Limor Livnat's career and developed a special brand of paranoia toward her which was even worse than her usual suspicion.

Livnat, for her part, no longer called the Netanyahu household. She found alternative ways to get messages to her boss. Whenever Netanyahu needed to talk to Livnat, he would call her himself and do his best not to let Sara know who was on the line. When the two women had to attend the same function, Netanyahu's people made sure that they were kept as far apart as possible. Livnat found this vaguely amusing, but Sara was only infuriated.

When the time came to appoint Limor Livnat a minister in the government of Israel, something totally unavoidable according to all the rules of the political game, Bibi had to send his friend Ya'akov Ne'eman to inform Sara of the fact. When the attorney arrived at the Netanyahu home with the news, he found Sara dressed in her holiday best, her hair newly streaked and teased. As expected, Sara threw a fit. She screamed and yelled and swore that she would not rest until she witnessed the complete and utter downfall of Limor Livnat.

In the end, Limor Livnat got the better of Sara Netanyahu: She was appointed minister of communications. Bibi managed to form a patchwork government with representatives from all the parties in his coalition. Israel's minister of education, a member of the National Religious party, vowed to instill "Jewish values" in the secular school system. (Most of Israel is secular, notwithstanding pronouncements made by the religious fanatics.) The minister of traffic came from the ultra-Orthodox sector, and the minister of labor from the Sephardic ultra-Orthodox community, many of whose members do not actually work, nor serve in the army, but feel that religious study is of supreme importance and should be supported by the state.

David Levy was made foreign minister, but has recently resigned and left the government because of the 1998 budget, which did not include allowances for social expenditures promised to him by Netanyahu in a signed document. Dan Meridor was the first finance minister in Netanyahu's government. Ariel Sharon became a minister of infrastructure; Avigdor Kahalani, minister of internal security; Benny Begin, minister of science, though Begin resigned shortly after taking the post. Eliyahu Ben-Elissar, who is close to David Levy, and whom Netanyahu has never liked or respected, was sent to fill the important and sensitive post of Israeli ambassador in Washington. Netanyahu had wanted Zalman Shoval, a close associate who had filled this post in the past, but Levy refused to give in.

Problems started popping up almost immediately. Government ministers spoke about Netanyahu behind his back, saying that he had run a great election campaign but failed to prepare himself to function as prime minister.

Three months after his victory in the polls, an attempted political putsch was made against Netanyahu. A wealthy (and anonymous) Israeli businessman tried to unite Sharon, Peres, and Arye Der'i, the Shas leader, to bring about Netanyahu's downfall. All three had ample reason to participate. Sharon was one of the designers of Netanyahu's victory and the man who had delivered him the ultra-Orthodox religious leaders. He was disappointed because Netanyahu had reneged on his promise to appoint him minister of finance. At first Sharon found himself completely excluded from the government. Only a few weeks later, after Sharon's good friend David Levy threatened to resign from the government if no suitable job was found for Sharon, did Sharon receive a ministry of infrastructure appointment, custom designed for him. For a long time, however, Sharon did not forgive Netanyahu.

Shimon Peres was still reeling from the shock of his defeat. He could not reconcile himself to the voters' decision.

Arye Der'i was angry with Netanyahu for his apparent desire to turn over the Religious Ministry to the National Religious party, whose political strength came from the West Bank settlements.

The plan devised by Sharon, Peres, and Der'i was to initiate a no-confidence vote for Netanyahu's leadership and put together a majority of Knesset members to overthrow him. They would then arrange to have Shimon Peres appointed prime minister. The plan did not get off the ground. Der'i obtained the Religious Ministry for Shas in rotation with the National Religious party. He was not about to risk going to an early election, which would endanger the symbol of his party's enormous success—ten Knesset seats.

Netanyahu's government included two men, Benny Begin and Dan Meridor, whom the prime minister would have preferred to see out of the cabinet. Benny Begin had never been one of Netanyahu's supporters. Nor had Dan Meridor, a "prince" in the Likud family, an excellent attorney, and a man of political integrity. Selecting Meridor as finance minister was one of the more promising appointments in the new government. Yvette Lieberman, who had been appointed chief of staff of the prime minister's office, repeatedly advised his boss to put an end to Begin and Meridor's political careers so that they would no longer threaten his leadership. In Benny Begin's case, this would not be necessary. After the Hebron agreement, which called in part for Israeli withdrawal from the West Bank, Begin resigned. A right-wing ideologist, he saw the agreement as an act of treason against the State of Israel.

31

Too Many Promises

While navigating the political obstacle course of government appointments, Bibi also had to establish his own office. His associates, who had been with him throughout the wild race for prime minister, were now responsible for handing out jobs.

Danny Naveh gave himself the position of government secretary. He knew that Yossi Beilin and Dan Meridor had turned this position into a springboard for their political careers. Naveh had already tried his luck at getting elected to the Likud and failed. He was not a natural politician who promoted himself by shaking hands at weddings and bar mitzvahs. Naveh knew that his only chance of getting anywhere in Israeli politics was via the prime minister's office.

Yvette Lieberman's place in Bibi's office was a given. Yvette is Netanyahu's closest adviser. Netanyahu and Lieberman have shared many days and many secrets. Lieberman planned to handle the responsibilities of governing the state the same way he ran the Likud, and Netanyahu was pleased to make this possible.

Shai Bazak sought the position of press spokesman. Bibi had always shown complete confidence in Bazak, but hesitated before giving him the job. He was worried about Bazak's relative inexperience and his age—he was only twenty-nine. As a reinforcement, Bibi called in his old friend and confidant David Bar-Ilan, who was appointed head of information, ostensibly as Bazak's superior. In reality, Bar-Ilan, a pleasant and polite man, was only there to support Bazak and brief the foreign press. Communication with the Israeli press was left solely to Bazak.

Another appointment taken for granted was Dore Gold as Bibi's political adviser. Netanyahu admired Gold's talent for analysis and valued his widespread connections in the Arab world. Shortly after winning the election, Bibi sent Gold off on a mission to Gaza to meet with PLO chairman Yasser Arafat.

This, then, was Bibi's starting five—Lieberman, Naveh, Gold, Bazak, and Bar-Ilan. Some of them are more competent than others, some more suited to their jobs than others, but all have the quality most important to Netanyahu: blind devotion to the boss.

Eyal Arad, however, was no longer seen in Netanyahu's entourage. Arad had been with him for ten years, from his days as ambassador to the United Nations right up until his victory in the elections. Unfortunately for Arad, Sara Netanyahu had never forgiven him for what she perceived as his part in the "hot video" scandal. She openly blamed him for Bibi's affair with Ruth Bar, refusing to believe that Arad had no idea about the nature of the relationship between her husband and Ruth. Sara marked Eyal Arad, just as she had marked Limor Livnat and so many others.

During the election campaign, Sara demanded that Arad be thrown off the team when she discovered that he was her husband's leading strategist. At that time, however, it was explained to her that such a step would mean losing the elections. After the election, she put her foot down. "I will not have this man here any longer," she decreed.

Arad felt enormous fulfillment from winning the election, and decided to resign and enter the private sector. Bibi did not try to dissuade him. Had he remained, Arad would have been the natural choice to head the prime minister's office. Like Rabin's Eitan Haber or Peres's Avi Gil, he could have been a powerful figure in the prime minister's office, whispering in the boss's ear, telling him what he should and should not do, who to speak to and who to ignore.

Bibi wanted to create a position similar to the chief of staff in the American White House, someone who would be responsible for the operation of his office, an adviser and administrator who could be entrusted with authority and responsibility. He offered the post to his friend and personal attorney Yitzhak Molcho, but Molcho turned him down. As the head of a flourishing law office in Jerusalem, Molcho did not particularly relish the idea of becoming a civil servant. He was willing to do a lot for Bibi, but not give up his practice.

The first few months of Netanyahu's term in office were characterized by scandals, mistakes, and unflattering write-ups in the press. Netanyahu's dream of creating an efficient, presidential-style office that would give him the upper hand in matters of state and government was quickly disintegrating.

During his first few days in the prime minister's building, Yvette Lieberman made his rounds of all the offices and fired anyone he did not like. Among the casualties was the office's attorney, Ahaz Ben-Ari, a reserve army major general. Lieberman dryly informed him that he no longer needed to come to the office. "We are looking for people who think like us," Lieberman told Ben-Ari. As soon as Ariel Sharon learned of his departure, he took over Ben-Ari's office.

Ben-Ari was replaced by attorney Avi Halevy, who as it turned out was totally unqualified for the job. After a few months, Halevy left the office in disgrace. Had anyone bothered to check his credentials before his appointment, considerable unpleasantness could have been avoided. Situations like this were happening frequently in Bibi's administration.

In a very short time, Netanyahu lost much of the faith and credit he had cultivated in the Israeli public. His days of grace quickly elapsed as the euphoria of victory dissolved. Left in its wake was an inexperienced prime minister surrounded by power-hungry amateurs.

The official victory celebration in Jerusalem three days after the elections provided an early hint of the kind of government culture the country could expect during Netanyahu's term. The party, at which the expression "Heide, Sara" (Go home, Sara) was first coined, resembled a celebration of a football victory more than a political victory.

Later, Netanyahu took time off to thank all those who had helped him achieve high office. On June 20, he took part in a giant Habad event in Tel Aviv celebrating the Lubavitcher rabbi's release from prison. It soon turned into a giant victory celebration. Only Ariel Sharon, the man who had joined Netanyahu with the Habad movement, stayed home.

On July 2, Netanyahu visited Rabbi Kaduri, the renowned Kabbalist who had given him an enormously helpful blessing on the eve of the elections. As he had done with the Habadniks, Netanyahu said thank you and went home.

The elections, however, were a thing of the past, and the country needed leadership. During his first few months, Bibi was a hesitant, inexperienced prime minister who tried to abruptly change a deeply rooted government structure. Within three months, it was clear that the national security council he wanted would not be formed, that a supreme economic council would not be established, and this his freedom of action as prime minister was rather limited.

The clumsy efforts made by Dore Gold to act behind the back of Foreign Minister David Levy caused the first of many explosions between Levy and Netanyahu. Gold, a man who seems to keep secrets even from himself, made a habit of setting off on clandestine missions without informing the Foreign Office or the embassies.

In August 1996, Netanyahu paid a visit to King Hussein without bothering to take a representative of the Foreign Office along. Levy decided that he had had enough. He broke all contact with Netanyahu, and went on a protest vacation, in the middle of which he traveled to the United States to attend a private event, leaving the government and its prime minister confused and hoping for the best.

After two weeks, the foreign minister returned to his job, but only after receiving a clear promise from Netanyahu that he would not be left in the dark over the peace process and would be kept updated regarding every event, no matter how small.

At the end of his first year, Bibi still did not have faith in anyone except his small band of devotees. He felt that the Foreign Office, the Finance Office, the Justice Office, and the security system all belonged to the previous administration. In August, Knesset member Uzi Landau declared that there were senior officers in the security establishment who were operating "under orders of the previous government."

Bibi had criticized senior officers in the IDF for participating in political debates during the Rabin administration. In his government, he vowed, the IDF would remain outside the political arena.

Bibi's insistence on a separation between the military and political establishments caused a serious crisis. The prime minister, the chief of staff, the head of the Mossad, and the head of the Shabak all became embroiled in the conflict. The country's security chiefs, headed by the IDF chief of staff, Lt. Gen. Amnon Shahak, felt that Netanyahu and his young associates were trying to bypass their operational decisions because of their false belief that the chief of staff, the Shabak head, and senior IDF officers were trying to harm Netanyahu by supporting the Labor party. At one point, several officers considered resigning. To avoid this, Bibi was forced to break yet another vow, this time his declaration that the military would not be involved in politics. After several months, he agreed to consult army heads on issues connected to national security.

On August 8, 1996, justice minister Ya'akov Ne'eman resigned his post after it became known that he was being charged with attempting to interfere in legal processes in the Arye Der'i trial. About a year later, cleared of all blame, Ne'eman returned to the government as minister of finance after Bibi successfully caused Dan Meridor to resign.

The sense of chaos in the prime minister's office was worsened by the presence of the leader's wife. Stories about Sara's behavior were soon leaked to the press: her demand for her own office and staff; her frequent, unannounced visits; her hysterical phone calls to the office in the middle of the night; her demands of staff members for services not owed the prime minister's wife. In off-the-record conversations, even the most zealous of Netanyahu supporters did not deny that his wife's behavior caused problems.

At the beginning of 1997, Netanyahu visited Holland and Italy, taking his wife and small children with him. During the visit, Sara Netanyahu misplaced a coat. The prime minister's wife raised a ruckus, claiming that the coat had great sentimental value. She demanded that the prime minister's staff find it forthwith. By the time the missing coat was finally found, the fuss surrounding the coat had grown to the proportions of a full-scale diplomatic incident.

Since the famous "peace" between Bibi and Sara following the Ruth Bar affair, Bibi indulges all of Sara's idiosyncrasies, tolerates the embarrassing scenes she makes in public, and accepts her insensitivity to people and basic disregard for principles of protocol. He has no other choice.

Sara goes everywhere with the prime minister. She sits by her husband, leafing through highly classified material, taking an active part in matters of state. She accompanies him on all his official visits abroad, usually bringing the children along too. On one visit to the United States,

President Clinton invited the Netanyahu family to visit the Oval Office. Sara brought the two small children, and press photographs show an embarrassing scene with the two boys, completely out of control, throwing cushions around the president's office, while Clinton looks on with his arms crossed and a bemused expression. Sara, showing too much thigh in a very short skirt, looks on with the pride of a doting mother.

32

Shaking Hands With Arafat

Benjamin Netanyahu spelled out his political ideology in his book *A Place Among the Nations*, which was published in English in 1993. In it Netanyahu contends that the free world is obliged to honor the commitment made in 1917 by the British government to build a national homeland for the Jews in Palestine. According to Netanyahu, the Balfour Declaration, named after its author, the earl of Balfour, Britain's foreign secretary, is a contract that must be honored. As a disciple of Jabotinsky, Netanyahu believes that the historic Land of Israel, as it appears in the Bible, belongs to the State of Israel.

Furthermore, Netanyahu insists that the 1967 Six Day War, when the IDF liberated Jerusalem and captured the territories of Judea and Samaria up to the River Jordan, on Israel's eastern border, righted a historic injustice. This view is shared by the National Religious party, whose members have occupied most of the West Bank settlements since 1967.

The left in Israel, led by the Labor party, supports a territorial compromise in the West Bank as part of a permanent arrangement between Israel and the Palestinians. The first Oslo accord between Israel and the Palestinians, signed in 1993 by Yitzhak Rabin and Yasser Arafat, induced Israel to give up the Gaza Strip in the south, one of the most densely populated areas in the world and traditionally a hornet's nest of terrorism. Also included in the first accord was an agreement that Israel would relinquish Jericho, Ramallah, and Nablus.

The second Oslo agreement, reached in the summer of 1995, was an improved version of the first. It called for Israel's withdrawal from the Arab-populated parts of Hebron and other Palestinian lands, but not for the evacuation of Israeli settlements. The accord was formulated by Rabin and Arafat, with the intervention of President Clinton, Secretary of State Warren Christopher, and the U.S. special emissary to the Middle East, Dennis Ross.

The sudden rise to power of Benjamin Netanyahu in May 1996, in the wake of Rabin's assassination, in the most sensational, against-all-odds election victory in Israel's history, brought about a dramatic change in the political process. In his election campaign, Netanyahu had promised that if he were elected prime minister, Israel would honor all signed international commitments, including the Oslo accords, notwithstanding the fact that—in his opinion—the accords were a catastrophe for Israel.

From the moment he assumed office, however, Netanyahu did all he could to delay the peace process. He stated that Israel would honor the agreements signed with the Palestinian Authority, but only if certain conditions were fulfilled. Netanyahu demanded that the PLO publicly rescind the Palestinian charter which, in fact, had already been rescinded in 1996 at the Palestinian National Council in Gaza; he demanded the extradition of terrorists involved in attacks on Israel who had already been brought to trial in Palestinian courts of law; he insisted on a total war against Hamas and all sources of terrorist activity. Netanyahu relied on his magical political term—"mutuality." Without mutuality, he would allow no progress.

Netanyahu remains torn between Israel's political commitments and his own ideology, which holds that the Arabs have more than enough territory outside the boundaries of the State of Israel to solve the Palestinian problem. His policy on the accords has been delay. However, he knows that a breach of the accords could destroy Israel's favored relationship with the United States and the Clinton administration, both of them party to the accords.

Netanyahu also has a personal problem—his deep hatred of Arafat. As Israel's ambassador to the United Nations, Netanyahu built his career fighting Palestinian and international terrorism, which, as far as he is concerned, are the same. To Benjamin Netanyahu, Arafat was, and remains, the leader of a terrorist gang.

Netanyahu has never accepted that Arafat matured and gave up terror as a political instrument. Netanyahu believes that Arafat has the blood of hundreds of Israelis, Americans, and Europeans on his hands. Bibi has continually sought to highlight the Americans who became victims of terrorist activity. In the summer of 1985, when Palestinian terrorists took control of the *Achille Lauro,* an Italian cruise ship which was sailing in the Mediterranean, they murdered Leon Klinghoffer, an elderly and physically handicapped American Jew. At the time, Netanyahu was Israel's ambassador to the United Nations. This incident allowed him to stir American indignation at Arab terror. Netanyahu charged Yasser Arafat, whose men carried out the attack, with responsibility for the murder. He denounced Arafat from every platform and television screen possible.

During his election campaign, Netanyahu gladly approved Finkelstein's idea for a TV spot condemning Peres's relationship with Arafat. In the commercial, Peres and Arafat walk side by side up a flight of stairs against a background of glass which shatters into thousands of pieces—a symbolic reference to the idea that Peres's cooperation with Arafat would lead the State of Israel into disaster.

Netanyahu believed that he could continue to ignore Arafat even after being elected prime minister of Israel. However, pressure from Clinton and Christopher led him, against his better judgment, to meet Arafat on September 4, 1996, at the Eres checkpoint in the Gaza Strip. For Netanyahu, this was one of the most humiliating and degrading moments of his life. Some time later, he described his feelings at the time. He wondered what his father, Benzion Netanyahu, who raised him to hate Arab leaders, would think of him. Photographs show Netanyahu shaking Arafat's hand, both of their faces grim and filled with suspicion. The photos appeared on the front pages of the world's major newspapers. For as long as Netanyahu lives, he will never forget the moment he held Yasser Arafat's hand.

Arafat and Clinton had to wait seven months before Netanyahu finally persuaded the Israeli cabinet to approve a withdrawal from the Jewish quarter in Hebron, on January 15, 1997. The ominous forecasts of Hebron becoming a river of blood proved wrong, as things remained relatively quiet. The Hebron withdrawal demonstrated that coexistence between Israelis and Palestinians is possible if both sides want it.

The withdrawal did not, however, generate much political momentum for the peace process. The aftermath has been a political freeze of doubts, suspicions, and delaying tactics, despite the best efforts of the American mediator, Dennis Ross.

Netanyahu did not personally share the hopes of the Palestinians, and of a large number of Israelis, that the Hebron agreement would encourage cooperation between Netanyahu and Arafat. At his cabinet meetings, the prime minister said that as far as he was concerned, the Palestinians could wait. Meanwhile, tensions rose in the territories.

At the end of September 1996, Netanyahu was pressured by Irving Moskowitz, the Jewish-American millionaire from Miami, to open the Western Wall tunnel in Jerusalem. Moskowitz, a religious fanatic who believed in the right of the Jews to settle all the occupied territories, had donated large sums of money to Netanyahu's election campaign and to settlement activity in the West Bank.

As a religious zealot, Moskowitz had been excited by the discovery of the Western Wall tunnel by Israeli archaeologists several years earlier. Because of the tunnel's proximity to the Temple Mount, a place sacred to Moslems, the late prime minister Yitzhak Rabin had decided that the tunnel would be opened only at one end. The side leading to the Temple Mount would remain closed.

At a security cabinet meeting, Netanyahu raised Moskowitz's demand for the tunnel to be opened. He spoke hypothetically, making no mention of the fact that he fully intended to have the tunnel opened in the near future. Minister of Defense Itzik Mordechai, Chief of Staff Amnon Shahak, and the Shabak chief, Ami Ayalon, all agreed that unilaterally opening the tunnel without first consulting with leaders of the Wakf, the Moslem religious leadership in Jerusalem, could cause serious rioting in the city. Netanyahu listened to their warnings but made no response.

On the eve of Yom Kippur, the Day of Atonement, Netanyahu gave Jerusalem mayor Ehud Ulmert permission to open the tunnel, a surprise holiday gift for Irving Moskowitz. Netanyahu had faith in Moskowitz's prediction that opening the tunnel would bring millions of tourists to Jerusalem. They would all want to see with their own eyes the tunnel which, according to archaeologists, had served the Maccabees in their glorious war against the Greek rulers before the birth of Christ.

Not one of the senior military leaders was privy to Netanyahu's secret. Only his closest assistants—his chief of staff, Yvette Lieberman; his government secretary, Danny Naveh, and his devoted spokesman, Shai Bazak—knew what was about to happen. They had warned Netanyahu that the senior military establishment was contaminated by politics and pandered to the Labor party. Thus, to avoid political interference, Bibi made a major decision with serious security ramifications without involving or even informing Israel's military leaders or security heads. Having opened the tunnel, Netanyahu took off with Sara for London the following morning, the first stop on a state visit to Western Europe. That day, rioting broke out in Jerusalem, just as Bibi's security cabinet had foreseen. Netanyahu received reports of skirmishes in the occupied territories, but decided to continue with his planned visits to Bonn and Paris. Shabak chief Ami Ayalon's warning that opening the tunnel would cause the territories to explode like a barrel of dynamite had come true. By the time Netanyahu returned, twenty-six Israeli soldiers had been killed fighting with Palestinian police and civilians. More than one hundred Palestinians were dead. Hundreds were injured.

Israelis awaited the return of their prime minister in this time of crisis. Upon arriving, Netanyahu casually stepped down from the plane, hand in hand with Sara. He was unrepentant, blaming the Palestinians for the riots and defending his decision to open the tunnel. "The Western Wall tunnel is the rock of our existence," he said.

The Israeli media, public, and military elite were all furious at Netanyahu. The prime minister's office in turn criticized the military leaders for passing the blame. The rift between Netanyahu and the higher military echelons deepened. Israel had paid a high price for catering to Irving Moskowitz.

Beyond the death toll from the riots, the opening of the tunnel took a serious toll on the relationship between the prime minister and PLO leader Yasser Arafat. Overnight, Arafat changed from someone amenable to reconciling with Netanyahu into someone who refused to speak to him. It took a massive diplomatic intervention from the United States and an emergency summit meeting in Washington to rescue what remained of the peace process.

Bibi and Arafat's summit in Washington was much different from their first meeting at the Eres checkpoint in Gaza. Bibi seemed to have changed his outlook. Perhaps he had come to believe that Arafat could be his partner in peace. Their embrace on the White House lawn evoked memories of Rabin and Peres's meetings with the Palestinian leader. Bibi later spoke of Arafat with considerable enthusiasm. His tone of arrogance, denigration, and ridicule had completely disappeared. This apparent transformation led Barbara Walters to choose Benjamin Netanyahu as one of 1996's most fascinating personalities.

Netanyahu's government experienced another serious jolt following the "attorney general affair." On January 20, 1997, Netanyahu decided to appoint a new attorney general. Just as in the United States, the attorney general is considered one of the most important posts in the Israeli government. Netanyahu chose Jerusalem lawyer Roni Baron, a member of the Likud central committee and an avid football fan, for the job. The Israeli public was shocked by what they considered a poor and illogical choice for such an important office. Shock turned to outrage when Ayala Hasson, a Channel 1 reporter, alleged that the Baron appointment was part of an underhanded political deal whereby Baron would end the prosecution of Shas leader Arye Der'i, and in return Der'i would convince his party to vote with Netanyahu in favor of the Hebron agreement. The public outcry over this accusation forced Netanyahu to ask for a police investigation into the matter. After investigating, the police recommended trying Netanyahu for abuse of confidence, together with Arye Der'i and Lieberman.

The state attorney decided not to accept the police recommendation. An indictment was filed against Der'i, but Netanyahu's case was dropped due to insufficient evidence. He did, however, receive a reprimand from the attorney general. Netanyahu called on Arthur Finkelstein to devise a campaign to clear his name. Finkelstein advised Bibi to blame the media and the left.

For more than two months the country speculated as to who would be the new attorney general. Netanyahu eventually chose a man with whom he had clashed in the past, Elyakim Rubinstein. Rubinstein had years earlier been frustrated by losing the coveted appointment to the United Nations to Netanyahu. Later, in Washington, Netanyahu was the frustrated one when he led the Israeli delegation to the peace talks but felt that Rubinstein did all the real negotiating. Nevertheless, Netanyahu now set aside the personal in favor of the political, and, as he expected, the appointment of Rubinstein was met with approval across the political spectrum.

While the Baron affair was still in the news, Labor party chairman, Shimon Peres asked Netanyahu for a meeting. Peres had a tempting offer to pose: he would support the prime minister during these difficult days in return for Netanyahu's participation in a national unity government. Bibi was interested, and the two met a number of times. Bibi needed Labor's support to get through the attorney general crisis. Peres wanted to unify the government before June 3, 1997, the date set for primary elections for Labor party leadership. Negotiations progressed through March and April. Peres suggested party equality in the government, and Bibi agreed: six ministers from Labor, six from the Likud, a political-security cabinet, and Netanyahu as final arbitrator on matters of importance, including the economy.

Netanyahu offered Peres the post of finance minister, but Peres preferred to be appointed minister for peace. Bibi agreed. Foreign Minister David Levy was brought into the process. Netanyahu promised that negotiations with the Palestinians would remain his responsibility, with Peres assuming authority only for negotiations with Syria. Levy agreed.

Peres asked that Ehud Barak be appointed minister of defense. Bibi agreed. Itzik Mordechai, increasingly a thorn in Netanyahu's side, would leave the Defense Ministry and be appointed minister without portfolio and a member of the political-security cabinet.

Prime Minister Netanyahu and opposition leader Peres agreed on a platform. They committed themselves to persuading their separate parties to approve the arrangement by Passover. Surprisingly, it was Peres who met resistance within his own party. Both Ehud Barak and Yossi Beilin announced that they would not support any unity government headed by Netanyahu. Peres still believed he could get the deal approved by Labor—when the news surfaced that the police would recommend indicting Netanyahu. This put an end to all plans for a national unity government. Peres informed Netanyahu that he was voiding the deal because of the police recommendation. By the time it was determined that Netanyahu would not have to stand trial, it was too late to salvage the project.

Bibi went through a period of torturous uncertainty. His future lay in the hands of Attorney General Elyakim Rubinstein. If Rubinstein were to indict him, it would surely end Benjamin Netanyahu's political career.

One by one, Bibi called in each of his government ministers to ask for their support: Natan Sharansky, Avigdor Kahalani, Dan Meridor, Limor Livnat. Not one had ever seen Netanyahu in such an apologetic and humble state.

The meeting with Livnat took place in the afternoon. Security men, visibly nervous, surrounded the prime minister's office. They knew Sara was due to arrive at any minute. They also knew that she would throw a violent tantrum if she discovered that Livnat was in Netanyahu's office. Fortunately, she did not.

The attorney general's office finally published its report. Bibi read through the complicated legal jargon. "There is no recommendation to indict," he announced with great relief.

"We're okay," Danny Naveh agreed.

Netanyahu had escaped political ruin, but he still feared the possibility of resignations within his cabinet in the wake of the attorney general's report. Bibi knew, for example, that if Limor Livnat resigned it would cause a domino effect and the entire government would be in jeopardy.

Livnat was the first to call after the report was released. "There's no indictment. We've come out of it all right," Bibi told her.

"Okay, Bibi," Livnat replied. "But I want to read the report."

Meanwhile, Attorney General Rubinstein and Dvora Arbel, the chief prosecutor, held a press conference to discuss their report. Immediately afterward Bibi appeared on television with a rehearsed response. He took no questions from reporters.

For the first time as prime minister, Netanyahu admitted to having made a mistake. After promising to mend his ways, he launched into an attack on the media, especially Israel's public TV channel, for questioning his authority and attempting to interfere in the government in an undemocratic manner.

Livnat, Sharansky, Meridor, and Kahalani read the report. At eight o'clock that evening Livnat decided to remain in Netanyahu's government. The others had reached the same decision even earlier. Meridor deliberated the longest, as usual, even making up his mind to resign at one point, but in the end he chose to stay. Netanyahu's government stood.

Having survived the Baron affair, Netanyahu set out to destroy the career of his finance minister, Dan Meridor, whose excessive moralizing had exacerbated the controversy. Before long Netanyahu got his chance.

Meridor had become embroiled in a debate with the governor of the Bank of Israel, Professor Ya'akov Frankel, over an important economic issue. Netanyahu pounced on the opportunity. He came out strongly against Meridor and staunchly supported the governor's stand. He succeeded in undermining any hope of compromise between the two. Meridor had no choice but to resign from office and leave the government altogether. Professor Ya'akov Ne'eman, member of an eminent Tel Aviv law firm, was subsequently appointed minister of finance.

It seemed that Bibi had finally orchestrated the government of his dreams, with Dan Meridor and Benny Begin locked out. But problems continued to hound him. On September 25, 1997, the Israeli Mossad attempted to poison and kill Haled Mash'al, the Hamas leader in Jordan responsible for planning terrorist attacks and suicide bombings. Danny Yatom, the head of the Mossad, recommended the assassination of Mash'al, and Netanyahu authorized the operation. Minister of Defense Itzik Mordechai, IDF Chief of Staff Amnon Shahak, and Shabak head Ami Ayalon were all kept in the dark.

Two hit men, members of the Mossad's annihilation squad, found Mash'al on a main street in Amman. In broad daylight, one of the hit men injected a lethal poison into Mash'al's ear. Mash'al's bodyguards chased the Mossad agents and apprehended them. Consequently, Israel was forced to supply the antidote, which was given to Mash'al in time to save his life.

The botched attempt on Mash'al's life caused great tension between Israel and Jordan. King Hussein was furious with Netanyahu and refused to meet with him. The Israeli media and public were also up in arms over the embarrassing incident. In an attempt to address the outcry, Netanyahu convened a commission to investigate the incident. In the end, Bibi once again managed to avoid taking personal responsibility, as he made sure the blame was placed squarely on Danny Yatom, who eventually was forced to resign.

On November 8, 1997, a month and a half after the aborted Mossad attempt to kill a Hamas leader in Jordan, over half a million people poured into Tel Aviv's Rabin Square to participate in a memorial rally, two years after the assassination of the prime minister.

At the Likud Conference in November 1997, Bibi received a standing ovation from the Likud Center, which consists of 2,100 members of the

3,000-member Likud. Behind the scenes, Yvette Lieberman was attempting to rescind the primaries system of elections in which all members of the Likud party elect their representatives to the Knesset. Lieberman wanted to limit the elections to the Likud Center, which had received Bibi so warmly. Netanyahu had been one of the staunchest supporters of the primaries and was elected by a large majority according to this system, but he now changed his stance and adopted Lieberman's approach. He knew that his strength was greatest in the Likud Center.

By changing the election process, Lieberman aimed to weaken Itzik Mordechai, Dan Meridor, still a member of the Knesset, though no longer a cabinet minister, and Minister of Communications Limor Livnat, who was extremely popular among Likud voters.

Lieberman's efforts to do away with the primaries system caused a furor in the Likud. Netanyahu had promised the Likud ministers that he would prevent Lieberman from including such a proposal on the conference's agenda. In reality, Netanyahu was supporting Lieberman's initiative behind closed doors. The Likud Center held a vote and by a large majority chose to rescind the primaries system.

The Likud cabinet ministers felt backstabbed, so much so that they began to consider plans for ousting Netanyahu. Fearing a coup, Netanyahu called on his ace, American adviser Arthur Finkelstein. Finkelstein advised Bibi to pacify his colleagues by sacrificing Lieberman.

Bibi called a press conference. He announced that he would hold a referendum among all the Likud members to determine the voting system they liked best. Lieberman felt so betrayed that he resigned from Netanyahu's government. Bibi accepted his resignation "with sorrow." Today, Lieberman is a businessman and Likud activist.

By the end of 1997, only eighteen months after being elected prime minister, Netanyahu's popularity rating had fallen to below 30 percent, while his opponent, Labor leader Ehud Barak, saw his rating rise to 45 percent. Shortly after the Likud Conference, when Netanyahu went to London to meet Tony Blair, Great Britain's new prime minister, the visit received little mention in the British press. A small item appearing in Israel's *Yediot Ahronot*, informing its readers that Sara Netanyahu, who was not invited to meet Cherry Blair, took the children out for the day in London.

33

Bibi Netanyahu and Bill Clinton

Netanyahu first met Bill Clinton at Jerusalem's King David Hotel, in March 1996. Clinton had come to Israel to express his sympathy in the wake of a wave of terrorist attacks during February and March in which suicide bombers blew up public buses in Tel Aviv and Jerusalem and in one of Israel's largest shopping malls, Dizengoff Center. Clinton and Shimon Peres, then prime minister of Israel, called for an international conference on terrorism in response to the attacks. The conference was held at the Egyptian resort of Sharm el-Sheikh on the Red Sea coast of the Sinai peninsula.

While Clinton was in the region, he had a brief meeting with Benjamin Netanyahu, the Israeli opposition leader. As Clinton and Netanyahu parted, Bibi promised, "We'll meet again when I am prime minister of Israel."

Clinton smiled politely, but he did not believe that Netanyahu would ever be the prime minister of Israel.

In 1996, after his victory Netanyahu visited the White House as the new Israeli prime minister. Clinton had done everything he could to get Shimon Peres re-elected. At the White House, Clinton, realizing he had miscalculated Netanyahu's potential, tried to develop a friendly relationship with Israel's new leader.

There has never been much chemistry between the two. Clinton resents Netanyahu's friendships with his political enemies. Netanyahu is close with some of the president's severest critics, such as Newt Gingrich and Jerry Falwell.

As his term has progressed, Netanyahu has learned that he can defy the American administration without harsh repercussion. He does not believe that Clinton is willing to risk the friendship between the United States and Israel. This assumption has proven partly correct. Clinton has continued to speak warmly of Israel as America's ally. However, he has gradually developed a fundamental mistrust of Netanyahu.

When Netanyahu was in Los Angeles in November 1997 as the guest of honor of several Hollywood movie stars, including Kirk Douglas and Arnold Schwarzenegger, Clinton also happened to be in L.A. Clinton claimed he was unable to meet with Netanyahu, but found time to see Shimon Peres and Leah Rabin.

As he does at home when half the nation is against him, Netanyahu seeks support from the far right. In Israel, that means the settlers, the Likud, and the ultra-Orthodox fundamentalists. In the United States, he finds comfort among the Republicans and the conservatives.

When Madeleine Albright became the U.S. Secretary of State, Netanyahu figured that her Jewish origins and her family's losses in the Holocaust would make her a natural political ally. Albright, however, was not taken by Bibi's charm. She was quick to grasp the rules of the game in the Middle East, and realized that Netanyahu is no easier to deal with than Arafat.

Albright is less diplomatic than President Clinton in her dealings with Netanyahu. Both, however, seemed to have lost their patience with Bibi when, after sixteen months of negotiations, they gave him a deadline to agree to a 13 percent Israeli withdrawal from the West Bank, a percentage which Arafat accepted. From Netanyahu's point of view, this could be construed as a short-term victory, as he had forced the Clinton administration to relinquish the role of "facilitator" and become a direct negotiator with Israel, with Arafat on the sidelines. In this case, Bibi might have viewed himself as a biblical David who stood up to the United States, the world's greatest superpower.

Afterword

T wo years after his sensational victory over Shimon Peres, Netanyahu admits he was lacking in experience when he took office. A consummate campaigner, he was unprepared for the actual job of prime minister.

During Netanyahu's two years in power, many relationships have soured. King Hussein of Jordan severed his personal relationship with Netanyahu. President Mubarak of Egypt doesn't believe a word he says. Relations with Yasser Arafat are, at best, tense, as Netanyahu blames Arafat for not doing enough to combat terrorism. Netanyahu's relationship with President Clinton, who had arguably been more favorable to Israel than any of his predecessors, has cooled off considerably. Netanyahu is suspicious of Madeleine Albright's Middle East policy, and she believes he is frustrating and possibly jeopardizing the entire peace process. The only positive step Netanyahu has taken with regard to peace is the withdrawal from Hebron as outlined in the Oslo accords.

Netanyahu's decision to build a new Jewish settlement in Har Homa (Homa Hill) in East Jerusalem provoked the Palestinians and the world. Clinton, Albright, Arafat, and European leaders were furious. Netanyahu ignored their protests. Jerusalem, he told the world media, is the ancient capital of Israel and has been a Jewish city since biblical times. He quotes the stories of the Bible and promises that Jerusalem, the holy city, the capital during the reigns of King David and King Solomon, will never be divided again. When the British foreign minister, Robin Cook, visited Har Homa in Jerusalem and met with Palestinian leaders, Netanyahu immediately canceled an official dinner with him.

Today, the majority of the Israelis do not find Netanyahu credible. He knows this and promises to change it. His views on security and antiterrorism remain his guiding principles for leading Israel, and only after those issues are settled on his terms can final negotiations begin with the Palestinians.

As a hard-liner, Netanyahu believes that the Arabs and Palestinians still dream of driving the Jewish state into the sea. He is prepared to fight for every inch of land in the West Bank, which he calls homeland, not occupied territories. The Jewish settlers in the West Bank are his friends and allies. Whenever a crisis arises, he calls on the settlements for support and promises to invest more money in developing what he calls the security belt of Israel.

Netanyahu is currently willing to give the Palestinians a maximum of nine to ten percent of the land. Clinton's compromise calls for thirteen percent. According to Netanyahu's estimates, one percent is the equivalent of seventy miles of land (about the size of Tel Aviv).

After two years of Netanyahu, Israelis are divided in their opinion of him. Fifty percent support Netanyahu, an increase of twelve percent from the end of 1997. The fifty percent who oppose him contend he is risking the security of Israel by losing the peace.

Even those who think that Netanyahu is the worst prime minister in Israel's history admit that he is a survivor. He is ambitious, proud, firmly believes in his policies and ideology, and has the courage of his convictions. He is not afraid of Clinton or Albright. He knows that when he clashes with the president he can always get Congress on his side by turning to the Republican majority. He also believes that Clinton is more susceptible to pressure from Israel because he is so distracted by his personal affairs. Netanyahu doesn't know Monica Lewinsky, but he thinks that she and the other women accusing Clinton of various things appeared at the right time for Israel.

Netanyahu annoys Israelis by being immodest and patronizing and acting macho. He indulges himself with expensive Davidof's Cigars. Many feel he is not a cultured man or a man of vision.

He conducts his political life more like an American president than an Israeli prime minister. He tried to build a White House–style office. He promotes American-style capitalism. Some call him the first "American" prime minister of Israel.

Having done away with the direct election system that served him so well, Netanyahu is now dependent on his slim majority in the Knesset and on his ministers. Ariel Sharon is the most powerful man in his cabinet. A general, a war hero, and a right-wing hawk, Sharon supports the settlers and their demands. David Levy and Dan Meridor, the moderates, are out of power.

Netanyahu is proud of overseeing a reduction in inflation from ten percent to five percent, but unemployment is growing. Nevertheless, he is convinced that Israel has become a high-tech world power, which in fact it has.

While analysts warn that danger lurks in neighboring Syria and Iran, Netanyahu remains confident that Israel is strong enough to overcome any Arab security threat. He is also confident that he will win the next election and remain Israel's prime minister into the next millennium. His opponent will be Ehud Barak, the Labor party's new leader. A former chief of staff and a war hero, Barak won five medals for bravery in secret operations for the army. He was Netanyahu's commander in the elite Sayeret Matkel unit in the 1970s. During those years Netanyahu admired Barak. Now he is ready to fight him. In an interview Netanyahu explained, "I'm not afraid of anyone. I'm only afraid of myself."

Index